International Economics

Global Markets and Competition

4th Edition

International Economics

Global Markets and Competition

4th Edition

Henry Thompson

Auburn University, USA

 World Scientific

NEW JERSEY · LONDON · SINGAPORE · BEIJING · SHANGHAI · HONG KONG · TAIPEI · CHENNAI · TOKYO

Published by

World Scientific Publishing Co. Pte. Ltd.

5 Toh Tuck Link, Singapore 596224

USA office: 27 Warren Street, Suite 401-402, Hackensack, NJ 07601

UK office: 57 Shelton Street, Covent Garden, London WC2H 9HE

British Library Cataloguing-in-Publication Data
A catalogue record for this book is available from the British Library.

INTERNATIONAL ECONOMICS
Global Markets and Competition (4th Edition)

ISBN 978-981-4678-15-5
ISBN 978-981-4663-87-8 (pbk)

Printed in Singapore

Preface for Students

International economics has moved center stage as countries become more integrated with trade, foreign investment, and migration. As the world get closer due to better transportation and telecommunication, international economics will affect your private and business lives.

The foreign exchange market is the largest market in the world. Industries expand and collapse in the face of international competition. The World Trade Organization WTO, North American Free Trade Agreement NAFTA, and European Union EU have become fundamental forms of government.

Protection eases the pressures of international competition. Industries seek the protection of tariffs trying to secure profit at national expense. Governments hinder international trade and investment. Central banks interfere with the foreign exchange market. Such maneuvers impede international commerce and lower income.

This text is based on how international markets work. An economy is a collection of markets with links across borders. Comparative advantage is a fundamental concept for predicting international production and trade based on underlying production capacity.

Trade policy redistributes income toward favored industries and groups. Costs of protection outweigh benefits but industry and labor groups lobby for their own protection. Politicians respond to political support by granting favors.

International trade is the arbitrage of products from countries where prices are lower to where they are higher. Arbitrage makes profit and distributes products more economically. The interaction of supply and demand determines international production and trade.

The graphs, examples, applications, and problems are essential. There are hints for even numbered problems in the back of the book. I think you will enjoy reading and working through the text. Visit my website at *www.auburn.edu/~thomphl*.

Preface for Instructors

International Economics: Global Markets and Competition is a unique textbook:

- a one term text for students with principles background
- microeconomic models stress positive theory
- advocates free trade
- stresses general equilibrium theory
- boxed examples
- problems relate directly to theory in the text

This text applies tools of international microeconomics and macroeconomics. The foreign exchange rate and balance of payments are integrated throughout. Open economy macroeconomic models stress micro foundations.

The text does not assume background in intermediate intermediate theory. Numerous boxed examples introduce tools and concepts from scratch.

Technical points are made with examples and graphs avoiding "formulas" and algebraic symbols. Classroom presentations can be based on diagrams and algebra.

Problems were developed in the classroom. Hints for even numbered problems are in the Appendix. Calling on students to work problems at the board will improve their performance.

You will be surprised at how well your students learn with this accessible text. See my webpage at *www.auburn.edu/~thomphl* and contact me at *henry. thompson@anburn.edu*.

Thanks

Students and colleagues too numerous to mention have provided suggestions and comments. The staff at World Scientific are excellent.

Contents

TRADE AND PROTECTIONISM

Markets and International Trade

Preview

This first chapter introduces some fundamental concepts of international economics:

- Supply and demand in export and import markets
- Excess supply and demand in international markets
- The trade balance as net receipts from international trade
- Comparative advantage as the foundation of trade

INTRODUCTION

The most important tool of economics is the model of supply and demand. Goods and services are traded in markets that determine prices. Markets include grocery stores, the stock market, the foreign exchange market, the international market for cars, and so on. In market transactions, money changes hands between buyers and sellers at agreed prices.

An international transaction occurs when the buyer and seller are in different countries. The exchange rate is involved in international transactions with the buyer's currency traded for the seller's.

In international economics, governments can tax imports with tariffs or limit transactions with quotas or nontariff barriers. Governments can also subsidize exports. International economics is characterized by the lack of labor mobility across national borders. Capital and investment also find movement more difficult than within a country.

The balance of trade is a country's export revenue minus import spending. Trade deficits occur when import spending is greater than export revenue Trade surpluses occur when export revenue is greater. The trade balance is a major topic in international economics, regularly making headlines.

Comparative advantage is relative production efficiency. When a country produces a good, it pays the opportunity cost of a lost alternative. Efficient use of limited resources based on comparative advantage leads to higher income.

A.   INTERNATIONAL MARKETS

Everyone is involved in international markets every day. Everything we buy has some foreign component. Every job contributes to exports and uses imports, eithere directly or indirectly. Markets are the basis of international economics.

Domestic Demand

The law of demand states the price and quantity demanded of a good move in opposite directions. Car dealers, stores, and oil refineries offer discounts when their inventories are too high.

Figure 1.1 shows domestic demand D for manufactures. This demand curve represents the quantity demanded at various prices by domestic consumers. At $15 the quantity demanded is 100 units per month.

Demand curves slope downward for two reasons:

- substitution effect a higher price induces consumers to look for substitutes
- income effect higher price lowers real income

Some goods have readily available substitutes. If the price of beef rises with a quota on imported beef, consumers switch to chicken. If the price of Japanese cars rises with a voluntary export restraint, consumers switch to European cars. If the price of Dutch cheese rises with a tariff, consumers switch to Wisconsin cheese.

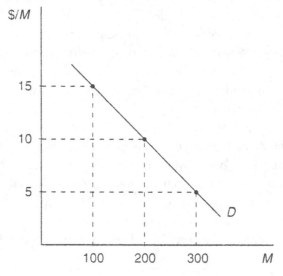

Figure 1.1
The Domestic Demand for Manufactures
Quantity demanded is inversely related to price.

Embargoes of the Organization of Petroleum Exporting Countries OPEC during the 1970s tripled the price of crude oil. Consumers began to substitute away from gasoline. Real incomes fell as the higher relative price of gas lowered purchasing power of income.

Demand curves slope downward due to substitution and income effects.

Various market influences shift demand curves:

- consumer tastes
- number of consumers
- price expectations
- income
- prices of related products

If tastes for a product increase, the demand curve shifts right. Consumers demand more at any price. A few decades ago, US consumers had little taste for foreign cars or imported beer. Tastes have changed.

As nations grow, there is increased demand for goods and services. When a country enters international trade, the number of consumers for its products increase. The North American Free Trade Area (NAFTA) increases demand for products in Canada, Mexico, and the US. If the US outlaws trade with Cuba, consumers lose. If Europe opens its protected agricultural industry to trade, the demand for US agricultural products will increase.

Expected higher prices induce consumers to buy now to avoid higher prices later, increasing current demand. With news that the Ukrainian wheat harvest will be poor, buyers of wheat increase demand right away.

Higher income raises demand for normal goods and lowers demand for inferior goods. As incomes rise in newly industrialized countries, demand for US exports of luxury goods like steaks rises while demand for inferior goods such as red beans falls.

Many goods are related in consumption. Demand for a good is positively related to the price of its substitutes. Coffee and tea are substitutes. The price of coffee rose in the early 1970s when the international coffee cartel restricted output, raising the demand for tea. Cars and gas are complements. Higher gas prices reduce the demand for cars.

Demand curves increase to the right or decrease to the left due to nonprice influences.

EXAMPLE 1.1   *International Trade Growth*

Since World War II international trade has steadily increased. Output has grown but not as fast as world trade. Business firms are becoming more involved in trade. Consumers enjoy products from around the world.

Domestic Supply

Supply curves are the marginal cost of production, the cost of producing more output. Marginal cost slopes upward for two reasons:

- Diminishing marginal productivity of inputs
- Increasing output bids up prices of inputs

Diminishing marginal productivity implies the additional output per unit of input declines as the input increases. The marginal product of additional workers declines after some point.

Output increases when price rises. There is a positive relationship between price and quantity supplied. Figure 1.2 shows the upward sloping domestic supply of manufactures such as cars, apparel, or computers. Supply curves differ across countries. Differences in the supply curve are due to

- technology
- the number of firms
- prices of inputs
- price expectations

Improved technology allows firms to produce more output with the same inputs. More efficient jet engines lower the cost of international air travel shifting supply to the right.

An increase in the number of firms increases supply. The original personal computers were made by a few companies that enjoyed high prices. Other firms entered the industry, foreign firms or domestic firms buying foreign components, increasing supply.

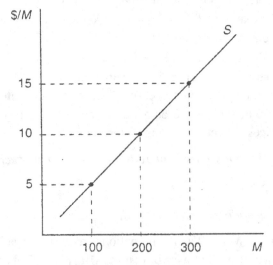

Figure 1.2
The Domestic Supply of Manufactures
The quantity supplied is positively associated with price.

Lower input prices increase supply. Immigration lowers wages, increasing the supply of agricultural goods and construction.

Price expectations shift supply. If firms expect lower prices, they sell inventories right away before price falls. If an OPEC meeting ends in agreement to restrict output, dealers expect higher oil prices. Oil in storage will be worth more in the future, decreasing supply immediately.

Supply curves slope upward, reflecting higher marginal cost associated with higher output. Supply curves shift due to nonprice influences.

Shifts in supply or demand are different from movements along the curves. A change in price causes a change in the quantity supplied or demanded along the curve. A change in a nonprice influence shifts the curve.

EXAMPLE 1.2   *A Relatively Closed Giant*

Relative to other countries, the US economy is a closed giant. The US produces about one sixth of world output. The US leads all countries in share of world trade but trade is a small share of US output. The ratio of export revenue plus import spending to output has grown to about 30% for the US. The ratio is similar for Japan but over 50% for the EU. For many countries $(X + M)$/GDP is much higher.

Markets and Market Clearing

The domestic market for manufactures is shown in Figure 1.3. The domestic price is $10 determined where the quantity domestic buyers are willing to consume equals the quantity domestic suppliers are willing to produce, 200.

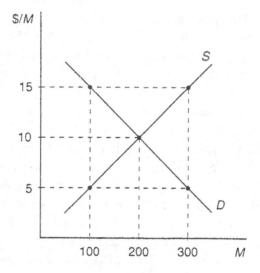

Figure 1.3
The Domestic Market for Manufactures M
Domestic supply S and demand D interact to determine the domestic equilibrium price $10 and the domestic equilibrium quantity 200. The equilibrium price equates quantity supplied with quantity demanded.

At any other price the quantities supplied and demanded are not equal. At $15, production is 300 and consumption 100. Suppliers would lower price to keep their inventories from accumulating. At $5 consumption at 300 is greater than production at 100 and the price is bid up.

Market clearing explains why government policymakers cannot set prices. Suppose a politician thinks a $5 price would be popular and sets a price ceiling. Buyers want 300 units but suppliers produce only 100.

At the other extreme, a $15 floor price would benefit the industry. Firms respond with higher output but consumers purchase only 100. The government may buy the surplus as happens with some agricultural products.

Markets clear at equilibrium prices that equate the quantity demanded with the quantity supplied.

EXAMPLE 1.3   *Ports for US Merchandise Exports*

Ports in California, Texas, and New York account for one third of US exports. California and Washington are located on the Pacific Rim and trade heavily with Asia. Texas trades heavily with Latin America. New York is on the Atlantic and trades with the EU. Michigan and Illinois have ports on the Great Lakes and trade with Canada.

International Markets

Producers and customers in different countries are involved in international markets. Figure 1.4 shows home and foreign markets for manufactures M. Asterisks indicate the foreign country. The equilibrium price in the home market is $10 and in the foreign market 250 yen.

When comparing prices, traders convert currencies. The exchange rate is the dollar prize of the yen or $/yen. In Figure 1.4, the exchange rate is $/yen=0.01 with each yen worth one cent.

This international market offers an opportunity for *arbitrage*. Traders buy the good in the foreign country at 250 yen or $2.50=250 × 0.01, less than the $10 domestic price. Arbitrage is the foundation of international trade.

A price of $5 clears this international market. The home country imports 200=300=100 units at a price of $5. Domestic production falls from 200 to 100. Domestic consumers enjoy the lower price and increase the quantity demand from 200 to 300. On the foreign side, production rises from 200 to 300 with the increase in price from 250 yen to 500 yen. Foreign consumers suffer higher prices, cutting their level of consumption from 200 to 100.

International trade seeks the price where excess demand from one country equals excess supply from the other.

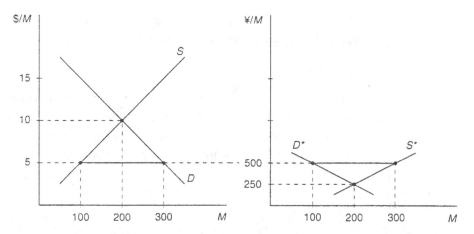

Figure 1.4
The International Market for Manufactures (M)
Free trade takes place where the excess demand from one country equals the excess supply from the other country. At a price of $5, the foreign country will export 200 units of manufactures to the home country.

International trade creates winners and losers. In an export market, firms are better off but consumers suffer. In an import market, industry suffers while consumers benefit.

International markets arise when prices vary across countries. International market prices equate excess demand with excess supply.

In practice, traders are concerned with transport costs that include costs of shipping, storage, insurance, and delivery. If each unit of M in Figure 1.4 cost $6 to transport, imported goods would cost $5+$6=$11. There would be no trade.

EXAMPLE 1.4   *Trade in Services*

World trade in services amounts to about a quarter of merchandise trade. The US is a major service exporter. Services include engineering, construction, banking, mineral exploration, insurance, shipping and education. More specialization in services can be expected in the US.

Section A Problems

A1. Draw the shift in demand for manufactures if the quantity demanded at every price in Figure 1.1 increases by 200. Find the new domestic market equilibrium price and quantity.

A2. Predict what happens to the international price and quantity traded of the manufactured good in Figure 1.4 with a domestic improvement in technology.

A3. Suppose the home wage rises with a new labor contract. Show what happens in the international market of Figure 1.4.

A4. Create a diagram similar to Figure 1.4, with home exports due to differences in supply. Do another diagram with home imports due to differences in demand.

EXAMPLE 1.5   *Trade Index*

The sum of export revenue plus import spending relative to output $(X+M)/$GDP is a gauge of trade. Singapore is the highest trading economy and Brazil the lowest. Singapore and Hong Kong are trade and shipping centers. The top 3 and bottom 3 countries are below with major US trading partners. The US index is 30%.

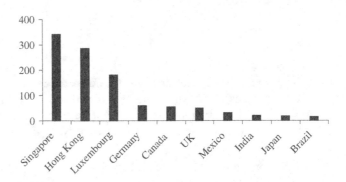

B.   EXCESS SUPPLY AND EXCESS DEMAND

Excess supply and demand simplify the analysis of international markets. The difference between quantity demanded and supplied in an importer is excess demand. The difference between quantity supplied and quantity demanded is excess supply. The international market is reduced to a simpler excess supply and demand diagram.

Excess Demand

The excess demand XD in Figure 1.5 is derived from the home market in Figure 1.4. At the domestic $10 market price *XD* is zero. At $5, *XD* is 200 with home firms producing 100 and home consumers buying 300. The home country imports 200 units at an international price of $5.

A shift in supply or demand shifts the *XD* curve. If increased demand drives the domestic price up to $12.50, excess demand increases. Decreased supply would also increase *XD*.

An increase in supply has the opposite effect. The home country becomes less willing to import. At any price *XD* falls. Decreased demand or increased supply would cause *XD* to fall.

Excess demand shows the quantity a country wants to import at every price. Excess demand shifts with its underlying supply or demand.

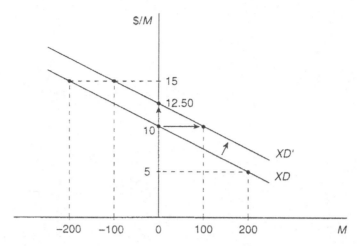

Figure 1.5
Home Excess Demand
Excess demand *XD* is inversely related to price. Increased demand in the home country shifts *XD* for to the right. Decreased supply of manufactures has the same effect.

EXAMPLE **1.6**   *Trade between DCs and LDCs*

Most exports come from developed countries DCs and most of that is exported to other DCs. Less developed countries LDCs account for about a quarter of world exports, shipped mostly to DCs. Newly industrial countries NICs such as India and Brazil are increasing their shares of world trade.

Excess Supply

Foreign excess supply in Figure 1.6 is derived from the foreign demand and supply curves in Figure 1.4. Foreign excess supply *XS** is zero at the foreign market price of 250 yen. At 500 yen *XS** is 200. Changes in foreign supply and demand shift foreign excess supply.

> *Excess supply shows the quantity a country wants to export depending on price. Excess supply shifts with its underlying supply or demand shifts.*

EXAMPLE **1.7**   *Largest US Ports*

The largest US ports and their main exports are below.

	Exports
New York	Primary metals
San Jose	Machinery
Seattle	Transport equipment
Detroit	Transport equipment
Los Angeles	Transport equipment
Chicago	Electrical equipment
Houston	Machinery

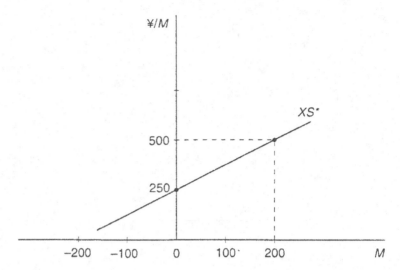

Figure 1.6
The Foreign Excess Supply of Manufactures
Excess supply XS is positively related to price. As price rises, quantity supplied by the foreign country rises and quantity demanded falls. At prices below 250 yen there is excess demand.

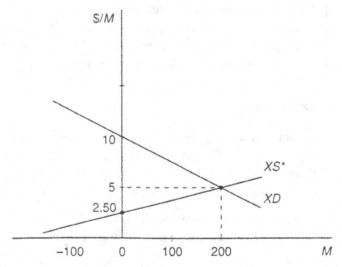

Figure 1.7
Large Economy International Market
In this international market for manufactures, the foreign country exports 200 units of M to the home country. The international equilibrium price of $5 equates XD with excess supply XS^*.

International Markets

International excess supply and demand determine the quantity traded and the international equilibrium price of the traded good. In Figure 1.7 the international price of the manufactured good is $5. Foreign excess supply is matched by home excess demand at $5. The two countries are large and affect the international price.

For any price below $5 there is a shortage. Exporters in the foreign country notice inventories decline. Foreign exporters to raise price to ration supply. If price is above $5, inventories accumulate. The way to eliminate the surplus is to lower price.

International markets clear at the price where excess demand from importers equals excess supply from exporters.

Transport costs can be crucial. Gravel and cement are heavy relative to value and not traded. At the other extreme, the ratio of weight to value is low for electronic components, drugs, and jewelry, goods that are heavily traded.

National borders impose costs of customs procedures and paperwork. Foreign exchange transactions, cross border insurance, and border delays raise costs. Charles Engel and John Rogers (1994) find that national borders effectively add as much cost as 2500 miles between US and Canadian cities.

EXAMPLE 1.8   *US Agriculture Trade*

The US has a trade surplus in agriculture. Major categories in US agricultural trade are below.

Export revenue share		Import spending share	
Animal products	21%	Animal products	19%
Oil seeds	19%	Fruits and vegetables	19%
Grains	19%	Coffee	10%

Shifts in Excess Supply and Demand

The exchange rate influences international prices and trade levels. The exchange rate of $/yen = 0.01 results in the international price of $5 and trade level of 200 in Figure 1.7. Dollar depreciation means the exchange rate $/yen rises.

Foreign producers supply less at every dollar price when the dollar depreciates. Dollar depreciation reduces XS^* in Figure 1.9. The dollar price rises and the volume of trade falls.

Any reduction in foreign supply would cause XS^* to fall as in Figure 1.8, as would an increase in foreign demand. A depreciating yen, an increase in foreign supply, or a decrease in foreign demand increase XS^*.

Turing to domestic excess demand, suppose domestic supply falls due to a new labor contract. Excess demand increases due to the reduced supply. There is an increase in the international price and a higher trade volume in Figure 1.9. The increase in XD could also be caused by any increase in domestic demand.

Anything that affects supply or demand shifts excess supply or excess demand, changing the international price and quantity traded.

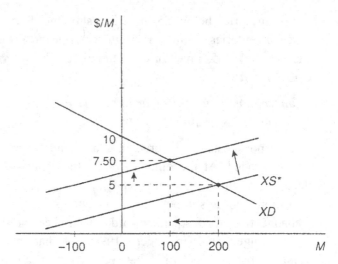

Figure 1.8
A Decrease in Foreign Excess Supply
Declining foreign excess supply raises the international dollar price and lowers the trade level.

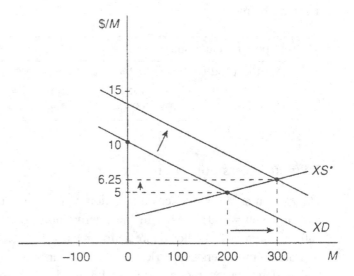

Figure 1.9
An Increase in Home Excess Demand
Rising excess demand *XD* from the home country increases the international price of manufactures and raises the level of trade.

EXAMPLE 1.9   *Trade and War*

A typical opinion is that democracies do not go to war with each other. In fact, trading partners do not go to war. Solomon Polachek (1997) examines the history of wars from 1800 to 1986 and finds democracy has no effect but the level of trade does. Countries do not want to attack their suppliers or customers.

EXAMPLE 1.10   *How to Trade*

> The Department of Commerce has a Trade Promotion Association with parctical information on trade. The Small Business Administration has an Office of International Trade that offers training conferences and counseling. The Service Corps of Retired Executives also provides advice to traders.

Section B Problems

B1. Show what happens in the international market for manufactures in Figure 1.7 if (a) foreign income falls; (b) home tastes for imported manufactures falls; and (c) home production technology improves.

B2. Illustrate the effects of a simultaneous decrease in domestic demand and increase in domestic supply on excess demand. Predict what will happen to the international price and quantity traded.

B3. Suppose Japan imports wood. Japanese supply rises when a forest matures. Show the effect on the international market for lumber assuming excess supply from NAFTA.

C.   THE BALANCE OF TRADE

Imports are products that we enjoy consuming without having to produce. Exports are goods a country has to produce but cannot enjoy consuming. Importing firms and consumers pay firms in the foreign country for imports. Millions of products are traded internationally among hundreds of nations. The balance of trade reports the net flow of trade.

International Transactions

A country pays for imports with the foreign currency it collects through exports. When a good is exported, the foreign importer converts currency to pay the exporter. This transaction involves a bank or foreign exchange dealer.

EXAMPLE 1.11   *The US BOT*

> The US has BOT deficits in trade with NAFTA, Japan, and the EU but surpluses with many small countries. BOT deficits are offset somewhat by surpluses in services trade.

Calculating the Balance of Trade

The *balance of trade* equals the difference between export revenue X and import expenditure *M*,

$$BOT = X - M = (P_{exp} \times Q_{exp}) - (P_{imp} \times Q_{imp})$$

The BOT regularly makes the news, a trade deficit when negative and a trade surplus when positive.

The balance of trade reports the difference between revenue from exports and spending on imports. The BOT is the international net flow of cash due to international trade.

The international market for agricultural goods with domestic excess supply and foreign excess demand is in Figure 1.10. The exchange rate is yen/$ = 100. In the foreign country the autarky price is 1500 yen = $15. Autarky means self-sufficient.

Excess supply comes from the home country, where the autarky price is $5. The international market clears at $10 = 1000 yen with 100 units of agricultural goods traded. Export revenue X is $10×100 = $1000. Suppose import spending on manufacturers is also $1000 as in Figure 1.7. Trade is then balanced at BOT = 0.

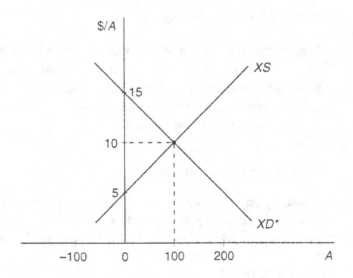

Figure 1.10
The International Market for Agricultural Goods
XS from the home country and XD* from the foreign country meet at the international price $10 with 100 units exported from the home country.

EXAMPLE 1.12   *US Merchandise Exports by State*

The top 4 merchandise exporting states in the US are below. California and Texas are the largest exporters. Washington is the most involved in export production, primarily aerospace.

	% Total
California	14
Texas	11
New York	6
Washington	5

Balanced trade almost never occurs with international markets for thousands of different goods. Suppose a bumper crop of agricultural goods is enjoyed in the importing country. Supply increases, lowering excess demand. Import spending M falls, creating a trade surplus. Export revenue X for the other country falls creating a BOT deficit.

A deficit in the BOT occurs when the country spends more on imports than it receives from exports. A trade surplus occurs if X is greater than M.

Chart 1.1 shows the merchandise balance of trade for the US in dollars per household. Manufacturing firms in the US like to suggest that the trade deficit is the cause of economic problems. Both exports and imports are growing as the US economy becomes more open. Before the 1970s the US had BOT surpluses. The quantity of exports is underestimated because there is no mandatory reporting or taxing of exports. There are automatic forces that create a tendency for an economy to move toward balanced trade.

Chart 1.1 US Merchandise Balance of Trade ($/household)

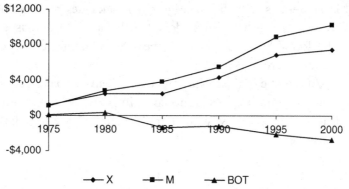

EXAMPLE 1.13   *The Big 3*

> NAFTA, the EU, and Japan account for half of world output and over half of world trade. The big three currencies are the dollar, euro, and yen. China, India, and Brazil are emerging as major economies.

Trade Deficits

If a country spends more on imports than its exports, the opposite must be true for another country. A country with a trade deficit may:

- Borrow and go into debt
- Spend wealth

Debt is essential for economic growth in low income countries. Firms borrow to invest in the capital equipment to increase production. Consumers borrow to buy a house or go to college. Nations as a whole borrow in order to grow.

Mercantilsim is the mistaken belief that deficits are bad. Adam Smith wrote over 200 years ago in *The Wealth of Nations* that wealth is not measured by the amount of money or gold amassed. Productivity is the measure of wealth. It is rational to go into debt to acquire capital. College students borrow to acquire human capital. Growing nations experience BOT deficits, importing capital machinery and equipment.

There is another good reason not to worry much over reported BOT deficits. They are not very reliable. Reported data are accumulated through surveys by the Department of Commerce. Nations keep better records of imports because of tariffs and quotas. The US underestimates its merchandise exports. Using Canadian data on imports from the US as the basis for underestimated export revenue, it is not clear whether the US had trade deficits at all. The sum of trade balances for all nations should be zero but it is a large negative number implying exports are underestimated.

Another mistake to avoid is to concentrate on bilateral trade. The US has BOT deficits with Japan. Figure 1.11 includes trade with the rest of the world ROW. The US has a trade deficit with Japan. Japan has a deficit with the ROW. The ROW has a deficit with the US. Bilateral deficits can be offset by other bilateral surpluses.

Automatic adjustment processes lead to balanced trade. A trade deficit leads to currency depreciation. Imports become more expensive. Money leaves the economy with a trade deficit, lowering the purchasing power of consumers.

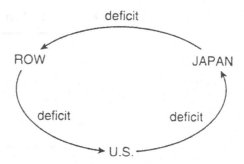

Figure 1.11
Multilateral Trade Balance
Imbalanced trade can be balanced for each country.

EXAMPLE 1.14   *Confusing Trade News*

Trade makes the news when monthly trade figures are released. The story below is edited from *USA Today* in November 1999. These monthly news reports contain bits and pieces of information but mislead by depicting deficits as bad news. It is a mistake to focus on any bilateral deficit. The "world currency crisis" refers to the depreciation of overvalued fixed exchange rates. China joined the WTO after decades of closed inefficienct command and control. This news report is confusing and unfocused.

* * * * *

WASHINGTON (edited from AP) The US trade deficit widened to $24 billion in September even though beleaguered American farmers saw their exports climb to the highest level in 19 months. America's deficits with China and Japan rose with China setting an all-time high. The latest deterioration in trade left the overall deficit running at an annual rate 56% above last year's record. Exports edged back reflecting declines in exports of airliners and autos. Imports hit a new high as the price of foreign crude oil shot up to the highest level in 31 months. American manufacturers have lost a half-million jobs since early 1998 as the world currency crisis has cut sharply into exports and contributed to a flood of cheap imports. The US deficit with OPEC set a record as the foreign oil bill climbed reflecting higher volume and price.

US Exports and Imports

The largest categories of US exports are machinery, agricultural products, aircraft, chemicals, and metal products. The largest categories of imports are capital goods, consumer goods, vehicles, oil, steel, and food.

The largest buyers of US exports and suppliers of US imports are in Table 1.1. NAFTA is the largest trading partner with about 1/3 of export revenue and import expenditure. The EU accounts for about 1/5 of each. NAFTA is growing

Table 1.1 US Trade Partners

NAFTA
EU
NICs
Japan
Americas
ROW

Table 1.2 US Manufacturing Trade

Product	% X	% M
Vehicles	8	13
Electrical machinery	11	9
Office equipment	7	8
Misc manufacturing	5	5
Telecommunication equip	4	5
Transport equip	8	4
Industrial machines	5	3
Power generation equip	4	3
Machinery	4	3
Apparel	0	4
Nonmetallic mineral mfg	0	2
Scientific instruments	4	0

in importance as a US trading partner while Japan and the EU are declining. Newly industrialized countries NICs supply about 1/5 of imports. Both X and M are increasing as the US economy becomes more open.

The largest categories of US manufacturing trade are in Table 1.2. Vehicles and electrical machinery are important. The top imports are typically consumer goods manufactured on assembly lines by unskilled labor.

There is good reason to focus on exported business services:

Accounting	*Construction*	*Motion pictures*
Advertising	*Consulting*	*Retailing*
Architecture	*Education*	*Shipping*
Banking	*Engineering*	*Tourism*
Computer services	*Insurance*	*Transportation*
Communications	*Lodging*	*Wholesaling*

These services represent about 3/4 of US jobs and 1/3 of US export revenue. These are activities in which US firms are efficient and competitive.

In 1900 most workers in the US were in agriculture. The service sector has grown from 30% to 70% while agriculture shrunk from 40% to 2%. Manufacturing has consistently accounted for about 30% of all jobs.

Trade in services accounts for about one quarter of world trade the US is the world's leader in service exports. Japan and Germany are net service importers. To explain evolving trade, service trade has to be included.

Section C Problems

C1. Find import spending with the increased excess demand for manufactures in Figure 1.9. Find the BOT with the export revenue in Figure 1.10.

C2. Predict what will happen to the BOT if excess supply of agricultural goods in Figure 1.11 increases with improved home technology.

EXAMPLE 1.15   *US BGS*

The two parts of the Balance on Goods and Services BGS are reported below in billions of constant 2004 dollars. The BOT was positive through the 1960s and 1970s but turned negative in the 1980s with imports of oil and labor intensive manufactures. The BOT fell substantially after 1995. The TS has been positive but smaller in magnitude offsetting about 1/4 of the BOT deficit.

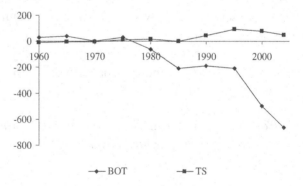

EXAMPLE 1.16   *Seattle Trade Battle*

WTO countries held a meeting Seattle in during December 1999. Major issues were agricultural protection and subsidies in the EU and Japan, labor issues in the LDCs, global environmental agreements, protection of local business services from US multinational firms, and dumping into the US. There were protests in Seattle from a colorful crowd including anti-globalists, protectionist reactionaries, US steelworkers, French farmers, clergy demonstrating for third world debt relief, radical political groups, Industrial Workers of the World, forest activists, and environmentalists.

D.   COMPARATIVE ADVANTAGE AND SPECIALIZATION

The slogan of international economics is specialize and trade. International economics faces arguments of domestic industries seeking protection from imports. Free trade leads to increased international specialization. This section introduces the principle of comparative advantage. Gains from specialization result from trade based on comparative advantage.

EXAMPLE 1.17   *Opening US Trade*

The US economy has become steadily more open to international trade since the 1950s with lower tariffs, more efficient international transport, and improved communication. The trade index $(X+M)$/GDP gauges trade relative to national income. The US has become much more dependent on international markets as the index rose from 7% to 30%.

Absolute versus Comparative Advantage

An absolute advantage in producing a good is lower input per unit of output. Absolute advantage means fewer resources are used to produce a unit of the good. Suppose a country has an absolute advantage in producing both manufactured goods and services It has more capital and more highly trained labor. Should it be totally self sufficient, consuming only its own products and not trading at all?

Comparative advantage is a lower opportunity cost in an activity. Opportunity cost of an activity is the cost opportunity to do something else. Comparative advantage is relative efficiency.

Countries consume more of all products when they specialize and trade according to comparative advantage.

EXAMPLE 1.18   *Regional Trade*

Most trade occurs between countries located close together. About 2% of world trade occurs between the Americas and Japan, and 3% between the Americas and the EU. Another 3% occurs between the EU and Africa. The rest is mostly between neighboring countries where there are low transport costs, cultural ties, and regional trade agreements.

Comparative Advantage

Suppose the inputs it takes to produce a unit of manufactured goods (M) or services (S) in the US and Mexico are:

	US	MX
S	2	3
M	3	4

The US has an absolute advantage in both products since fewer inputs are required to produce a unit of either.

The US is relatively more efficient in S. For the inputs to produce 1 unit of S, 2/3 M could be produced. In Mexico, 3/4 M could be produced. The opportunity cost of producing S is higher in Mexico. The US has the comparative advantage in services.

Competitive forces lead nations toward specialization according to comparative advantage. Global resources are used more efficiently and world output increases with specialization. This idea is one of the oldest in economics.

Comparative advantage abstracts from the details of supply and demand to provide a more fundamental explanation of trade.

The original example of comparative advantage by David Ricardo involves the labor required to produce wine W and cloth C in Portugal and England,

	PORT	ENG
W	80	120
C	90	100

Portugal has the absolute advantage in both goods. With the labor to produce one W, 8/9 C can be produced in Portugal and 6/5 C in England. The opportunity cost of wine is lower in Portugal. Portugal has the comparative advantage in wine.

EXAMPLE 1.19   *China Trade*

China is opening to trade and finance after decades as a closed planned economy. China remains an LDC but foreign investment and export of manufactures are increasing. Exports of labor intensive apparel have increased with imports of textiles and yarns to make cloth. Imports of machinery go into production. The Pacific Rim has become a major part of world production and trade.

Main Exports	Main Imports
Clothing	Chemicals
Textiles	Electrical machinery
Electrical machinery	Textiles
Telecommunication equipment	Machinery
Chemicals	Oil

Comparative advantage predicts the pattern of trade between countries. Firms look for profit opportunities as consumers look for goods and services at lower prices. International trade occurs as these agents act in their own self interest.

No matter how inefficient a country might be in an absolute sense, it has comparative advantage in some activities. Comparative advantage works between nations, regions, states, cities, neighborhoods, and individual people as well.

EXAMPLE 1.20   *Infrastructure and Trade*

Infrastructure includes roads, bridges, utilities, telecommunication, airports, ports, water, and sewage. Infrastructure facilities international trade. Spiros Bougheas, Panicos Demetriades, and Edgar Morgenroth (1999) uncover evidence that better infrastructure lowers transport costs and increases the trade level inside the EU.

Section D Problems

D1. You are a whiz and can clean the bathroom in 15 minutes and the kitchen in 30, while your roommate takes 20 and 45 minutes for the two tasks. Find who has the absolute and comparative advantages.

D2. Determine the absolute and comparative advantage in this example between the US and Canada.

	US	CN
S	2	3
M	3	2

EXAMPLE 1.21   *LDCs and Global Trade*

The US and the EU account for a large share of world output and exports although Asia is growing. LDCs have almost 80% of the world's population but produce only 40% of world output and 2% of exports.

EXAMPLE 1.22   *Fresh Tomato Imports*

The quantity of fresh tomatoes consumed in the US has risen over recent decades. Domestic quantity supplied QS kept up pace with quantity demanded QD until NAFTA in the early 1990s when imports from Mexico began to grow. Tomato prices have been steady. Most US tomatoes are grown in California, Florida, and Texas by migrant Mexican workers.

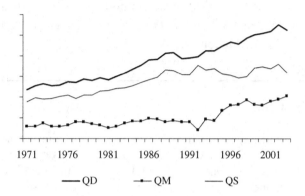

CONCLUSION

International markets adjust to determine trade and prices of traded products. Market fundamentals are critical to anticipate changes in trade and commerce. Consumers enjoy imported goods and services. Firms and industries export, import intermediate products, and face import competition.

Terms

Absolute advantage	Import spending
Arbitrage	International price
Autarky price	Mercantilism
BOT	Normal versus inferior goods
Comparative advantage	Opportunity cost
Diminishing marginal productivity	Specialization
Excess supply	Substitution and income effects
Exchange rates	Transport costs
Export revenue	Price Expectations

MAIN POINTS

- International markets for small countries face world prices.
- International markets for large countries clear at prices where excess demand from importers equals excess supply from exporters.
- Shift in domestic demand or supply affect trade levels.
- The balance of trade equals export revenue minus import spending. A trade-deficit (surplus) means import spending is greater (less) than export revenue.
- A country has a comparative advantage in a product if its opportunity cost of production is low.

REVIEW PROBLEMS

1. Diagram what will happen to the price and quantity of oil traded when OPEC restricts supply with a diagram similar to Figure 1.4.
2. By tradition, Japanese businesses deal only with Japanese banks. As Japanese businesses begin dealing more with foreign banks, show what will happen in the international market for banking services.
3. Illustrate what will happen in the international market for cars as income rises in China.
4. Russia imports wheat. Diagram what will happen in the market for wheat between the US and Russia when Russia has a poor harvest.
5. Illustrate what will happen if the Buy American campaign aimed at US consumers decreases domestic tastes for imported apparel.
6. The US exports business services and is trying to get other nations to lower their protection. Show what will happen in the international market if foreign nations lower protection. Explain what happens to domestic consumers of services.
7. Diagram what will happen in the international market for cars if the US announces a lower tariff on imports that will take effect after one year.
8. Show what will happen in the international car market if technology for auto production improves in the importing countries.
9. Illustrate what will happen in the international market for gold if news of war causes buyers and sellers to expect higher gold prices.
10. Suppose US and Venezuelan demands for steel are approximately the same. The domestic and

foreign autarky prices are $500 and 18,000 bolivars. The exchange rate is bol/$=45. Determine the likely exporter. Illustrate international excess supply and demand when the international price is $475, the volume of trade 100, US production 100, and Venezuelan production 300. Find consumption in each nation.

11. In Problem 10, find US import spending on steel. How many bushels of wheat would the US have to export at $2.50/bu to balance trade? At $2/bu?
12. Explain whether you think a BOT surplus or deficit should be preferred. Should governmental policy help attain this goal?
13. Consider the following pattern of inputs between the US and the EU. Who has the absolute and comparative advantage in each product? Predict the trade pattern.

	US	EU
S	2	3
M	3	4.5

14. Justify your opinion about which products on this list the US has a comparative advantage: oil, insurance, new cars, thread, accounting, textiles, engineering, clothing, olive oil, economic forecasting, chemicals, wheat, telecommunications, warm winter vacations, cool summer vacations, citrus fruits, fast food, architectural design, education, internet service.

READINGS

Jeffrey Schott (1996) *WTO 2000: Setting the Course for World Trade*, Washington: Institute for International Economics. Framework of the WTO.

Kenneth Pomeranz and Steven Topik (1995) *The World that Trade Created: Society, Culture, and the World Economy, 1400 — The Present*, New York: M.E. Sharpe. Lively history.

Khosrow Fatemi, ed. (1996) *International Trade in the 21st Century*, New York: Pergamon. Articles on trade issues.

Lynden Moore (1985) *The Growth and Structure of International Trade since the Second World War*, Sussex: Wheatsheaf Books. Descriptive study.

John Adams (1979) *International Economics: A Self-Teaching Introduction to the Basic Concepts,* Wellesley Hills: Riverdale. Drills on international economics.

Joseph McKinney and Keith Rowley, eds. (1989) *Readings in International Economic Relations*, Champaign: Stipes. Trade policy, international finance, multinational firms.

CHAPTER 2

Gains from Trade

Preview

Topics on the gains from trade are:
- The production possibility frontier
- Gains from trade
- Trade in less developed countries
- Industrial trade policy

INTRODUCTION

Firms and industries are constrained in production by limited labor, capital, and natural resources. These factors of production play a critical role in the pattern of production and trade.

There are different skills of labor. Capital machinery and equipment come in varieties. Natural resources are as different as Kansas farmland, Kuwaiti crude oil, Colombian mountain slopes, and sunny Mediterranean beaches. Technology to combine these imputs into goods and services continually improves.

When prices change, resources move between industries. The limits to what can be produced are described by the production possibilities frontier. If output in an industry increases, resources must come from the rest of the economy. The opportunity cost of a good increases as its output increases.

Consumers choose between available products according to prices, making choices subject to budget constraints. When the relative price of a product increases, consumers choose substitutes. Relative prices determine output through the interaction of supply and demand in the economy.

Goods and services that a country can produce cheaply or better are exported. One measure of gains from trade is whether consumers can afford more of every product. Another measure is social utility. Free trade brings overall gains but adjustments have to be made. Firms expand output in some industries but reduce output in others. Business is risky business. Workers are forced to retrain or relocate.

Trade plays a vital role in development as an engine of growth. The US is a prime example. Cheap agricultural products based on abundant natural resources were exported during early US history. High tariffs on manufactured imports were the main source of government revenue.

A.   THE PRODUCTION FRONTIER AND REAL INCOME

The production possibilities frontier PPF shows the potential to produce and lays the foundation for the gains from trade. This section develops increasing opportunity costs and utility as the gains from trade.

Production in an Economy

Prices and quantities are determined in markets. Prices of the factors of production (labor, capital, natural resources) are determined in factor markets where owners sell to firms. Firms sell outputs to consumers who have earned income supplying their factors of production.

Economic activity is summarized in Figure 2.1. Solid arrows show the flow of goods and services, and dotted arrows factor markets. Payments flow in opposite directions. Some firms sell intermediate products to produce other products. The government hires factors and provides services collecting revenue through taxes.

Figure 2.1 is a flow diagram for an open economy. International economics studies transactions that cross the national boundary. Foreign firms sell to domestic firms, consumers, and government, and buy intermediate inputs from domestic firms. Domestic firms make similar international transactions. Factor owners can supply their labor, capital, and natural resources to foreign firms or governments.

EXAMPLE 2.1   *Expanding Services Output*

Investment in the US since the 1950s has tended toward services. Over half of all investment during the last half of the 20th century went to services, over 70% during the 1970s, and over 90% during the 1980s. About 80% of the stock of capital is in services. Service output has grown to about two thirds of output in developed countries.

Increasing Opportunity Costs

In Figure 2.2 the economy at point C produces 300 units of manufactured goods M and no services S. All resources go to manufacturing with complete specialization. As the economy moves along the PPF toward point B, resources are bid away from manufacturing by higher payments in services. Firms in services hire inputs that are more productive in services production.

The economy reaches B when service output climbs to 50 while output of M drops 275. The *opportunity cost* of the first 50 units of S is the lost 25 units of M. From point C to B, $1/2M$ is given up for every S produced.

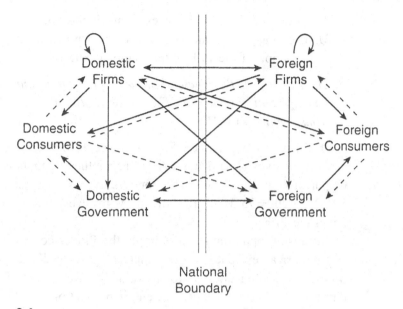

Figure 2.1
Circular Flow of Economic Activity
International economics studies transactions that cross the national boundary.

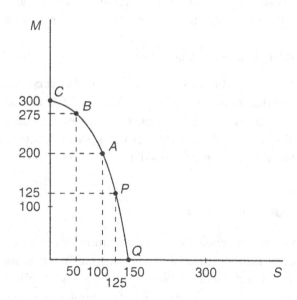

Figure 2.2
Production Frontier with Increasing Cost
Increasing opportunity costs of production imply a concave PPF. The opportunity cost of additional production of S rises from 0.5 between C and B to 5 between P and Q.

The slope of the PPF is an estimate of the opportunity cost of S in terms of M. The tangent at point B estimates how much M an extra unit of S would cost. The slope of the PPF is the marginal rate of transformation (MRT).

The PPF shows the potential of the economy to produce with full employment and efficient production. The slope of the PPF is the marginal rate of transformation (MRT).

If the relative price of S rises, more resources shift into services. The economy moves toward point A where another 50 units of S are produced and output of M drops to 200. The opportunity cost of these additional 50 units of S is $275-200=75$ M, or 1.5 units of M for every unit of S. The MRT increases down the PPF.

Increasing opportunity costs imply the PPF is concave to the origin. Theory and empirical evidence suggest increasing costs due to diminishing marginal productivity. The marginal product or addition to output of an extra unit of input diminishes as more of the input enters production.

Increasing costs of production and a concave PPF are due to diminishing marginal productivity.

Consumers choose a point on the PPF according to demand. The interaction of consumer and producer choice determines prices of the two products. Factor markets in the background determine prices of labor, capital, and natural resources. All markets in the economy are linked in this general equilibrium.

EXAMPLE **2.2**   *Global Growth: Who's Hot*

Yearly growth rates in income per capita vary over time and location. The fastest growing region in the world has been the Pacific Rim with its free trade while the slowest growing region has been Africa due mainly to corrupt governments. NAFTA and the EU have grown steadily. Latin America suffered declines during the 1980s but has rebounded.

Consumer Choice

Consumers choice is pictured with indifference curves. Consumers equally value combinations of M and S along indifference curve I in Figure 2.3. Similarly, consumers equally value any point along indifference curve II. Consumers prefer any point on II to any point on I. Indifference curve III represents a higher level of utility.

In autarky, consumers choose a point on the PPF. Bundles B or P on indifference curve I would be inferior to point A on indifference curve II. Consumers would like to be on indifference curve III but it lies beyond their PPF. The optimal choice is point A where utility is maximized subject to the PPF.

The slope of an indifference curve is the marginal rate of substitution MRS. The MRS indicates how many units of one good consumers are willing to sacrifice for an extra unit of another. At the optimum, the MRS equals the MRT.

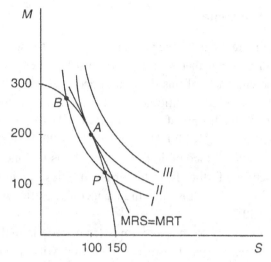

Figure 2.3
Maximizing Utility
Indifference curve I represents a low level of utility, II an intermediate level, and III a high level. Consumers maximize utility subject to the PPF. Point A represents the optimal consumer equilibrium where the MRS equals the MRT.

Consumers value an extra unit of S exactly the same as its opportunity cost of production at point A.

At point B the MRS is greater than the MRT. Consumers value an extra unit of S more than its opportunity cost in production. At point P consumers value an extra unit of M more than its opportunity cost in production.

> *In market equilibrium, the MRS equals the MRT. Markets lead the economy toward this general competitive equilibrium.*

EXAMPLE **2.3**   *Investment Across Countries*

Countries that invest more produce more in the future. Investment relative to output varies across countries. Higher growth can be anticipated in countries that invest a larger percentage of income.

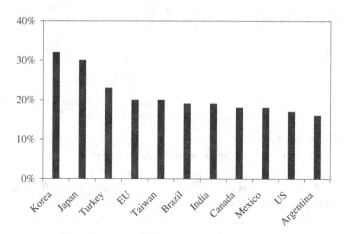

Real Income

In Figure 2.4 the slope at point A equals rise over run or –400/200 = –2. The negative sign indicates that 2 units of M must be given up for the extra unit of S at point A. The endpoints of this domestic price line indicate real income.

The value of national income at point A is 400 M. Consumption is 200 M and 100 S. Each unit of S is valued at 2 M so the 100 S are worth $2 \times 100 = 200$ M. Real income is 200 $M + (2 \times 100\ S) = 400$ M. Real income also equals 200 S.

National income in terms of goods is real income. At the same relative price, a price line farther from the origin implies higher income. The price line at 500 M in Figure 2.4 illustrates higher income. National income is 25% higher at 500 M or 250 S.

One way to measure gains from trade is real income at autarky prices. Trade produces gains if consumers end up with a bundle of goods valued higher at autarky prices. Gains from trade are also indicated by higher utility.

EXAMPLE **2.4**   *Expanding PPF and Specialization*

The US production frontier has expanded as production shifts toward services due to specialization. Patricia Beeson and Michael Bryan (1986) estimate the ratio of services to manufacturing output rose from 2.8 to 3.5 between 1950 and 1985. Output in services rose 252% while manufacturing output rose 178%. The relative price of services rose 26% over the period according to Lynn Brown (1986). DCs are specializing in the production of services as countries with lower production wages specialize in manufacturing.

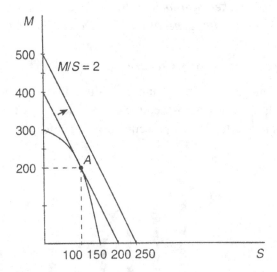

Figure 2.4
Relative Price Lines and Real Income
Production and consumption take place in autarky at point A. The line tangent to the PPF is the relative price line. National income is 400 M or 200 S. The parallel shift in the price line shows an increase in national income.

Section A Problems

A1. Diagram a production possibility frontier with points $(M,S) = (100,0)$, $(90,25)$, $(70,50)$, $(40,75)$ and $(0,100)$. Show the increasing opportunity costs.
A2. From the diagram of A1 *estimate* the MRT when consumption is $(M,S) = (90,25)$. What is the value of consumption in terms of S?
A3. *Estimate* the change in relative price needed to shift consumption from $(90,25)$ to $(40,75)$ along the PPF in A1.

B. SPECIALIZATION AND THE GAINS FROM TRADE

A trading economy opens its markets to international prices that rearrange production. Production of exports expands but import competing industries shrink. This section stresses that specialization and trade lead to overall gains. Real income increases as consumers enjoy increased utility.

International Prices

The supply side of an economy is pictured by its production frontier with efficiency and full employment. The demand side of consumer preferences is summarized by indifference curves. The interaction of supply and demand determines prices, production, consumption, and national income.

There are two ways to increase consumption and income. One is economic growth, the other international specialization and trade.

Consider the economy with the autarky relative price of services $M/S = 2$ at point A (for autarky) in Figure 2.5. The economy produces and consumes 200 M and 100 S. In the international market each unit of services is worth $4M$. If the economy opens to free trade, the higher price is the incentive to export services.

Figure 2.5 shows the international price of $M/S = 4$. The economy is small, not affecting the international price.

Industry responds to the higher price of services through specialization. Capital labor, and natural resources shift into services and output rises to 125 at point P as manufacturing output drops to 125.

EXAMPLE **2.5**   *The Nirvana Economy*

With both NAFTA and the WTO in the 1990s protectionists warned of a giant sucking sound that would drain jobs from the US. Instead, the US economy transformed and specialized. The Associated Press ran a series of articles called "The Nirvana Economy?" during October 1999. One article "Transforming Middletown USA and the Nation" focuses on Muncie, Indiana. Blue collar workers became programmers and switched from making jet parts to semiconductor equipment and software. Jobs in the rust belt switched from manufacturing to services.

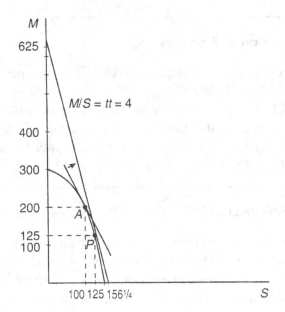

Figure 2.5
International Prices and Specialization
The line $tt=4$ is the international price of services, higher than the domestic relative price. An open economy specializes and moves from A to P.

Real Gains from Trade

In Figure 2.6 the economy takes the terms of trade tt, adjusts production to point P, and trades to the most demanded point T.

Consumer choice determines point T on the highest indifference curve along tt. At point T the marginal rate of substitution along indifference curve III equals the terms of trade. Consumption at T has higher utility than at autarky A.

With trade consumption takes place where the marginal rate of substitution MRS equals the terms of trade tt.

With trade 205 units of M and 105 units of S are consumed. Production takes place at P where $(M,S) = (125,125)$. Exports of services are $125-105 = 20$ S. Imports of manufactures are $205-125 = 80$ M. Trade reflects the terms of trade, $tt = 80/20 = 4$ M/S.

The shaded triangle in Figure 2.6 is the trade triangle. Point T is northeast of point A. Consumers can consume more of every good with trade.

International prices determine the pattern of production and trade for a price taking small open economy.

The *real gains from trade* are found valuing consumption at autarky prices. The autarky relative price of M is 2 from Figure 2.4. Each unit of M consumed is valued at the domestic autarky price of $1/2$ S. With trade in Figure 2.6 the

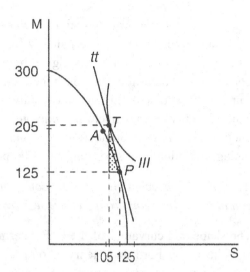

Figure 2.6
Production and Consumption with Trade
With international specialization at P, consumers at point T move to a higher utility
level than in autarky.

value of consumption in terms of services is $105\,S+(205\,M\times 1/2)=207.5\,S$. The
gains from trade are $7.5\,S$. Gains can be also calculated in terms of M.

*The real gains from trade in a commodity show the increased value of
consumption.*

EXAMPLE **2.6**   *From Autarky to Free Trade in Japan*

Before 1858 Japan was an isolated feudal economy with no trade when a fleet
of US warships arrived to pry it open. Over the next 30 years, the level of
trade in Japan increased 70 times according to Richard Huber (1971). Japan
exported silk, tea, copper, dried fish, and coal. Prices of these exports rose by
one third. Japan imported sugar, cotton, and metals as these prices fell 40%.
World prices for these commodities were not affected by Japan's trade. Hubor
estimates national income rose over 50% with free trade. Daniel Bernhofer and
John Brown (2005) estimate a somewhat smaller income gain.

Production Adjustment

Domestic import competing firms face competition when the economy opens to
free trade. Foreign firms have a cost advantage in the products a country imports.
When an economy opens to trade, it adjusts along its PPF toward products with
higher international prices.

The economy in the example exports its high priced services in exchange for
cheap manufactures. Importing firms buy cheap manufactures from abroad to
sell in the domestic market.

Some manufacturing firms go out of business and some workers have to retrain and relocate. Stockholders in the industry lose and only the more efficient firms survive. Adjustment costs are outweighed by the efficiency gains from free trade.

The friction of adjustment can push the economy below its PPF as in Figure 2.7. Resources in manufacturing may not readily transform into services. Labor with specialized skills or manufacturing equipment may not be suitable for service production in services. Some resources may have to relocated. The costs of retraining, retooling, and relocating must be paid.

As firms in an economy open to competition, they adjust to world market conditions. The gains from free trade may involve transition costs.

The shape and curvature of the PPF determines how much outputs and factor prices adjust. Jon Ford and Henry Thompson (1997) find the PPF is relatively flat. Price changes have large effects on output. Complete specialization and industrial shutdowns are likely outcomes of specialization and trade. Input prices also undergo adjustments but outputs adjust more.

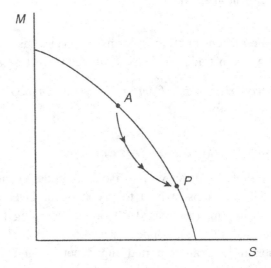

Figure 2.7
Adjustment Frictions
Production may be forced to take a path below the production frontier in its adjustment. These adjustment costs, push the economy below its long run potential.

EXAMPLE 2.7   *Free Trade Fallacy?*

The NAFTA debate brought free trade into the headlines. Ravi Batra (1992) and Batra and Daniel Slotje (1993) present evidence that increased trade since the 1970s caused a decline in US wages. Declining wages were due in part to increased import competition. Sugata Marjit (1994), Farhad Rassekh (1994), and Channing Arndt and Thomas Hertel (1997) disagree that free trade was a fallacy. Free trade may cause wages to fall in high wage countries but investment and training can offset losses.

Section B Problems

B1. Evaluate the real gains from trade in terms of manufactured goods in Figures 2.4 and 2.6.

B2. Starting with Figure 2.4 suppose the terms of trade tt are $0.9\,M$ for every S. Illustrate the specialization.

B3. At $tt=M/S=0.9$ suppose production moves to point B in Figure 2.2. Diagram the trade triangle if 72 units of M are exported. Find consumption with trade.

B4. If the domestic autarky price in Figure 2.2 at point A is 2, find the real gains from trade in terms of S.

EXAMPLE **2.8**   *Compact Pickups*

Compact pickup trucks were first imported to the US from Japan during the late 1960s. Protectionist tariffs increased from 4% to 25% in response. The trucks proved durable and imports increased in spite of the tariff. Robert Feenstra (1988) estimates the consumer gains from imported trucks were about 20% of price. The tariff reduced consumer gains by 2/3, lowered the quality of US produced trucks, and raised prices for US consumers.

C.   TRADE AND GROWTH

International trade is indispensable for raising incomes through economic growth.

Trade Policy and Growth

Economies grow by increasing or improving their capital and labor. Human capital is acquired through education and training. Capital equipment and machinery are accumulated with investment spending. There is little capital in the typical less developed country LDC. Economic growth is a gradual process with no shortcuts.

Growth is pictured by an expanding PPF. A growing economy can produce more of every product.

Trade plays a role in growth. As an economy specializes, workers intensify training to compete in international markets. Export led growth occurs when growth is biased toward its export sector. Policy aimed at pushing the economy toward specialization is export promotion.

Governments of many LDCs have tried import substitution replacing imports with domestically produced goods. The basic motivation is that the economy should provide for itself. Tariffs to protect domestic industry. Protected industries operate inefficiently but survive with subsidies and price supports.

The US imposed high infant industry tariffs after the Great Tariff Debate of 1888. Democratic President Grover Cleveland opposed tariffs. Agriculture favored free trade with Europe. Republican Benjamin Harrison favored tariffs to protect US manufacturing in the North. The Civil War was due in part to high tariffs favoring the industrial North. Cleveland won the popular vote but Harrison won the electoral vote. High tariffs in the 1890s followed. Douglas Irwin (1998) makes the point that protection on iron impeded US industrialization when steel and iron prices were falling. The high tariffs were a drain on the economy.

Figure 2.9 illustrates losses due to import substitution. Suppose the economy is operating with free trade at production point P, specializing and exporting agricultural goods A. Import substitution policy moves the economy toward the autarky point to point IS. The economy trades at the international terms of trade along line tt' parallel to tt.

Consumption with free trade is T and consumption with import substitution T'. Consumers are forced to a lower level of utility and real income falls with import substitution.

The direction of development is determined by the availability of capital, natural resources, and labor. Mineral deposits, fertile land, and climate are critical natural resource inputs. Capital, management, labor, entrepreneurship, and infrastructure are involved in production. Infrastructure refers to roads, telecommunications, police, public health, airports, and sea ports.

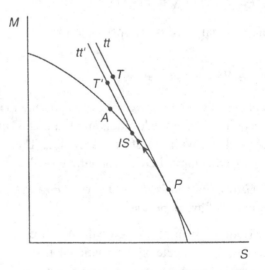

Figure 2.8
Import Substitution
Import substitution encourages the economy to shift from point P to point IS. Trade occurs along the terms of trade line tt'. Consumption point T' is below T with consumers losing utility.

EXAMPLE **2.9**   *Evidence on Trade and Growth*

Countries that specialize and trade grow faster. Zhenhui Xu (1996) presents evidence that increases in exports stimulated output in 17 of 32 LDCs between 1960 and 1990. Wenshwo Fang, Wenrong Liu, and Henry Thompson (2000) examine evidence for Taiwan between 1971 and 1995 and find both imports and exports stimulated output.

Export Led Growth

Figure 2.9 shows economic growth led by export of manufactures. The production frontier expands and favors manufacturing. The terms of trade *tt* determine production for the open economy.

The economy starts at point P and trades to point T. As the economy grows, its potential to produce manufactures grows more rapidly than its potential to produce agriculture A. This bias can be due to international investment, labor skills, or technology.

With growth, the economy produces at point P′ and trades to point T′. Consumers enjoy a higher level of utility and higher real income.

Production frontiers expand faster with export led growth. When an LDC trades freely there is increased incentive and opportunity to expand.

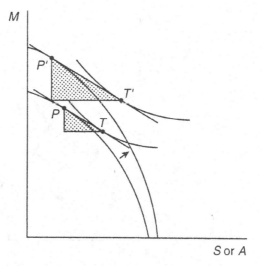

Figure 2.9
Export Led Growth
Concentrating on export production of manufactures can lead to increased potential illustrated by a PPF that expands toward the export.

The developmental gains from trade are the enhanced growth in the production frontier with specialization.

The US provides a classic example of export led growth as agricultural exports to Europe dominated US export revenue during the 1800s.

Growth biased toward export has the potential to lower the price of the exported good when the economy is a major supplier on the international market. Examples may be Chile and copper, Bolivia and tin, Saudi Arabia and oil, South Africa and diamonds, and Colombia and coffee. If the terms of trade fall enough the exporter may end up worse off with *immiserizing growth*.

Figure 2.10 pictures immiserizing growth. Before growth production is point P and consumption point C. With increasing exports, the terms of trade fall to *tt'*. The terms of trade fall to *tt'* with production ending up at P' and consumption at C', below C. Immiserizing growth is not much of a problem in practice.

Foreign Investment and Growth

The potential to specialize is an incentive for investing in exports. LDCs typically depend on DCs for initial investment. For instance, rapid development in the US began with foreign investment in railroads during the early 1800s. Many countries have limited foreign ownership, curtailing multinational investment. Such restrictive policy restricts production potential. Foreign investment leads to expanded export industries and higher income.

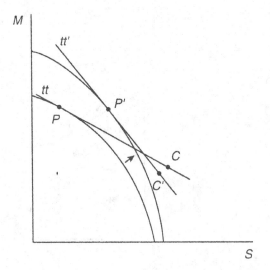

Figure 2.10
Immiserizing Growth
Increased export can lead to a fall in the terms of trade if the economy is a major supplier on the world market. The fall in the terms of trade to *tt'* forces the economy to an inferior bundle at C'.

Robert Lucas (1993) examines the importance of human capital and learning on the job. Workers in fast growing economies quickly learn how to produce more sophisticated products.

EXAMPLE 2.10   *LDCs — DCs — NICs*

LDCs have much lower income per capita and the highest labor growth. DCs specialize in service production. Investment is risky but returns higher in the LDCs. The DCs use energy intensively. Newly industrialized countries NICs produce manufactures for export. Brazil switched from an exporter of agricultural products during the 1970s. Korea was an agricultural economy up to the 1960s but now earns almost all export revenue from manufactures. Mexico slowly emerged as a supplier of manufactures and now earns about half its export revenue from manufactures. The NICs have moderate wages, good infrastructure, and foreign investment.

Less Developed Countries and Newly Industrializing Countries

Less developed countries LDCs are typically agricultural with subsistence farming. Newly industrializing countries NICs rely on manufactured exports. A large share of worldwide assembly line production takes place in NICs. Developed countries DCs have high wages and cannot compete with low manufacturing wages in the NICs.

LDCs would like to become NICs but are often stuck on import substitution. The infrastructure in NICs is generally better than in LDCs.

The DCs protect manufacturing. The LDCs and NICs view this protection as a hindrance to export and growth. Tariffs on DC imports can keep LDCs from selling in the large DC markets. Protection of basic industries such as textiles, apparel, and footwear remains high in the DCs. Protection is high for precisely the products that would be exported by LDCs and NICs.

EXAMPLE 2.11   *Rice and Fertilizer Trade in Vietnam*

Vietnam has a large agricultural sector with poor households. Vietnam liberalized trade in rice and fertilizer between 1993 and 1998 during a period of market reform from socialism. The poverty rate fell by half. Ganesh Seshan (2005) finds that the free trade in rice and fertilizer accounts for about half this reduction in poverty.

Section C Problems

C1. Brazil grows trees and exports plywood. Illustrate export led growth with a PPF.

C2. With growth biased toward manufactures what happens to the opportunity cost of a unit of manufactures when the ratio of outputs is constant? (Hint: The ratio of outputs is constant along ray from the origin.) How does this changing opportunity cost reflect biased growth?

C3. Growth can be unbiased across sectors. Illustrate unbiased growth showing what happens to the level of trade when there is unbiased growth.

EXAMPLE **2.12** *Capital Production and Growth*

Capital machinery and equipment are essential for growth. Countries with abundant productive capital grow faster as Bradford DeLong and Larry Summers (1990) show in a study of 61 countries. Japan invested 12% of its income in new capital between 1965 and 1980 leading to yearly output growth of 5%. At the other extreme Argentina invested only 2% of its income and grew at a 1% rate. Protection of domestic machinery and equipment industries slows economic growth.

D. INDUSTRIAL TRADE POLICY

Industrial trade policy is government effort to manage trade and support favored industries. Exports are encouraged with subsidies, monopoly franchises, free trade zones, and free enterprise zones.

Export Promotion

Governments devise ways to promote exports of favored industries. Import competing industries are sheltered with protection. *Industrial trade policy* is based on political support and contributions to politicians.

A subsidy lowers the cost or increases the revenue of a firm. The simplest export subsidy is a direct payment per unit exported. Other subsidies include reduced taxes, wage subsidies, or waivers on tariffs of imported intermediate goods. Government sponsored research and development R&D can lower cost in export industries. Foreign aid given to poor countries often results in the export of domestically produced goods. The US offers military aid tied to the purchase of US weapons, amounting to subsidies for weapons firms. The Export-Import or Ex-Im Bank of the US Department of Commerce makes loans at low interest rates to exporting firms.

Cost reducing subsidies enable exporting firms to sell at lower prices on international markets. Foreign competing firms view these subsidies as unfair.

Export subsidies aim to make exports cheaper and increase competitiveness of exporting firms.

Export subsidies involve spending tax revenue to make goods cheaper for foreign consumers. Export subsidies tax domestic consumers to subsidize foreign consumers.

EXAMPLE 2.13   *Production Subsidies*

Governments support favored industries with subsidies, direct payments, subsidized loans, and R&D. The OECD estimates the level of subsidies as a percentage of total output across DCs.

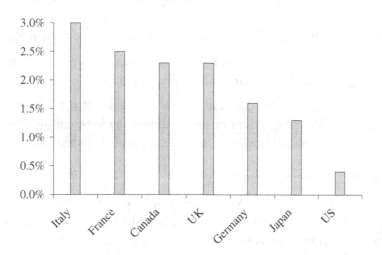

Costs of Export Subsidies

An export subsidy lowers the cost of production. In Figure 2.11 the domestic supply of exports increases from S to S' with the subsidy. At the international

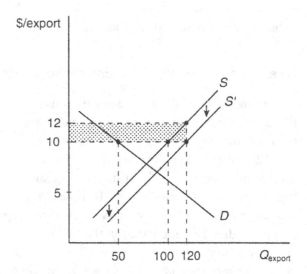

Figure 2.11
Subsidy Burden
A subsidy increases domestic supply from S to S'. At an international price of $10, production increases from 100 to 120 and exports increase from 50 to 70. The subsidy costs domestic taxpayers the shaded rectangle, $2 \times 120 = $240.

price of $10 output increases from 100 to 120 units. Domestic quantity demanded remains at 50. Excess supply increases from 50 to 70, and export revenue from $500 to $700.

The industry benefits from the subsidy but the subsidy does not come from thin air. Taxes are levied to pay the subsidy. A subsidy of $2 per unit, the distance between S and S', costs taxpayers $2 for every unit produced. The tax burden of the subsidy in Figure 2.11 is $240, the shaded rectangle.

Costs as well as benefits of a subsidy have to be considered. The tax burden may outweigh gains to producers.

A subsidy can lead to long run gains if it biases growth toward an industry with rising prices on international markets. Subsidies generally have not been successful, however, in targeting growth industries.

EXAMPLE 2.14   *Wartime Industrial Policy*

During World War II economic policy funnelled resources toward wartime production but disrupted markets. *Business Week* (23 October 1943) reported price ceilings on corn caused shortages of animal feed. Imports of Canadian wheat substituted for the lost corn but these imports displaced iron ore shipping on the Great Lakes. The wheat had been used to produce alcohol and synthetic rubber. To replace the lost wheat, alcohol producers substituted molasses imported from the Caribbean. Those freighters had been carrying petroleum products from the Gulf Coast, leading to petroleum shortages. Meanwhile, hog farmers substituted skim milk for feed, leading to a shortage of adhesives since casein made from skim milk is used in adhesives. Casein then had to be imported from Argentina. Arbitrary trade policy always has such unintended market consequences.

Free Trade Zones and Free Enterprise Zones

Free trade zones FTZs are exempt from tariffs and taxes on foreign investment. FTZs encourage foreign multinational firms for export production. FTZs increase trade by skirting protectionist policy.

FTZs are close to ports and airports. Goods are brought for storage, reshipping, and manufacturing. Costly customs procedures are avoided. US manufacturers began using FTZs during the 1970s based on a law dating to the Smoot-Hawley Act. Jafar Alavi and Henry Thompson (1988) report that 3% of US production occurs inside FTZs. Industries in the US enjoy inverted tariff structures that protect production of intermediate goods. Production in an FTZ avoids the inverted tariff since intermediate goods are imported without duty, assembled, and shipped into the country at the lower tariff rate for finished goods. The first automobile firm to become an FTZ in the US was Honda. All auto plants are now FTZs. Almost all of the goods shipped from FTZs in the US are sent into the country.

Consumers can shop inside a free enterprise zone FEZ where protectionism is relaxed. Goods and services are traded without tariffs, quotas, or customs hassle. Hong Kong and Singapore are FTZs.

"New" Trade Theory

The debate continues over industrial trade policy such as export subsidies, protection, and other measures to manage trade. "New" trade theory is based on imperfect competition and intelligent policy makers aided by economists with sophisticated models who can outguess foreign competition. Good luck.

This "new" trade theory is as old as political economy. The debate over protectionism gave rise to economics. Taxpayers would be unlikely to support export promotion when they realize they are subsidizing some politicians, favored industries, and foreign consumers.

Any policy should have to pass the economic test of costs versus benefits. Economic theory and evidence from history strongly oppose industrial trade policies.

EXAMPLE **2.15**   *Deadly Industrial Trade Policy*

Two instances of import substitution in pharmaceuticals trade led to deadly consequences. US drug companies developed a test for HIV and a method to decontaminate blood for transfusions in 1985. French health officials would not import the products and waited for their Pasteur Institute to develop its own. As a result 1200 hemophiliacs received tainted blood and over 250 died. In another story Japanese government officials would not import a highly reliable vaccine for measles, mumps, and rubella from a US drug company as the Japanese Ministry directed three companies to develop a vaccine. Numerous cases of meningitis, encephalitis, paralysis, brain damage, and death resulted.

Section D Problems

D1. How is a currency devaluation similar to an export subsidy? How is it different?

D2. As a consumer, would you prefer to live inside an FTZ or an FEZ? As a firm, where would you want to locate?

D3. Predict the effects of a subsidy for an import competing industry in a small open economy.

D4. If two trading economies both subsidize their export industries, analyze the possible outcomes.

EXAMPLE **2.16**   *Productivity and Exporting*

> Exporting firms perform better than non-exporters in productivity. Good firms may become exporters, or export competition may make firms better. Andrew Bernard and Bradford Jensen (1998) uncover evidence that good firms in fact become exporters.

EXAMPLE **2.17**   *Gains from Used Car Trade*

> In 1993 Cyprus began to allow the import of Japanese used cars more than two years old. Japan has an excess supply of three year old cars due to a warranty renewal system. Steering wheels are on the right hand side in both countries. Safronis Clerides (2005) finds consumers in Cyprus substituted toward the higher quality used car imports with gains of a few hundred dollars per consumer.

CONCLUSION

International trade leads to overall gains. Regardless, every nation hinders trade with tariffs, quotas, foreign exchange controls, export subsidies, and other trade policy. Protectionism is the oldest topic in economics and remains relevant. "New" trade theory advocates active trade policy but successful practice has yet to emerge. The next chapters analyze the redistribution caused by trade, protection, and industrial trade policy.

Terms

Developmental gains from trade	Indifference curves and utility
Diminishing marginal returns	Industrial trade policy
Diversification	LDCs, DCs, NICs
Domestic relative prices	Marginal productivity
Export promotion	Marginal rate of substitution
FTZs and FEZs	Marginal rate of transformation
Gains from trade	Nominal prices
Human capital	Production possiblity frontier
Immiserizing growth	Subsidies
Import substitution	Terms of trade
Increasing opportunity cost	Trade triangle

MAIN POINTS

- The production possibility frontier illustrates limited resources and increasing opportunity costs. Relative prices determine outputs.
- Specialization and trade allow a country to increase utility, the gains from trade.

- Economic growth is an expanding production frontier. Export led growth focuses on trade and creates higher income.
- Industrial trade policy of export promotion and import substitution that has not proven successful.

REVIEW PROBLEMS

1. If income rises to $220\,S$ in Figure 2.4 with the same relative price of S, find real income in terms of M.

2. From Example 2.1 of the US production frontier, sketch the PPFs and outputs in 1950 and 1986. Discuss the underlying rise in the relative price of services.

3. Sketch a PPF with constant costs of production and maximum manufacturing output of 200. What is the relative price of M along the PPF?

4. Sketch a PPF with increasing costs of production and outputs of 200, 150, 100, 50, and 0 M. Show the opportunity costs. What determines where production takes place?

5. Suppose the domestic autarky relative price $M/S = 1$ and autarky consumption takes place at $(M,S) = (100,100)$. Production with free trade takes place at $(M,S) = (50,160)$ with 50 units exported and 60 units imported. Find the consumption bundle (M,S). Sketch the trade triangle. What are the terms of trade?

6. In the previous problem, find the gains from trade in terms of M and the percentage gains from trade.

7. Illustrate consumer choice and the welfare gains in the previous problem with indifference curves.

8. Comparing unbiased growth with biased growth, which leads to higher gains from trade? Which leads to higher national income?

9. Distinguish between the gains from trade and the developmental gains from trade.

10. There is a large FTZ in McAllen, Texas on the Mexican border. Workers pass freely in both directions. If you were organizing a firm, what would you consider in deciding whether to operate in the FTZ or across the border in Mexico?

11. Suppose the entire state of Texas declares itself an FEZ. What would be the effects? What would be the effects on the rest of the US?

12. The most heavily subsidized industry in developed countries is agriculture. What would happen to the pattern of trade if these agricultural subsidies were eliminated?

READINGS

Robert Barro and Xavier Sala-i-Martin (1999) *Economic Growth*, Cambridge, The MIT Press. Excellent textbook.

Robert Solow (2000) *Growth Theory: An Exposition*, Oxford, Oxford University Press. A concise presentation.

Douglas Irwin (1996) *Against the Tide: An Intellectual History of Free Trade*, Princeton: Princeton University Press. The free trade argument through history.

Peter Morici (1995) Export our way to prosperity, *Foreign Policy,* Winter. How the US has gained from trade.

Paul Krugman (1991) Myths and Realities of US Competitiveness, *Science*, November. Popular misconceptions of competitiveness and trade.

Robert Lawrence (1983) *Can America Compete?* Washington: Brookings Institution. Changing structure of US industry.

Anne Krueger (1984) *Trade and Employment in Developing Nations: Synthesis and Conclusions*, Chicago: University of Chicago Press. Summary of trade and development.

Gerald Meier (1989) *Leading Issues in Economic Development*, Oxford: Oxford University Press. Readings on economic development.

David Landes (1999) *The Wealth and Poverty of Nations*, New York: Norton. A big picture of history and economics.

CHAPTER 3

Protectionism

Preview

The protection of import competing production is a central issue in international economics. This chapter considers:
- Tariffs on imports
- Quotas and other nontariff barriers to imports
- Distortions due to protection
- The political economy of protection

INTRODUCTION

Government protection of domestic industry from foreign competition leads to a debate on free trade. International economists consistently advocate competition and free trade. Protectionism alters the pattern of production and trade, creating gains for some but larger losses for others. Those who enjoy the gains pay the government for protection. Theory and evidence suggest free trade raises income while protection restricts the benefits of specialization and trade.

Tariffs, quotas, and other nontariff barriers are common policies. The owners and workers in the protected industry are organized and willing to lobby and pay politicians. Consumers do not realize the extent of their losses. The benefits of protectionism are concentrated but larger costs are thinly spread.

A. IMPORT TARIFFS

A tariff is a tax on a product imported across a national border. As with every tax, the consumer pays a higher price. Tariffs are inconspicuous, easy to collect, and beneficial for the protected industry. Tariffs remain a popular way for governments to raise revenue.

The US government earned more than half of its revenue from tariffs until 1870, and more than a quarter until the 1920s. Income taxes account for most government revenue in developed countries but LDCs rely on tariffs.

The average tariff rate in the US is about 4%, falling from 15% in the 1950s. This reduction is due to negotiations organized under the General Agreement on Tariffs and Trade GATT and the World Trade Organization WTO. Countries are committed to lowering their protection through GATT. The WTO oversees the agreement and acts as a court for trade disputes.

GATT sprung from the desire to restore international trade following World War II. Average tariffs worldwide have fallen from 40% to below 10%. High tariffs remain on some products in every country and nontariff barriers have become more popular.

The Escape Clause allows the US Congress to enact temporary protection in the "national interest" for an industry that can prove to the International Trade Commission ITC it has been damaged by imports. The vague criterion leads to persistent protectionism.

EXAMPLE 3.1   *US Tariff History*

High tariffs in the 1800s on manufactures reduced income in the agricultural South leading to the Civil War. Slavery was becoming uneconomical due to mechanization. Tariffs provided over a quarter of government revenue until income taxes were made constitutional in the 1920s. The high tariffs of the Smoot-Hawley Act of 1930 stopped international trade and led to the Great Depression as discussed by Alfred Eckels (1998). In 1934 the Reciprocal Trade Agreement Act allowed the President to negotiate tariff reductions and laid the foundation for progress toward free trade. GATT and NAFTA have recently decreased tariffs. The average tariff has steadily declined since World War II but quotas and other nontariff barriers have replaced tariffs to some extent.

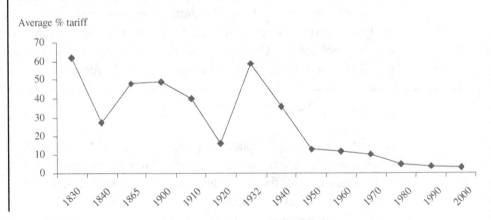

The Cost of a Tariff

Some idea of the price effects of tariffs are in Table 3.1 from Murray Weidenbaum and Michael Munger (1983). The higher price is a windfall for the domestic industry. The government receives revenue by taxing consumers.

Tariffs can be levied on finished products such as cars or they can be hidden in imported intermediate goods such as electric motors. These components and

Table 3.1 Estimated Price Effects of Tariffs

	Free Trade	Protectionism
Cars	$22,500	$30,000
Box of candy	$6	$15
Bluejeans	$45	$54

intermediate products are imported and included in goods labeled "Made in the USA" even if only minimal value is added inside the US.

The effective rate of protection includes protection on intermediate inputs as well as quotas and other nontariff barriers. Quotas are quantitative restrictions on imports. Nontariff barriers are other devices such as voluntary export restraints or numerous regulations that limit imports.

Effective protection is the net percentage of domestic value added shielded by tariffs. *Domestic value added* refers to the share of the price of a final product accounted for by domestic inputs. Domestic value added is V. If P^* is the international price of the finished good and t its tariff rate, the tariff raises price inside the country by $1 + t$.

Domestic producers may use foreign intermediate inputs. Suppose the international price of a shirt is $20 and the tariff on shirts is 10%. A domestic shirt maker imports materials worth $12 to make a $20 shirt, adding domestic value of $8. The $2 tariff protects domestic value added by $2/$8 = 25%. A 5% tariff on imported textiles taxes the shirt maker by $12 \times 0.05 = $.60$, reducing the effective rate of production ERP to ($2.00 - $.60)/$8 = 17.5%$. A tariff of 20% on imported textiles raises their cost by $2.60 = 0.2 \times 12 making the ERP negative: ($2.00 - $2.60)/$8 = -7.5%$.

Estimates of the ERP in Table 2.2 from Alan Deardorff and Robert Stern (1984) compare the US, Japan, and Europe. ERPs are much higher than the average tariff of 4%. These rates have fallen some under WTO and NAFTA but overall tax rate paid by US consumers is well over 5%. Howard Wall (1999) estimates US imports were 26% lower in 1996 than they would have been without protection.

Protectionism costs consumers due to higher prices.

EXAMPLE 3.2   *Tariff Duties Per Capita*

The percentage of tariff free goods has slowly increased as tariff rates have fallen. In the US over 50% of imported goods are duty free. There has been little decline, however, in average duties paid per capita.

Table 3.2 Effective Rates of Protection

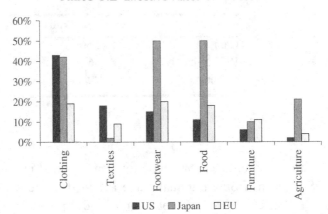

Market Analysis of a Tariff

The effects of a tariff on a domestic market are shown in Figure 3.1. the international price of the manufactured good M is $p^* = \$5$. The economy is a *price taker* in this international market. The difference between quantity demanded 300 and quantity supplied 100 is imports.

A tariff increases the domestic price. With a 20% tariff $t = 0.2$ and the domestic price rises to $\$5 \times 1.2 = \$6$. Consumers respond by switching to substitutes and reducing the quantity demanded to 270. Domestic producers respond with an increase in the quantity supplied to 120. Imports drop to $270 - 120 = 150$.

Tariff revenue for the government is $150, the tariff per unit $\$1 = 0.2p^*$ times the level of imports 150. Tariff revenue in Figure 3.1 is rectangle A.

When the price is $5 the quantity demanded is 300. Consumers back along the demand curve would pay more than $5. The first units of M could be sold at just under $15. At $5 consumers up along the demand curve acquire the good for less than they would be willing to pay. The triangle A + B + C + D + F + G measures the gains to consumers from buying at $5. This triangle is the consumer surplus, below the demand curve and above price. The consumer surplus equals $1/2\ [(\$15 - \$5) \times 300] = \$1500$.

Consumers lose A + B + C + D when the price rises from $5 to $6 with the tariff. This lost consumer surplus is a measure of the loss to consumers. Some consumers are squeezed out of the market and those remaining pay a higher price. With the tariff, consumer surplus falls to area F + G equal to $\frac{1}{2}[(\$15 - \$6) \times 270] = \$1215$. The loss in consumer surplus due to the tariff is $285.

The area above the supply curve and below price measures gains for firms as *producer surplus*. Producers gain area D with the tariff since they sell more

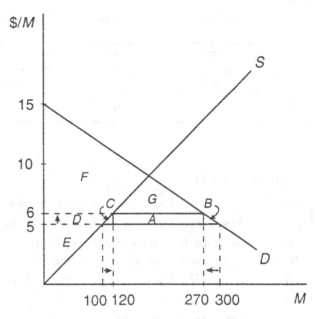

Figure 3.1
Market Effects of a Tariff
A 20% tariff raises the domestic price from the world price of $5 to $6. Imports drop to 150 and the government gets tariff revenue of $150 in area A. Domestic firms enjoy increased producer surplus area D $110. Consumer surplus falls with the tariff by area A + B + C + D = $285. Deadweight loss of the tariff is triangles B + C = $15 + $10 = $25.

goods at a higher price. Firms already in the market enjoy the higher price. Other firms may enter the industry, attracted by the higher price. Firms up along the supply curve sell at a price above what they would be willing to accept. When the price is $5, producer surplus is area E, ½($5 × 100) = $250. When the price rises to $6 with the tariff, producer surplus increases to E + D equal to ½($6 × 120) = $360. The gain in producer surplus area D is $110.

Triangles B and C are the deadweight loss from the tariff, consumer losses not offset by government tariff revenue or producer surplus. Rectangle A of the consumer loss goes to the government as tariff revenue, and D goes to domestic industry. Losses amount to B = $15 plus C = $10, a total deadweight of $25. Table 2.3 summarizes this income redistribution.

Tariffs are taxes that redistribute income and cause net deadweight losses due to inefficiency and price distortion.

Gene Grossman and Jim Levinshon (1989) find evidence that tariffs increase the value of the stocks of firms in protected industries. Shareholders have an interest in keeping their industry protected. There is also some empirical evidence that protection supports wages in protected industries.

Winners from a tariff find it worthwhile to spend money lobbying for protection. Government officials are happy to accept the money and favors. Political support and payoffs explain the bias toward protectionism.

Table 3.3 Income Redistribution from the Tariff in Figure 3.1

Consumer Loss	Producer Gain	Government Revenue	Deadweight Loss
A + B + C + D	D	A	B + C
$285	$110	$15	$15 + $10 = $25

EXAMPLE **3.3**   *Costs of Protection*

Protection for one industry hurts other industries. The following partial list of protected US industries from Gary Hufbauer, Diane Berliner, and Kimberly Elliott (1986) rank industries by yearly cost per job saved. The date of the law, the primary region of the world hurt, the price increase, and the cost per job saved are listed. The US would be better off paying these workers not to work and allowing free trade.

Industry	Year	Region	Price Increase	Cost/Job
Steel	1969	Argentina, Brazil	30%	$750,000
Shipping	1789	Global	60%	$270,000
Dairy	1953	Global	80%	$220,000
Glassware	1922	Europe	19%	$200,000
Ceramic tiles	1930	Brazil, Italy	21%	$135,000
Books	1891	Asia	40%	$100,000
Sugar	1934	Global	30%	$60,000

Protection versus Free Trade

Economists estimate deadweight losses from tariffs. Murray Weidenbaum and Tracy Munger (1983) estimate annual losses of $1200 per capita in the US.

Inefficient production results from tariffs. Valuable labor, capital, and natural resources are wasted making products available at cheaper prices on international markets. Instead of concentrating on profitable export production, the economy produces what it should be importing.

There are also losses due to the lobbying efforts of industry and labor groups. Protected industries employ lobbyists who give money and favors to politicians. It is better to face international competition. Protectionism is a quick fix that undermines economic efficiency.

Tariffs are inefficient but remain part of the political economy because the winners pay politicians. Protection is for sale.

Developed countries have witnessed declines in basic manufacturing industries including iron and steel, footwear, nonferrous metal, and apparel. These industries have been forced to face increasing competition from LDCs and NICs where wages are lower.

Since the 1950s manufacturing employment has dropped from over 1/3 of the US workforce to less than 1/5, while employment in services has risen from 1/2 to 3/4. This trend reflects underlying comparative advantage with increased specialization and trade.

In the DCs manufactures have shifted toward skilled labor. Unskilled wages have fallen, an incentive for education and job training.

President Reagan said he was a free trader but his administration turned the US back toward protectionism. The first President Bush advocated NAFTA, signed by President Clinton. The second Bush imposed large steel tariffs. President Obama imposed tariffs on Chinese products. The oldest issue in economics promises to remain one of the most pressing.

EXAMPLE **3.4**   *NAFTA Tariffs and Wages*

NAFTA eliminated protection between Canada, Mexico, and the US beginning in 1994. Mexican tariffs on US products had dropped from 10% to 2% and US tariffs on Mexican products from 4% to 0.5%. Mexican exports are generally labor intensive but some trade is based on natural resources. Incomes per capita and manufacturing wages are below.

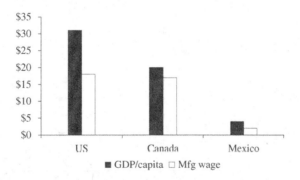

Section A Problems

A1. Suppose a 40% tariff is levied on imported manufactures in Figure 3.1. Find imports, tariff revenue, changes in producer surplus and consumer surplus, and the deadweight loss.

A2. Why is steel protected in the US while toys and games are not?

A3. Explain the negative effective rate of protection on cars.

A4. If demand is less elastic and supply more elastic than in Figure 3.1 explain how producer and consumers surplus would differ.

A5. Show the gains from trade in an import market with total surplus..

A6. Show the gains from trade in an export market.

EXAMPLE 3.5   *Transport Costs*

Transportation costs partly determine trade. Donald Rousslang and Theodore To (1993) find that total transport costs are about as large as tariffs for US imports. For imported consumer products tariff rates are 6%, international freight 3%, and wholesale costs 9% of the final price.

B.   QUOTAS AND NONTARIFF BARRIERS

A quota is a quantitative restriction on the level of imports. If domestic supply or demand change, quotas force adjustment onto price. Other nontariff barriers are similar to quotas.

Market Analysis of a Quota

Figure 3.2 shows a quota of 150 units. The international price is $p^* = \$5$. With no quota 200 units of M are imported. The quota pushes domestic price to where

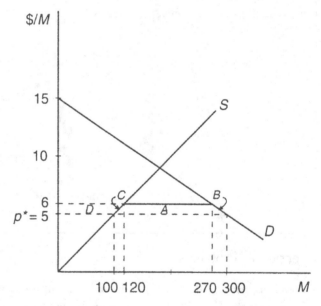

Figure 3.2
Import Quota
A quota of 150 pushes the domestic price up 20% from the world price $5 similar to 20% tariff a but without tariff revenue. The deadweight loss is A + B + C = $175 compared to B + C = $25 for a tariff.

quantity demanded minus quantity supplied is 150. Domestic price rises above the international price leading to inefficient production and costing consumers.

Consumer surplus falls by area A + B + C + D. Producer surplus gains D. Area A + B + C is the deadweight loss from the quota. With the equivalent tariff, the government would gain tariff revenue A.

Foreign exporting firms sell at the higher $6 price. Before the quota, foreign export revenue was $5 × 200 = $1000. With the quota, foreign export revenue falls to $6 × 150 = $900.

The deadweight loss from the quota is $175. Quotas are more costly than tariffs because the deadweight loss is greater. This quota costs the economy $150 compared to the equivalent tariff that costs the economy $25.

Governments may raise revenue auctioning quotas to firms selling at the artificially high domestic price. If foreign firms were forced to bid for the right to export, the government could appropriate A.

EXAMPLE **3.6**   *Costly Quotas*

The cost of a quota can be estimated. David Tarr and Morris Morkre (1987) estimate deadweight losses due to various US quotas are equivalent to a 19% tariff. The average cost to benefit ratio of all quotas is 35 to 1.

Market Adjustments with a Quota

Market adjustments with a quota is forced entirely onto price. Consider increased domestic demand increases as in Figure 3.3. With a quota of 150, increased demand forces price to rise to $7. Imports remain at 15. Domestic production is spurred to 14. Consumers are worse off with the quota than with a traiff.

Quotas do not produce tariff revenue and force all adjustment onto price.

Protected industries prefer quotas when the international price is falling, domestic demand is rising, or domestic supply is falling. In these circumstances the domestic industry maintains output with a quota.

Protected industries would favor tariffs over quotas when the international price rises, domestic demand falls, or domestic supply rises. In these circumstances a quota is nonbinding.

Quotas can lower the quality of domestic output. George Sweeney, Randy Beard, and Henry Thompson (1997) show that a quota lowers domestic quality when there are high quality imports. Domestic firms relax when imports fall, and compete less with quality. Foreign quality rises, another reason to avoid quotas.

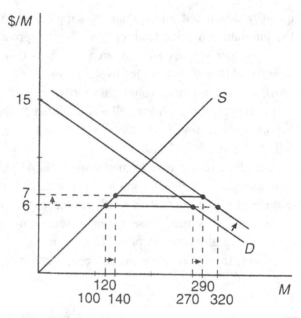

Figure 3.3
Market Adjustment with a Quota
With a quota of 150 an increase in demand forces adjustment onto price. Only 150 units of M can be imported. Price rises from $6 to $7.

EXAMPLE **3.7**   *The Customary Custom Hassle*

The American Association of Exporters and Importers was founded in 1921 to lobby for free trade and offer technical assistance to traders. The AAEI publishes *US Customs House Guide*, a formidable tour of US trade policy. The following tariffs illustrate the custom hassle:

Dolls representing only human beings and parts thereof:

Dolls, whether or not dressed	
Stuffed	12%
Other	12%
Parts and accessories	8%

Dolls dressed or stuffed should be imported in at least two parts. Dolls not representing human beings are another story evidently.

Other Nontariff Barriers

Developed countries are committed to lower tariffs under GATT and the WTO. Regional free trade agreements lower tariffs. Nontariff barriers NTBs are popular because they is difficult to estimate. Governments under pressure for protection devise methods to skirt free trade agreements.

A popular NTB is the voluntary export restraint VER. Japanese car exporters "voluntarily" limit exports to the US under threat of tougher US protection against Japanese imports. The US auto industry puts pressure on the US government, which puts pressure on the Japanese government, which puts pressure on Japanese automakers.

A VER has the same basic effects as a quota discriminates between trading partners. European auto producers benefit from the Japanese VER because they are not subject to quantity restrictions, and prices inside the US increase.

VERs create a cartel for exporters. Japanese automakers restrict competition among themselves in the US market. The VER gives market power to the foreign industry.

Import quality upgrading occurs with a VER or quota. If Japanese automakers agree to export a limited number of cars, they sell higher quality cars.

Japan has recently entered into voluntary import expansion VIE program on US goods. Computer chips, coal, beef, and construction industries in the US have benefited. Such VIE programs discriminate against other countries.

Legal trade restriction are designed to favor domestic firms. Lawyers, doctors, and other professionals restrict practice across borders. Telecommunications and electric utility industries are government franchises protected from foreign competition.

Health laws are selectively applied to foreign goods. Fruits from South America were banned when a test showed evidence of insecticides but foreign exporters suspected contaminated fruits were placed in samples. Other examples are banned British exports of beef during the "mad cow" scare and banned EU imports of genetically engineered crops.

Licensing also restricts competition. Constant monitoring is necessary to ensure fair application of product standards. International law handles claims of unfair trade practice and is a growing legal field.

US firms complain that the transportation industry in Japan does not deliver their goods. The "Buy American" campaign sponsored by US producers tries to prejudice consumers against foreign goods, presumably when they are better or cheaper.

Quotas and other nontariff barriers NTBs are as protectionist as tariffs.

Jong-Wha Lee and Phillip Swagel (1994) examine the causes of NTBs for 41 countries. They find governments tend to protect large declining industries facing import competition. Governments use a combination of tariffs, NTBs, and exchange rate controls.

EXAMPLE **3.8**   *Quota Losses*

Japan's voluntary export restraint VER on car exports to the US raises the price of cars and benefits exporters in other countries. Car firms in Europe enjoy higher export prices. Elias Dinopoulos and Mordechai Kreinin (1988) estimate the average price of a European car sold in the US was 53% higher due to the Japanese VER. Each of the 22,000 jobs saved cost over $300,000. Bee Yan Aw and Mark Roberts (1986) examine US shoe imports and find the quota agreement with Korea and Taiwan resulted in a 12% increase in the price of shoes. Korea and Taiwan shifted to exporting higher quality shoes with more profit per pair.

EXAMPLE 3.9   *Lobby Spending*

The US steel industry has a long history of protection. In 1998 it began a program to buy protection. Four years later President Bush invoked tariffs. Douglas Brook (2005) documents the large sums the steel industry spent on Congress and government regulators.

Section B Problems

B1. Calculate the deadweight loss from the quota after the demand increase in Figure 3.3.

B2. Compare market adjustment with a quota versus a tariff when domestic supply decreases due to a higher wage in a new labor contract.

B3. Compare adjustment with a quota versus a tariff when there is a decrease in demand.

EXAMPLE 3.10   *Winners and Losers with Protection*

The effects of protection vary across industries and regions. Linda Hunter (1990) finds the largest industrial winners in the US are textiles, autos, steel, chemicals, mining, plastics, and utilities, and the largest losers furniture, fixtures, and construction. Regions winning with protection are the Southeast and East with losses spread across the Midwest and West.

C.   PROTECTION AND PRODUCTION

Losses from protection include inefficiency in specialization on the production frontier and restricted consumer choice on the indifference curves.

Tariffs and the Production Frontier

Along the production possibilities frontier PPF in Figure 3.4 there is full employment of all resources. The slope of the PPF is the marginal rate of transformation MRT telling how many units of manufactures M are given up to

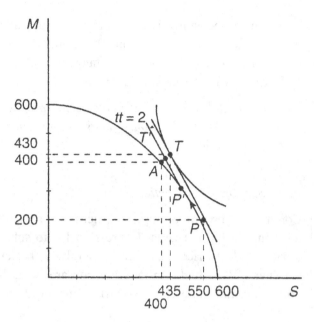

Figure 3.4
Specialization and Trade
A high international price of services induces the economy to specialize at P. Consumers choose point T that maximizes utility along the terms of trade line *tt* = 2. The economy exports 115 units of *S* in exchange for 230 units of *M*. A tariff pushes the economy to P'. Consumers are forced to the lower *tt* line and consumption falls from T to T'.

produce an additional unit of services *S*. As the relative price of services rises, the economy moves toward more *S* and less *M* production.

Without trade, consumers pick the point they most prefer on the PPF. Autarky production and consumption is point A in Figure 3.4. Consumers maximize utility subject to the PPF. In autarky 400 units of each good are produced and consumed.

If the price of services on the international market is higher, the economy opens to trade, specialization moves the economy from A to P. Resources shift to production of *S*. At point P the MRT equals the terms of trade, *tt* = *M/S* = 2.

From P the economy trades at world prices, importing 2 units of *M* per unit of *S* exported. Consumers maximize utility subject to the terms of trade line at T tangent to the indifference curve. The slope of the indifference curve is the marginal rate of substitution MRS. With trade *tt* = MRT at P and *tt* = MRS at T.

More of both goods are consumed at T compared to A. Consumers are better off with higher utility. The indifference curve tangent to T lies above the autarky level of utility at A.

A tariff lowers the relative price of services. Production moves to P'. This production distortion wastes resources on the protected production of *M*.

When the economy is at point P′ it trades along the lower terms of trade line. The new *tt* line from point P′ lies below one from point P. Consumption falls to T′. The indifference curve tangent to *tt′* at T′ lies below the one tangent at T. The tariff reduces consumer utility.

From a global perspective, inefficient production occurs with tariffs that discourage specialization. Tariffs reduce consumption possibilities leading to lower utility.

EXAMPLE **3.11**   *Farm Support as Protection*

Commodity programs support prices for agricultural products. Agricultural lobbying during the Great Depression led to subsidies for milk, sugar, cotton, tobacco, wheat, rice, corn, grain, sorghum, barley, peanuts, and wool. Bruce Gardner (1987) finds imported goods are more likely subsidized. Price supports have the same effect as tariffs, namely higher price, lower imports, and taxed consumers.

Tariffs and the Terms of Trade

A tariff may improve the terms of trade for a country that consumes a large share of the world market. Demand falls when a large country imposes a tariff causing the world price to fall. With better terms of trade, the country imposing the tariff might benefit. In Figure 3.4 the terms of trade could improve enough so the new *tt′* swings beyond T.

Conditions for such an optimal tariff are difficult to find. Even if conditions for are found, it could lead to a tariff war. Other nations retaliate with tariffs of their own, and the conditions that led to the optimal tariff are washed away.

The most famous tariff war occurred during the 1930s when countries raised tariffs to prohibitive levels. The Smoot-Hawley Tariff Act created very high US tariffs. More than 1000 economists protested, inducing a senator to claim that "professors in ivory towers do not make an honest living by sweating". International trade came to a halt, prolonging the Great Depression.

EXAMPLE **3.12**   *Smuggling*

Smuggling is illegal trade aimed at avoiding protection or prohibition. Smuggling is about 10% of international trade. A smuggler considers benefits as well as costs including the probability of being caught and penalized. Smuggling increases international specialization and trade but uses more resources than free trade because the goods are more costly to transport.

Section C Problems

C1. Explain the relative price of S in autarky and with trade for the open economy of Figure 3.4. Illustrate the effects of a tariff.

C2. What will happen if the relative price of S in the world exactly equals the autarky price in Figure 3.4? What would be the effect of a tariff?

EXAMPLE **3.13**   *Tariffs as Tax Surcharges*

Those with lower income pay a higher percentage of their income as tariffs, making tariffs a regressive tax. Basic items such as food, clothing, autos, and shoes cost more because of tariffs. Susan Hickock (1985) estimates the tax burden of tariffs as a percentage of income taxes. Lower income groups pay higher percentage surcharges, up to 40% while high income groups pay less than 10%.

D. POLITICAL ECONOMY OF PROTECTION

Economic arguments against protection are the inefficiency and misallocation of resources. Consumers suffer lost utility. Economists have been making these arguments for 200 years, and business people have pursued gains from trade since the dawn of history. The question is why protection persists.

EXAMPLE **3.14**   *Who is WTO?*

The General Agreement on Tariffs and Trade GATT has lowered protection on manufactures since the end of World War II. Services were added in 1994 but many countries maintain protection of government monopolies in telecommunications, utilities, postal service, banking and finance. The World Trade Organization WTO began in 1993 as the judicial branch deciding damages from complaints about protection.

Rent Seeking Protection

Protected industries and workers pay for protection. Congressional representatives and senators are paid to pass tariffs and nontariff trade barriers. Political contributions are tied to representative voting on tariffs.

Industries hire lobbyists and pay politicians for protection. Union labor groups lobby for protection of their industries. This rent seeking adds to the waste of resources. Representatives trade votes by logrolling to gain support for their tariffs. Politicians may say they are global free traders but they are local protectionists.

Industries lobby to buy tariff protection. Consumers suffer but are disorganized and unable to alter political protectionism.

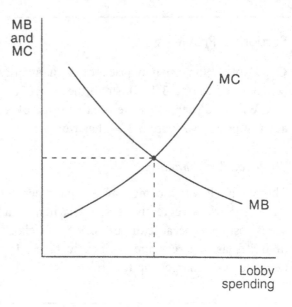

Figure 3.5
Optimal Lobby Spending
The marginal benefit MB to industry of lobbying is the protection of higher tariff rates. The marginal cost MC of lobby spending determines the optimal lobby spending where MC = MB.

The marginal benefit of lobby spending determines the amount spent by industry as shown in Figure 3.5. Every dollar spent creates benefit but marginal benefits diminish. The optimal amount of lobbying occurs where the marginal cost MC of lobbying equals the marginal benefit MB.

Political parties gain support of voters with tariffs. Workers in a protected industry support political candidates who deliver tariff protection for their jobs. Stockholders and local business interests want protection for their investment.

Tariffs create distortions as importing firms are disrupted, prices increase, national income falls, and votes are lost. These losses are the marginal cost MC of lost votes. At a tariff of 5% the MB of an increase in the tariff is greater than the MC. The optimal political tariff is the one that maximizes votes gained by the protectionistic party where MC = MB at a 10% tariff.

Industries lobby and political parties set tariffs according to costs and benefits in the political economy of protection.

EXAMPLE **3.15**   *An Appeal for Protection*

The following appeal might be heard in Congress this week:

Our domestic industry faces unfair foreign competition. They flood the domestic market and steal our customers, killing an important branch of industry. We cannot win this contest. Our workers need tariff protection.

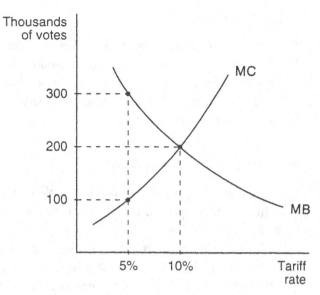

Figure 3.6
Optimizing Votes with a Tariff
A tariff gains votes from those who benefit but loses votes of those who suffer. If the tariff is 5%, the marginal cost MC of an increase in the tariff is 100,000 lost votes while the marginal benefit MB is 300,000 gained votes. The political party has incentive to raise the tariff to 10%.

This appeal is actually a satire by Fredric Bastiat written in the early 1800s. Bastiat favored a prohibitive tariff to shut all "windows, openings, and fissures" to support the domestic candle industry from the foreign rival, the sun!

EXAMPLE 3.16   *Chinese Apparel Quotas*

When apparel manufacturers in China recently faced quotas on their exports to the EU, China retaliated with export taxes. Chinese apparel manufacturers then shifted production to other countries.

Dumping: Unfair Competition?

Industries in the US can file claims of unfair trade competition with the International Trade Commission (ITC). Foreign firms thought to be selling temporarily below cost to drive out competition may face a hearing with the ITC. Subsidies by foreign governments to their export industries are considered unfair even though foreign taxpayers are subsidizing domestic consumers.

The President can award dumping damages and restrictive quotas can be put in place. Since the 1990s there has been a large increase in the volume of claims and value of awards. Dumping typically cannot be proved but dumping awards are made for political reasons.

EXAMPLE 3.17   *Dumping the ITC*

The WTO oversees dumping. Over a thousand dumping cases are filed per year. The ITC makes decisions on alleged dumping based on incomplete evidence. Foreign firms avoid exporting even on rumor of an ITC hearing. Joseph Stiglitz (1997) finds US trade law protectionist. Costly rent seeking adds to the losses as industries spend on lobbying.

Eliminating Import Restrictions

Protectionism distorts international production and wastes resources. Consumers lose due to higher prices. Costs to benefits are estimated and range from 4:1 to 10:1.

Even if consumers were aware of the costs of protection, they would find it difficult to lobby. Industries and labor unions, on the other hand, lobby every day.

The only sure way to remove inequities associated with protectionism is to eliminate it completely. It is constitutionally illegal to tax exports in the US. The bias against export duties in the US dates from colonial days when the King of England kept the export tax revenue from the colonies. Outlawing tariffs would eliminate inefficiency and rent seeking.

The protectionism debate is not new, as this 1696 quote from Charles D'Avenant (*An Essay on the East India Trade*) illustrates:

> "Trade is in its nature free, finds its own channel, and best directs its own course; and all laws to give it rules and directions, and to limit and circumscribe it may serve the particular ends of private men, but are seldom advantages to the public."

The temptation to pursue narrow local interests would be removed if protectionism were illegal. Protection offers temporary remedy but leads to dependence and inefficiency.

Developed countries should lead the way toward increased global efficiency by outlawing import tariffs.

EXAMPLE 3.18   *Union Pocketbook*

Labor unions pursue their goals in trade policy. The AFL-CIO circulates *The Pocketbook Issues* aimed at increased protection. Some of its recommendations are

- Bilateral trade deficit reductions
- Eliminate unfair trade practices
- Domestic content laws
- Policy to process raw products before export
- Increase share of cargo on US merchant ships

Section D Problems

D1. Why are large firms and industries more protected than small ones?

D2. Why might senators favor protectionism less than Congress members? Presidents less than senators?

D3. Some industries claim they must be protected because their products are essential for national defense. If you were president, which products would you allow national defense tariffs?

EXAMPLE 3.19   *Buy American, Regardless*

> The Crafted with Pride in the USA Council promotes domestic products. One large retailer conducted an experiment with identical jeans sold side by side, one "Made in USA" and the other with foreign labels. More of the domestic jeans sold. Surveys have shown that consumers consider country of origin. In the long run, however, quality and price are critical.

EXAMPLE 3.20   *Shrimp Dumping and Soybeans*

> Shrimp is a leading seafood in the US due to efficient farming techniques and global competition. US shrimpers won a dumping case with the ITC in 2004 and were awarded tariffs of 100% on imports. There was no evidence of predatory pricing by exporting Asian countries. The money to pay for the ITC filing came from disaster relief for shrimpers. Congress also awarded the shrimping industry the tariff revenue in violation of WTO rules. The US exports soybeans to Asia for shrimp food, Soybean farmers lobbied to repeal the shrimp tariffs. The only sure winners are lawyers, and government officials receiving lobby payoffs from all sides.

CONCLUSION

Protection is the oldest issue in economics and a vital contemporary issue. Protectionism will continue as long as the benefits to protected industries outweigh the costs of lobbying. In a large economy, protection may affect international prices. The next chapter shows how the terms of trade are determined between large economies, and how tariffs may improve the terms of trade.

Terms

Antiprotection	Production distortion
Deadweight loss	Protection
Dumping	Quality upgrading
Effective protection	Quota license

Fair trade   Quotas
ITC   Rent seeking
Logrolling   Tariffs
Nontariff barrier (NTB)   Voluntary export restraint (VER)

MAIN POINTS

- Tariffs impose deadweight losses that benefit the protected industry at the expense of the economy.
- Quotas and other NTBs have become popular due to the mandated lower tariffs in the WTO.
- Protection shifts production away from export industries and creates efficiency losses.
- Protection occurs when benefits to the protected industry outweigh cost of lobbying. Consumers would benefit from free trade. Antiprotection occurs when industries that export or buy imported intermediate products lobby for free trade.

REVIEW PROBLEMS

1. Problems 1 through 9 are based on the domestic demand $D = 100 - P$ and domestic supply of $S = -10 + P$ for sports shoes. Diagram the domestic market. Find imports if the world price is $30.

2. Suppose a 50% tariff is put on imports at the international price $30. Find and diagram the change in imports.

3. Find the tariff revenue and the deadweight loss with the 50% tariff.

4. Find the *prohibitive tariff rate*.

5. With an international price of $30 suppose a quota of 10 is imposed. Find the domestic price with the quota.

6. Find the total loss with a quota of 10.

7. Find the producer surplus of domestic shoe producers with the quota of 10. Compare it to free trade.

8. Suppose foreign shoe producers voluntarily agree to limit their exports to 30. Find the domestic price with this VER. Compare total losses with the quota of 10.

9. With free trade, suppose all shoe imports come from countries, A and B. Each supplies half of imports. Under political pressure, country A agrees to a VER of 15 units and country B agrees not to increase export. Find the price, imports, and the change in export revenue of both foreign countries.

10. Diagram the PPF of a closed economy where the relative price of manufactures is higher on the international market than at home. In which direction will the economy specialize if it moves to free trade? Describe the direction of trade. Illustrate the effects of a tariff on production.

11. Consider an economy producing services, manufactures, and agricultural goods. Describe its PPF. What determines which goods are imported or exported? What are the effects of protection?

12. If all congressional representatives were elected at the state level rather than from particular districts, explain whether there would be more or less protectionism.

READINGS

Ron Jones and Anne Krueger, eds. (1990) *The Political Economy of International Trade*, London: Blackwell. Readings on the economics of protection.

Forrest Capie (1994) *Tariffs and Growth*, Manchester: Manchester University. History of tariffs from 1850 to 1940.

Gary Clyde Hufbauer and Howard Rosen (1986) *Trade Policy for Troubled Industries*, Washington: Institute for International Economics. Potential of policy for US industry facing foreign competition.

William R. Cline, ed. (1983) *Trade Policy in the 1980s*, Washington: Institute for International Economics. Applied studies of trade policies.

I.M. Destler (1986) *American Trade Politics: System Under Stress*, Washington: Institute for International Economics. Analysis of the domestic politics of US trade policy.

Dominick Salvatore, ed. (1987) *The New Protectionist Threat to World Welfare*, Amsterdam: North-Holland. Studies on policy issues.

Inside US Trade, Inside Washington Publishers, Washington, DC. Weekly newsletter on government trade policy.

Jagdish Bhagwati, *Protectionism* (1988) Cambridge: MIT Press. A lively look at the oldest issue in political economy.

Stephen P. Magee, William A. Brock, and Leslie Young (1989) *Black Hole Tariffs and Endogenous Policy Theory*, Cambridge: Cambridge University Press. Political theory of protection.

Robert Baldwin, ed. (1988) *Trade Policy Issues and Empirical Analysis*, Washington: NBER. Articles on empirical analysis of trade policy.

Martin Wolf (2005) *Why Globalization Works*, Cambridge: Yale University Press. Excellent survey of arguments for free trade.

CHAPTER 4

Terms of Trade

Preview

Large countries can affect international prices. The terms of trade is the relative price of imports in terms of exports. This chapter presents:
- Offer curves and the terms of trade
- Optimal tariffs
- Strategic tariff gains
- Resource depletion and trade

INTRODUCTION

Some countries are large exporters in world markets. Examples are South Africa in diamonds, the US in airplanes, Canada in lumber, Saudi Arabia in oil, Japan in autos, Germany in machinery, and Greece in tourism. Other countries have market power buying imports, the US in oil, Japan in food, Latin America in machinery, and China in cotton. Changes in these countries affect international prices.

When an economy is large, it can affect the international price. Such a country is a price searcher in the international market. If two economies trade two products, the production frontier and preferences of each country determine the terms of trade. Offer curves illustrate this interplay between trading partners.

A tariff that lowers global demand lowers the international price. A large country can impose a tariff to improve its terms of trade. Each country adjusts tariffs resulting in a "game" with the outcome depending on strategies. Game theory predicts what will happen in such tariff games.

There are large international markets in nonrenewable resources such as oil and minerals. Depletion is a critical issue as these markets. Offer curves provide background for international resource markets.

A. OFFER CURVES

Offer curves show how the terms of trade and level of trade are determined. Gains from trade occur when two economies differ in production potential or consumer preference.

Trade Triangles and Offer Curves

Consider the economy in autarky at point A in Figure 4.1. The production frontier and consumer preferences lead to 100 units of each product. Consumer utility is maximized on the highest attainable indifference curve I tangent to the PPF. The autarky relative price at A is the marginal rate of transformation MRT on the PPF and the marginal rate of substitution MRS on the indifference curve.

If the international relative price of services is higher, production shifts toward S. At $M/S = 2$ produces at point P where $(M,S) = (50,135)$. The economy trades along the terms of trade line to the highest indifference curve II at point T where consumption is $(M,S) = (110,105)$. The shaded trade triangle shows exports of 30 S and imports of 60 M.

If the terms of trade improve to $tt = 3$ the economy increases specialization. Production moves to P′ in Figure 4.2 where $(M,S) = (25,145)$. Exports of 35 S are traded for 105 M. More is exported in exchange for increasing imports at the better terms of trade.

Figure 4.3 summarizes this response to better terms of trade. Imports of M and exports of S are plotted on the axes. The ray from the origin represents the terms of trade, the number of imports per unit of export. The trade triangles in Figure 4.1 and 4.2 are in Figure 4.3. Connecting imports and exports leads to the offer curve H.

Every point on the offer curve H represents a potential international equilibrium. Improving terms of trade creates larger gains from trade and expands the volume of trade along the offer curve.

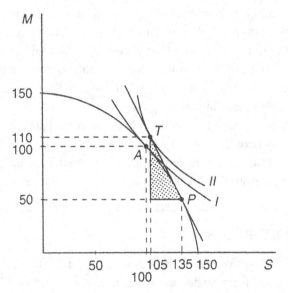

Figure 4.1
International Specialization
When $tt = 2$ the economy specializes in services and consumes at T. The level of trade grows from zero at autarky A to the shaded trade triangle. Consumers increase utility from I to II.

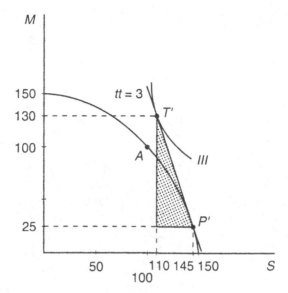

Figure 4.2
Increased International Specialization
If *tt* rises to 3 the economy specializes more in services and consumes at T′. The level
of trade grows with the larger trade triangle. Utility increases to III.

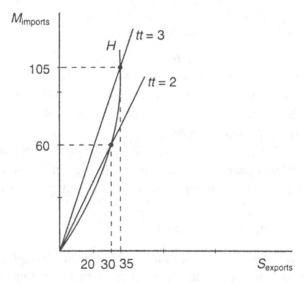

Figure 4.3
Home Offer Curve
The offer curve shows the level of exports and imports for any terms of trade.

*An offer curve shows the exports a country offers depending on the terms of
trade. Consumers enjoy gains from trade moving out the offer curve.*

Figure 4.4 shows the foreign offer curve. The autarky relative price of *S* in the
foreign country is 3. If the terms of trade are 2 the foreign country will specialize
in *M*, exporting 60 *M* in exchange for 30 *S*. At *tt* = 1 the foreign country exports
80 *M* for 80 *S*.

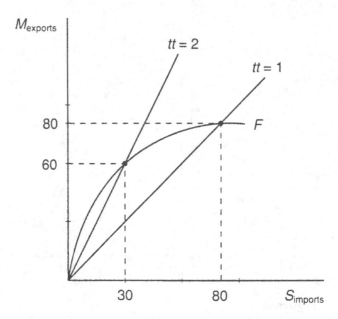

Figure 4.4
Foreign Offer Curve
As the terms of trade improve for the foreign country the level of exported M increases.

EXAMPLE **4.1**   *Trends in the Terms of Trade*

The terms of trade tt for oil importing countries fell during the 1970s due to OPEC oil embargoes but improved after 1980 and especially during the 1990s. Oil prices rose and tt fell during the 2000s with opposite moves during the 2010s before crashing in 2015. Improving tt for DCs is also due to cheaper manufactured imports.

A higher relative price for M induces more specialization and trade for the foreign country. Underlying the foreign offer curve are its PPF and indifference curves. The foreign offer curve bends away from its export axis.

International Terms of Trade

With two countries, home imports equal foreign exports and vice versa at the international equilibrium terms of trade. In Figure 4.4 with $tt = 3$ no trade is offered by the foreign country because its exports are too cheap. In Figure 4.3 with $tt = 1$ no trade is offered by the home country. Autarky prices in each country determine the limits to the terms of trade.

At the equilibrium terms of trade the quantities offered by each country match. Home and foreign offer curves in Figure 4.5 illustrate the international equilibrium.

The terms of trade and the level of trade are determined where offer curves intersect.

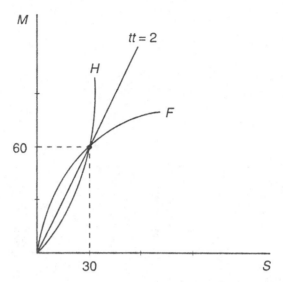

Figure 4.5
International Equilibrium
The terms of trade and level of trade are determined where the home offer curve H meets the foreign offer curve F. At any other terms of trade, exports from one country do not match imports for the other country.

If the international relative price of services were lower at $tt = 1.5$ would be there an international shortage of S. This shortage puts upward pressure on the price of services. There is also a surplus of M putting downward pressure on the price of M. The markets are stable because the terms and level of trade tend toward the equilibrium.

EXAMPLE **4.2**   *The tt of the LDCs*

International trade continues to grow. While trade in the LDCs is increasing, their terms of trade have been falling over recent decades. As nonrenewable resources become scarcer the *tt* for LDCs will improve. LDCs will also become more involved in the production of manufactures improving their terms of trade.

Shifts in the Terms of Trade

Offer curves change with production or preferences. Suppose manufacturing labor unions secure a new contract with higher wages and benefits. Manufactures would become more expensive to produce and the importing home country more open to trade.

Figure 4.6 pictures this expansion of the home offer curve. For each level of imported M, the home country offers more exported S. Expansion of the home

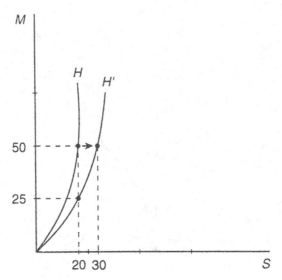

Figure 4.6
An Expanding Home Offer Curve
The home offer curve expands due to higher manufacturing costs or increased demand for M. The economy becomes more open to trade.

offer curve can result from decreased supply of manufactures, increased demand for manufactures, decreased demand for services, or increased supply of services.

The expanded home offer curve will lower the international price of services. In Figure 4.7, the terms of trade *tt* fall for the home country to 1.75. Home exports rise to 40 *S* and imports to 70 *M*. The trade triangles expand.

An expanding offer curve lowers the terms of trade and raises the level of trade.

Improved capability to produce services exports has a similar effect on the home offer curve. With investment or improved production technology in the export industry, the economy becomes more open to trade. The volume of trade increases but the terms of trade decline. Increased efficiency in export industries lead to falling terms of trade, similar to the effect of expanding supply.

A contraction of the offer curve occurs due to falling import demand, reduction in export supply, increased demand for exported products, or increased supply of imported products. The terms of trade improve but the level of trade falls.

EXAMPLE **4.3**   *US Terms of Trade*

The US terms of trade have been fairly constant over the past few decades as prices of imports and exports have both trended upwards. The price of oil can raise import prices but raise cost of production for exports. Other smaller economies specialize in particular products and are more exposed to changes in their terms of trade.

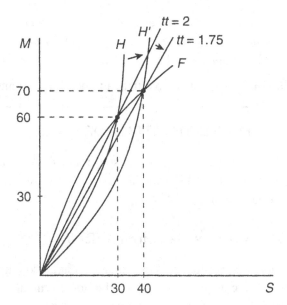

Figure 4.7
An Expanding Offer Curve and the Terms of Trade
A large economy that wants to expand trade will suffer falling terms of trade. As the home offer curve expands from H to H′ the terms of trade fall from 2 to 1.75 while the level of trade increases. Expansion of the offer curve could be due to lower tariffs or increased efficiency in the export industry.

Section A Problems

A1. Sketch the production possibility frontier and community indifference curves that lead to the offer curve in Figure 4.4.

A2. Show the offer curves two countries that would not trade.

A3. Explain why the equilibrium in Figure 4.5 is stable starting with a relative price of 2.5.

A4. Diagram the shift in Figure 4.5 if foreign demand for services decreases. What happens to the terms of trade and level of trade?

A5. Show and explain what happens to the international equilibrium in Figure 4.5 if home export supply increases.

EXAMPLE **4.4**   *Alfred Marshall and the tt*

Alfred Marshall, an English economist at the turn of the 20th century, developed many of the principles of microeconomics. Marshall expanded the frontiers of economic theory and wrote on economic issues. These edited remarks of Marshall (1926) are relevant today.

> *Before another century has passed there may remain only a few areas of rich minerals and raw products. Oil is a good example. With increasing scarcity,*

sellers will have the upper hand in international markets. Acting together, sellers will have a monopoly and restrict output to charge monopoly prices. This situation makes me regard the future of England with grave anxiety.

Discovery of oil in the North Sea turned England into an oil exporter after the 1980s.

B.   TARIFFS AND THE TERMS OF TRADE

When a large country imposes a tariff, demand for the import falls on the international market and the terms of trade improve. As a result a large country can gain with a tariff.

Large Country Gains from a Tariff

Figure 4.8 illustrates the potential of a large country to increase utility with a tariff. Autarky consumption and production occur at point A. With trade the country specializes in services, producing at P and trading up along the terms of trade line to T. Consumers enjoy increased utility with free trade compared to autarky.

A tariff protects domestic manufacturing pushing the economy away from specialization to point P′. The reduced international demand for *M* lowers the price of *M*. The terms of trade improve to *tt′*.

The economy trades up along the new terms of trade line *tt′* from P′. Consumers pick point T′ tangent to the domestic price line including the tariff. Real income and the level of utility increase.

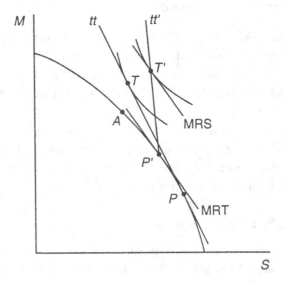

Figure 4.8
Improved Terms of Trade with a Tariff
Autarky production and consumption occur at A. With free trade the economy produces at P and consumes at T with *tt*. A tariff pushes the economy to P′. The relative price of exports rise on the world market to *tt′*. The economy trades up along *tt′* to T′. At P′ and T′, MRT = MRS < *tt′*.

The terms of trade line tt' is not tangent to the PPF at P′ since the tariff drives a wedge between prices inside and outside the country. The relative price of manufactures is higher inside the country.

A large country has the potential to improve its terms of trade with a tariff and raise utility compared to free trade.

EXAMPLE **4.5**   *Britain as a Large Open Economy*

In the early 1800s Britain protected its agriculture with the Corn Laws, tariffs on grain imports. Economists argued that Britain should move to free trade but recognized the terms of trade would fall since Britain was a large economy. Douglas Irwin (1988) finds that lowering tariffs in 1841 from an average of 35% to 25% lowered the terms of trade 3.5% and national income 0.4%. Efficiency gains were outweighed by the falling terms of trade. By the 1880s British tariffs had fallen to 14%. When Europe and the US followed the British example, world specialization and trade increased.

The Optimal Tariff

A large economy gets better terms of trade with a tariff. It can search for the optimal tariff that maximizes utility. A tariff reduces efficiency but improves the terms of trade. The marginal benefits from improved terms of trade may outweigh the marginal costs of lost efficiency.

Exports must be produced but are enjoyed by foreign consumers. Figure 4.9 illustrates trade indifference curves. More exports have to be offset by more imports implying trade indifference curves slope upward. As exports rise, consumers want increasing imports implying trade indifference curves bend away from the export axis.

Trade indifference curve I represents the autarky level of utility. Indifference curve IV is the highest. The large home economy can maximize utility subject to a fixed foreign offer curve. Suppose the home offer curve goes through point FT with free trade. The optimal tariff shrinks the home offer curve to go through the foreign offer curve at point OT. The highest level of utility on indifference curve IV is not attainable.

The optimal tariff maximizes utility subject to a given foreign offer curve.

Quotas and the Terms of Trade

A quota can have the same effect on the terms of trade as a tariff by lowering the demand for imports on the international market. If the home country imposes a quota, its offer curve is horizontal at the quota level. This restricted offer curve results in the same trade equilibrium as a tariff.

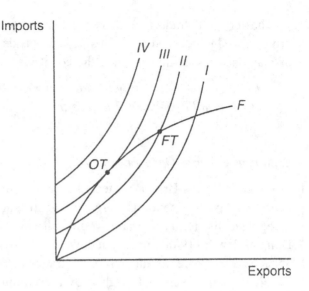

Figure 4.9
Trade Indifference Curves
Trade indifference curves I through IV represent increasing preferences. An optimal tariff shifts the home offer curve through the optimal point OT on the foreign offer curve.

There is no tariff revenue, however. Deadweight losses are higher at the same terms and volume of trade. If market conditions change all adjustment is forced onto price with a quota.

Tariff Wars

If the home country imposes an optimal tariff, the foreign country can retaliate with an optimal tariff of its own. This retaliation shrinks the foreign offer curve F. Foreign consumption of home exports falls, reducing demand and price for home exports. The terms of trade turn against the home country.

In a tariff war, the volume of trade shrinks with each round of tariff retaliation. Figure 4.10 shows a tariff war. The home country fires the opening shot, imposing an optimal tariff based on offer curve F and shrinking its offer curve to H'. The international equilibrium moves from A to B as the terms of trade improve for the home country. The foreign country then imposes an optimal tariff of its own based on home offer curve H'. The foreign offer curve contracts to F', the international equilibrium moves to C, and the terms of trade shift in favor of the foreign country.

The home country then imposes another optimal tariff based on foreign offer curve F' restricting its offer curve to H'', and so on. Tariff wars result in little change in the terms of trade but diminished trade. Trade ceases when prohibitive tariffs are reached.

Optimal tariffs create gains at the expense of trading partners, reduce the level of trade, and invite retaliation.

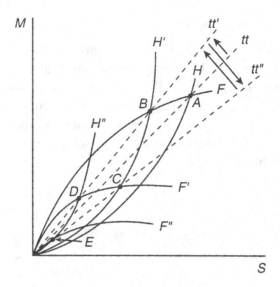

Figure 4.10
A Tariff War
The home country opens the tariff war by imposing a tariff that shifts its offer curve from H to H′ pushing the terms of trade in its favor from *tt* to *tt′* and reducing the level of trade from A to B. The foreign nation retaliates with a tariff improving its terms of trade from *tt′* to *tt″* but lowering the level of trade to C. Subsequent retaliation lowers the level of trade to D and E.

EXAMPLE **4.6**   *Canada/US Tariff Wars*

Canada and the US have regular tariff wars. Alok Bohara, Kishore Gawande, and William Kaempfer (1998) examine the pattern of tariff retaliation from 1868 to 1970. When the US initiated tariffs, Canada reacted with its own tariffs. When Canada initiated tariffs, it backed away and the US did not react. Internal political forces determine tariffs. The Canadian/US Free Trade Agreement and NAFTA have reduced these tariff wars.

Optimal Tariffs in Practice

The WTO dominates international political economy. Nations are committed through the GATT treaty to low tariffs and protection. Any country stepping out of line is noticed by competing industries. These institutional constraints have led to falling tariffs over recent decades.

The economic calculation and rational policy required to apply optimal tariffs do not exist. The political process of protection is anything but scientific. Industries have the incentive to lobby for protection. Tariffs benefit the protected industry that pays politicians protectionist laws.

Small countries have less incentive to impose tariffs. LDCs are exempt from WTO rules and are allowed to set their own tariffs. LDCs are typically small and their optimal tariff is zero.

EXAMPLE **4.7**   *US Energy Imports*

These figures show US consumption and imports of energy during the late 21st century. US energy sources are coal 40%, natural gas 27%, oil 18%, and hydro/nuclear 14%. Due to international environmental agreements, coal will decline and natural gas rise over the coming decades. Alternative backstop energy sources will eventually become economical as the price of nonrenewable fuels rise. Nuclear power is a backstop but with political and waste disposal problems.

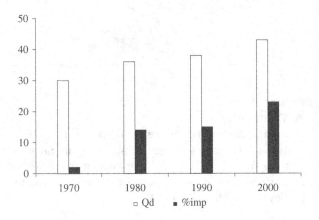

Section B Problems

B1. Illustrate foreign gains from a tariff on services in a production frontier diagram similar to Figure 4.8.

B2. Illustrate how a tariff war could eliminate trade.

B3. What is the analogy between the optimal tariff and the optimal price for a monopoly?

C. TARIFF GAMES

Players in game theory have conflicting goals and make choices based on strategy. The outcome depends on strategies. Board games, cards, and sports are strategic games. This section looks at tariffs as a game between large open economies.

Tariffs in the Prisoner's Dilemma

Consider two countries that trade in a two party game. The two countries can gain with a tariff through improved terms of trade but only at the other's expense.

If one's gains are exactly offset by the other's losses, the game is a zero sum game. Tariffs are a negative sum game since total losses outweigh gains.

Suppose each country decides whether to impose a tariff that lasts one year. The choices are free trade or a 10% tariff. Choices are announced simultaneously.

With free trade income is 100 in each country in the payoff matrix Table 4.1. A tariff increases income by 20% if the other country does not retaliate. A 10% home tariff with no foreign tariff results in home income of 120 but foreign income of 60. The home 20% gain is more than offset by foreign 40% loss.

If the foreign country imposes a tariff and the home country does not retaliate, the foreign country enjoys 120 income while home income falls to 60.

If both nations impose tariffs, they each lose 20% relative to free trade. The outcome with multilateral tariffs is income of 80. Globally, more income is lost with multilateral tariffs than with a single tariff.

If this tariff game is repeated, each country develops a strategy to decide whether to impose a tariff. The nations would be better off if they both choose free trade. If both countries have tariffs it would cost to unilaterally remove a tariff. If one country promises to remove its tariff, the other might not trust it. This situation is similar to a prisoner's dilemma.

In the prisoner's dilemma, police separate two suspected partners in crime and offer each a reduced sentence to squeal on the other. If they both keep quiet they go free. The police offer a reduced sentence for a confession and tell each separately their partner has already confessed. The prisoners may not trust each other. Tariffs are the dominant strategy in Table 4.1 since income with a tariff is larger regardless of the opponent's choice.

Multilateral tariffs are the Nash equilibrium defined by mathematician John Nash when each player makes the best choice given a correct guess about the opponent's choice.

The prisoner's dilemma illustrates why WTO negotiations are crucial to promote free trade. Each country is more willing to lower tariffs if it is assured that the other will do the same.

A country can signal a desire to move to free trade by unilaterally removing its tariff. This means a temporary loss of income if other countries keep their

Table 4.1 Symmetric Negative Sum Tariff Game
(foreign income, home income)

		Home tariff	
		0%	**10%**
Foreign tariff	**0%**	(100, 100)	(60, 120)
	10%	(120, 60)	(80, 80)

tariffs but they might follow suit with free trade. Free trade is an unstable equilibrium due to the temptation to gain at the other's expense.

The persistence of tariffs may be due to the prisoner's dilemma. Free trade is optimal only if every country eliminates tariffs.

EXAMPLE **4.8**   *MFA and the Shirt Off Your Back*

The Multifiber Agreement was an international market sharing plan for textile and apparel trade. The MFA began in 1961 between Japan and the US and grew to encompass a wide range of products and many countries. Its quota schemes were inconsistent with WTO rules. Irene Trela and John Whalley (1995) point out that the quota allocation system awards existing firms. This "lock in" effect makes it difficult for new firms to enter the international market. The end of MFA resulted in increased competition and lower prices.

Equilibrium Tariffs

Each country has an optimal tariff given the other's tariff. The process of arriving at equilibrium tariffs can be pictured by the reaction functions in Figure 4.11.

The home reaction function H shows the optimal home tariff on the horizontal axis for any given foreign tariff. With no foreign tariff the optimal home tariff is 2%. If the foreign tariff is 12% the optimal home tariff is 8%. The foreign reaction function F shows the optimal foreign tariff for any home tariff.

The home reaction function has a positive slope because a higher foreign tariff turns the terms of trade against the home country and requires a higher optimal tariff in response. Where the two reaction functions intersect, there is an international tariff equilibrium at point N. The equilibrium tariffs are 6% and 8%.

Reaction functions shift with changing market conditions. If the home country becomes more efficient producing exports, increased supply drives down the price of home exports. The falling terms of trade shifts the home reaction function to the right. The home country chooses a higher tariff regardless of the foreign tariff. Increased demand for imports in the home country causes a similar shift. Decreased supply of exports or decreased demand for imports would shift the home reaction function left and lower both tariffs.

EXAMPLE **4.9**   *US and Canadian Equilibrium Tariffs*

Canada and the US trade but bicker over tariffs. James Markusen and Randall Wigle (1989) evaluate the impact of free trade between the two countries. Equilibrium tariffs are estimated at 18% for the US and 6% for Canada. Tariffs are lower in the US than in Canada. The countries avoid the prisoner's dilemma in NAFTA.

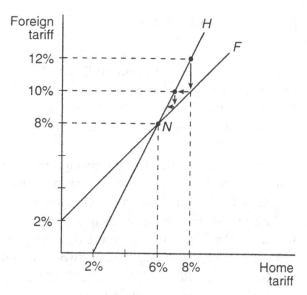

Figure 4.11
Reaction Functions and Equilibrium Tariffs
Each nation reacts to a tariff from the other with its optimal tariff. Starting with a 12% foreign tariff, the home nation sets its tariff at 8%. The foreign nation responds to with 10% tariff. The adjustment process continues until the Nash equilibrium is reached at N with a 6% home tariff and 8% foreign tariff.

EXAMPLE **4.10**   *Shipping Cartel*

Shipping rates for LDCs add to the tariffs they face. The two add about 15% to the price of exports. International shipping prices are controlled by cartels set at "conferences" with rates posted on the internet. Constant monitoring ensures cartel members do not cheat. Such monopolistic practices would be illegal inside the US but are allowed for shipping.

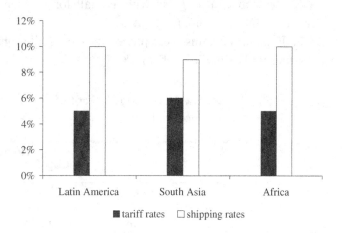

Mixed Strategy Tariff Games

A tariff game may not have an equilibrium. In Table 4.2 a tariff would help the home country given a foreign tariff with home income increasing from 97 to 98. If the foreign country has no tariff, a home tariff could lower home income from 100 to 99. When there is a foreign tariff, a home tariff improves the terms of trade. When there is no foreign tariff, a home tariff has little effect on the terms of trade.

The situation of the foreign country is reverse. A tariff hurts the foreign country if the home country has a tariff. If the home country does not have a tariff, a foreign tariff raises foreign income.

This mixed strategy game has no equilibrium. If the foreign country chooses free trade, the home country would benefit following suit. If the home country picks free trade, the foreign country would benefit with a tariff.

The game in Table 4.2 is called chicken. The countries vacillate between free trade and tariffs. It would be optimal to pick a mixed strategy, randomly choosing free trade versus a tariff.

The outcome of a tariff game depends on payoffs and strategies. A tariff equilibrium can be stable or unstable, and there may be no equilibrium.

EXAMPLE 4.11   *Eliminating Tariffs*

Eliminating tariffs would benefit some countries but hurt others. Alan Deardorff and Robert Stern (1984) estimate exports for industrial countries would rise 4% with worldwide tariff elimination. Incomes would increase slightly, less than 1% in the US. Income in the EU would fall due to falling terms of trade. LDCs would face modest losses. Japan, Australia, and Canada would enjoy small gains.

Section C Problems

C1. Develop a tariff game with a small foreign country and show the optimal tariff for the large home country.

C2. Explain the adjustment process to the equilibrium at point N in Figure 4.11 starting with a home tariff of 4%.

Table 4.2 Mixed Strategy Tariff Game
(foreign income, home income)

		Home tariff	
		0%	**10%**
	0%	(100, 100)	(95, 99)
Foreign tariff			
	10%	(101, 97)	(93, 98)

C3. Show and explain the effect on international equilibrium tariffs of an increase in foreign export supply.

EXAMPLE **4.12**   *Tariffs in the Great Depression*

The cause of the Great Depression was an international tariff war and drastic reductions in the money supply. International trade was decimated by the Smoot-Hawley Tariff Act that raised average US tariffs to 60%. Alfred Eckels (1998) examines the political history. Other countries followed suit with prohibitive tariffs. Republican president Hoover favored the act but Democrat Roosevelt followed with a push for free trade. More recently Republican Reagan advocated free trade but increased protection. Republican Bush favored free trade and initiated NAFTA following Mexico's lead. Democrat Clinton signed NAFTA in spite of labour union opposition. Republican W Bush talked free trade but imposed steel tariffs. Democrat Obama increased tariffs. Both parties say they favor free trade at least if it is "fair" but squirm under the politics of protection. In spite of the melodrama, average tariffs in the US have been declining since 1950 due to GATT and the WTO. Increasing trade continues to stimulate and transform the US economy.

D.   TERMS OF TRADE IN NATURAL RESOURCES

The terms of trade for natural resources are subject to tariffs and trade policies. A basic characteristic of nonrenewable resources is their limited available stock. Renewable resources regenerate depending on the rate of harvest. This section examines the price paths of resources. International resource cartels try to influence their terms of trade.

EXAMPLE **4.13**   *The Fuel Bill*

OPEC tries to increase profit by restricting oil supply to keep the price high. New discoveries and better technology increase supply and lower price. Demand changes with weather and economic activity. The bottom line is that oil prices should climb slowly over coming decades but might move up and down. James Griffin and David Teece (1982) estimate a long term oil import elasticity of 0.73 making oil imports inelastic. Rising oil prices will increase oil import spending, creating trade deficits for oil importers and higher export revenue for oil exporters over the coming decades.

Nonrenewable Resource Prices

Nonrenewable resources loom large in international economics and political relations. The OPEC oil embargo caused economic upheavals during the 1970s and 1980s leading to changes in production and redistribution of income.

Owning a nonrenewable resource is similar to owning other assets such as stocks, bonds, or real estate. An asset produces its rate of return, the ratio of return to asset value,

$$ROR = return/value$$

Money in the bank that pays 3% interest with no inflation, increases purchasing power 3% yearly. A perpetuity bond that pays $50 per year when the rate of return is 3% has a present value of $50/.03 = $1667. The perpetuity bond is equivalent to $1667 in the bank.

An oil well valued at $1 million with return this year of $30,000 has rate of return of 3%. A crucial issue in deciding how much oil to sell this year is what you expect to happen to its price in the future. If the price is $100 per barrel and the rate of return on other assets is 3% an expected price of $103 next year will leave you indifferent between selling oil this year and waiting to sell next year. Oil in the ground is then "money in the bank".

The price of oil is defined by its opportunity cost as an asset. Owners deplete their oil to increase the price of oil at the rate of return on other assets. As the stock of oil is depleted, its price rises and depletion falls.

The rate of return determines the expected price paths for nonrenewable resources. The value of the stock of the resource increases at the rate of return of all assets.

EXAMPLE **4.14**   *Oil Depletion*

During the 1970s OPEC was so successful restricting production that prices jumped from $10 to $120 per barrel, leading to efficient cars and energy conservation. Rising oil prices conserve oil in the ground. Proven oil reserves would last centuries at the current rate of consumption. Rising prices and improved technology will lower consumption. Fossil fuels are the source of mechanical motion and chemical change, a chief input in industry, the material source of energy, and part of everything we do. As we exhaust fuels, it is worthwhile to consider the quantities remaining. This may sound like a contemporary energy economist or environmental activist but it is an abridged quote from Stanley Jevons in his book *The Coal Question* published in 1864.

Abundant fossil fuels are the source of mechanical motion and chemical change, a chief input in industry, the material source of energy, and part of everything we do. As we exhaust the fuels, it is worthwhile to consider the quantities remaining on earth.

Energy Substitutes as Backstop Resources

As the price of a nonrenewable resource rises the incentive to find substitutes increases. Doomsayers base pessimistic predictions of depleted resources on current prices and consumption, disregarding the conservation of markets. As a resource becomes more scarce, its price rises and consumption falls.

Backstop resources are close substitutes that can serve the purpose of a depletable resource. Solar, nuclear, wind, geothermal, natural gas, and coal are backstop resources for oil. Natural gas and coal are nonrenewable fuels with large reserves.

Over time technology for backstop resources improves. OPEC oil embargoes led to accelerated backstop technology.

US energy policy during the oil embargoes encouraged "energy independence" policies of subsidized nuclear investment, increased coal consumption, and increased depletion of US oil reserves. The US has no tariff on oil imports unlike most other importing countries. A strategic oil tariff would improve the terms of the trade and encourage backstop technologies.

EXAMPLE **4.15**   *The Real Price of Oil*

The real price of oil in terms of gold or other goods has been about constant since the 1880s. Increases in demand have been met with increases in supply, leading to increased quantities but steady prices. Reserves of oil increase with the price of oil and improved exploration, drilling, and extraction. The price of oil and related products from fuels to plastics depend on oil prices.

Resource Cartels and the Terms of Trade

Oil producers formed OPEC to improve their terms of trade by restricting exports. Figure 4.12 represents trade between OPEC and OECD. The Organization for Economic Cooperation and Development is a "club" of developed countries. The terms of trade *tt* and volume of trade at point A are based on optimal oil depletion. At point A, the expected return on oil is the same as the expected return on other assets.

Suppose OPEC imposes an output restriction. The OPEC offer curve is cut off at the cartel quota. The terms of trade improve for OPEC to *tt'*. The relative price of oil increases on the international market and the volume of trade falls.

Oil revenue might rise or fall with the quota since exports fall. There is evidence from the OPEC oil embargoes that revenue rose for the first few years but fell back to over a decade.

International cartels find it difficult to agreeing on the quantities each member is allowed to sell under a quota. A surplus occurs in Figure 4.12 at *tt'* if the quota is broken. The high price *tt'* make it tempting to cheat on the cartel.

Cartels in rubber, coffee, tea, bananas, and various minerals have broken down because of the inability to maintain quotas. The war between Iraq and Kuwait stemmed from disagreement over OPEC strategy and their common pool of oil.

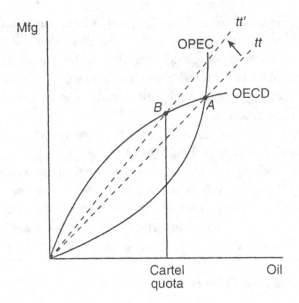

Figure 4.12
Cartel Quota and Price
A cartel quota imposes the terms of trade improve for the cartel but the trade level falls to B. The cartel must maintain restricted output to avoid a surplus on the international market at the high *tt'*.

Oil exporters and importers use economic policy to influence the price of oil. Embargoes, production subsidies, tariffs, subsidized R&D for energy research, auto efficiency standards, and emission standards affect the international oil market. Similar trade policies influence other international resource markets.

EXAMPLE **4.16**   *Global Oil Production*

World oil output has steadily increased over recent decades. Saudi Arabia is the largest single producing country. Other OPEC countries are Iran, Venezuela, Algeria, Indonesia, Iraq, Kuwait, Libya, Nigeria, and the UAE. China, Mexico, and Norway supply about 5% of world output. The US share of world output declined since the 1970s but has recently increased due to hydraulic facturing or fracking.

Rates of Resource Utilization

Resource utilization varies across countries according to their time preferences. LDCs are concerned with the immediate future and want income. This desire for quick income creates a high discount rate and faster resource depletion. Rich DCs discount the future at a lower rate and are more conservative with resources.

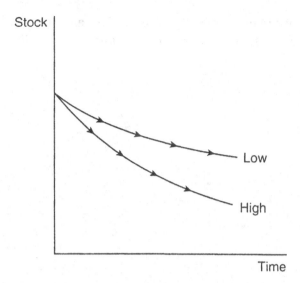

Figure 4.13
Depletable Stocks and Discount Rates
A higher discount rate means quicker depletion of a natural resource.

Figure 4.13 illustrates the depletion of a resource in a country with a high discount rate versus one with a low discount rate. The country with a low discount rate realizes the higher prices in the future and is willing to wait. The country with a high discount rate is not willing to wait. Starting with equal stocks, the country with a higher discount rate depletes its resource faster.

The discount rate of a resource owner determines how quickly the resource will be depleted.

Oil exporters with different discount rates may form a cartel, but importers can impose optimal tariffs in retaliation. The cartel goal is to maximize its wealth by restricting output. Cartels conserve resources by restricting output. Cartel members with high discount rates may agree to slower depletion if subsidized by others in the cartel.

EXAMPLE **4.17**   *The Price of Oil*

The international price of oil will rise as oil is exhausted but reserves have increased with improved technology. Large areas of the world have not been explored due to political and environmental issues. This chart shows the real price per barrel of crude oil in 2003 dollars. Price was stable through the 1950s and 1960s with adequate supplies and refining capacity. The price spikes in the 1970s and 1980s were due to oil embargoes. Prices stabilized from 1986 through 2002 before beginning a climb due to rising world demand, market uncertainty over the Middle East and the war in Iraq, and limited refining capacity. In 2015 the price crashed back below $30.

Section D Problems

D1. The interest rate is 4%, the present value of an oil well is $800,000, and the current price of oil is $100 per barrel. How many barrels are sold this year? How many barrels would be sold at a price of $120?

D2. Find the path of prices over the next 10 years if the present price of oil is $100 and the real rate of return is 6%. Compare this path with the example in the text of a 5% real rate of return.

EXAMPLE **4.18**   *Major Oil Importers*

Japan, the EU, and the US are the major oil importers. The % imports below is the percentage of consumption imported. %OPEC is the percentage of imports from OPEC and %PG is the percentage of oil from the Persian Gulf. The US gets imports from Mexico and Venezuela.

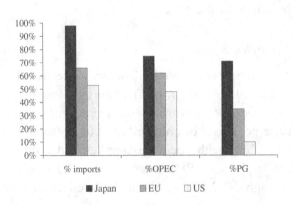

EXAMPLE **4.19**   *Resource Curse?*

Countries with an abundance of natural resources tend not to invest in physical and human capital, relying instead on resource income. This "resource curse" slows economic growth and leaves income in the hands of the resource owners. Thorvaldur Gylfason (2004) examines data across countries and finds that resource rich countries have less trade, foreign investment, income equality, political liberty, education, and investment. Oil exporting Norway is an exception, but was a developed country when oil was discovered. Processing primary products has a positive effect on growth as shown by Zhenhui Xu (2000).

CONCLUSION

The terms of trade contribute to determining national income and utility. Tariffs and other trade policies are not generally successful in improving the terms of trade. Strategic tariff policy assumes the other country is less skillful, a dangerous assumption in any game. Trade policies designed to influence international resource markets result in inefficiencies. In practice, trade policies are unlikely to improve the terms of trade.

Terms

Backstop resource	Optimal tariff
Cartel	Prisoner's dilemma
Discount rate	Real rate of return
Dominant strategy	Repeated games
International equilibrium	Smoot-Hawley Tariff Act
Nash equilibrium	Strategic games
Offer curve	Tariff wars
Optimal depletion rate	Unilateral tariff removal

MAIN POINTS

- The terms of trade are determined between large countries through international supply and demand.
- Tariffs can improve the terms of trade for a large country by decreasing the international demand for its imports. Large countries may maximize utility with optimal tariffs.
- If a country imposes a tariff its trading partner may follow suit leading to a tariff war. The outcome of tariffs games depends on strategies and choices. Free trade is optimal but tariffs may present a prisoner's dilemma.
- The time paths of international prices of nonrenewable resources depend on how resource owners discount the future. Resource cartels conserve resources by restricting depletion.

REVIEW PROBLEMS

1. Show and explain what happens to trade when the utility from imports increases in a large home country.
2. Show and explain what happens when foreign consumers increase their demand for home exports.
3. Show and explain what happens to offer curves with increased investment in the foreign export industry.
4. Show and explain what happens when the foreign country supply of its export falls due to higher input prices.
5. Evaluate what happens if both the home and foreign countries increase import demands.
6. Explain the remark "The 1950s tariff on oil imports was a policy of Drain America First."
7. Suppose the terms of trade start at 1 and are improved 10% by respective tariffs. If each country responds to the other's tariff with a tariff of its own, find what happens to the terms of trade after 5 rounds. Under threat of a trade war, should the home country wait for the foreign country to impose its tariff?
8. Suppose the foreign country has a policy of imposing a 4% tariff regardless of other countries. Diagram its reaction function. Given the home reaction function in Figure 4.11 describe the adjustment process if the home country enters with a tariff of 3%.
9. Illustrate the shift in the foreign reaction function when foreign demand for the home export falls in Figure 4.11. What happens to tariffs?
10. Illustrate a tariff equilibrium with free trade in a payoff table.
11. In Table 4.1 suppose payoffs to both countries with tariffs are ($80, $110). Predict and explain the outcome.
12. Show what happens in Figure 4.12 if OPEC imposes a tariff on manufactures. How is the outcome different from the cartel quota?
13. Why is it easier for cartels to form on primary products like oil, copper and minerals, than on cars or engineering services?
14. The price of oil is $100 per barrel and 80,000 barrels are sold. If the interest rate is 2% find the value of the oil deposit. Explain the difference if the interest rate is 3%.
15. Countries A and B each have oil reserves of 1 billion barrels. Discount rates are 10% for A and 2% for B. How much oil will each country sell this year?

READINGS

Max Corden (1997) *Trade Policy and Economic Welfare*, Oxford: Clarendon Press. Neoclassical analysis of trade policy.

Bernard Hoekman and Michel Kostecki (1995) *The Political Economy of the World Trading System: From GATT to WTO*, Oxford: Oxford University Press. Analysis of different interests at work in evolution of trade agreements.

Robert Barro (1998) *Determinants of Economic Growth*, Cambridge: The MIT Press. Short book on economic growth.

Daniel Verdier (1994) *Democracy and International Trade: Britain, France, and the United States, 1860–1990*. History of the ideals of trade.

International Financial Statistics, Washington: IMF. Trade data, price data, international financial data.

James Griffin and Henry Steele (1986) *Energy Economics and Policy*, New York: Academic Press. Economies of exhaustible resources.

Ferdinand Banks (2004) *Energy Economics*, New York: Springer-Verlag. Sensible book on energy economics.

Farhad Rassekh (2004) The interplay of international trade, economic growth and income convergence: A brief intellectual history of recent developments, *Journal of International Trade and Economic Development*. Excellent review of the theoretical and empirical literature.

PRODUCTION AND TRADE

CHAPTER 5

Constant Cost Production and Trade

Preview

Comparative advantage was discovered over 200 years ago by David Ricardo who sought the causes of trade. Ricardo developed a model of production with constant input per unit of output. Applications of this constant cost model remain useful in economics. This chapter covers:

* Constant cost production and trade
* Gains from trade with constant costs
* Labor productivity and international wages
* Applications of the constant cost model

INTRODUCTION

Mercantilism was a popular economic doctrine that wealth is the stockpile of gold and other assets. Mercantilists in the 1700s believe exports create wealth but imports squander it, and recommend policy to promote exports and restrict imports. Some have a similar view today.

Adam Smith argued against mercantilism pointing out that wealth is the capacity to produce goods and services. Smith advocated specialization based on cost advantage and trading for cheap products on international markets. Smith believed international competition would lead to wealth.

Ricardo realized there are gains from trade even for a country inefficient in producing every product. To enjoy gains from specialization and trade, relative efficiency is sufficient. Every country has comparative advantages in some activities.

Production lies at the heart of trade. In Ricardo's model, labor per unit of output is fixed implying constant opportunity cost. Countries gain through specialization according to comparative or relative efficiency advantage.

This chapter presents fundamental relationships among wages, labor productivity, and exchange rates. Applications and tests of constant cost theory support Ricardo's model. Comparative advantage and the gains from specialization and trade remain sound principles.

A.   CONSTANT OPPORTUNITY COSTS

Labor in the Constant Cost Model

Assume the only input is labor. With fixed the amount of labor required to produce a unit of output does not vary. Suppose the amount of labor it takes to produce a unit of services is 2 and the amount of labor it takes to produce a unit of manufactures is 3,

$$a_{LS} = 2 \quad \text{and} \quad a_{LM} = 3.$$

These labor inputs are the constant cost technology.

Let S be the output of services. Labor employed in services production is $2S$. If output of services is $S = 30$, labor input must be $60 = 2 \times 30$.

Labor is fully employed. The quantity of manufactures is M. If it takes 3 workers to produce a unit of output in manufactures, $3M$ workers are employed in manufacturing. If the total amount of labor L in the entire economy is 120 then

$$L = 120 = 2S + 3M$$

The economy is constrained in the outputs it can produce. With a given labor force and constant labor inputs, more of one output implies less of the other.

EXAMPLE **5.1**   *Labor Productivity*

Capital raises labor productivity. As the ratio of capital to labor K/L in the US grew during the last half of the 20th century, labor input per unit of output fell. Investment is not a fast process but a sure one.

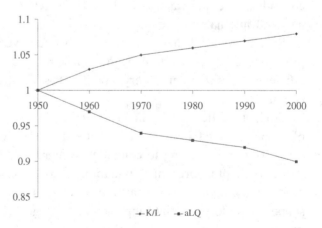

Constant Cost Production Frontier

In Figure 5.1 if the entire labor force worked in manufacturing, service output S would be zero and $120/3 = 40$ units of M could be produced. If no M were produced, $120/2 = 60$ units of S could be produced.

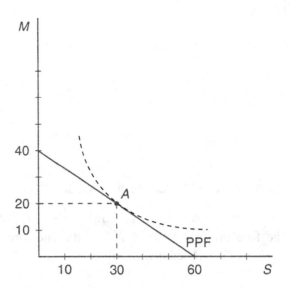

Figure 5.1
Constant Cost Production Frontier
Opportunity cost is constant along the linear PPF. The labor force is $L = 120$ and inputs are $a_{LS} = 2$ and $a_{LM} = 3$. At point A production is $(M,S) = (20,30)$.

Each unit of S costs the same amount of M along the linear PPF. The opportunity cost of one added unit of S in terms of M is constant.

The domestic relative price of services is the PPF slope, $|-40/60| = 2/3$. This much M must be given up to produce one additional unit of S. This constant cost PPF is much simpler than the increasing cost PPF.

Consumers maximize utility subject to the PPF. Consumers choose point A where $M = 20$ and $S = 30$. Consumers then spend half their income on each good. Half the labor force works in each sector.

EXAMPLE **5.2**   *Labor Productivity and Technology*

Improved technology increases labour productivity. A startling example is long distance telephone calls per operator, rising in the US from 64 per day in 1970 to 1300 in 1994. The ten telecommunication firms in the US that cut the most jobs during the 1990s had an increase of 25% in labor productivity due to investment in improved technology.

EXAMPLE **5.3**   *Labor Productivity and Human Capital*

Investment in human capital increases labor productivity. One success story is Japanese manufacturing where labor input per unit of output fell dramatically in the chart between 1955 and 1995.

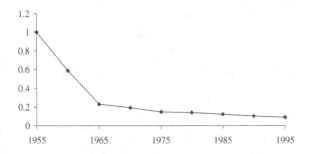

International Differences in Production

The foreign country has unit labor inputs, $a_{LS}^* = 6$ and $a_{LM}^* = 4$. The foreign labor force is $L^* = 240$. The foreign production frontier PPF* is in Figure 5.2. Its endpoints are $60M^*$ and $40S^*$. The equation of the PPF* is

$$L^* = 240 = 6S^* + 4M^*$$

The foreign relative price of services is $M/S = |{-60/40}| = 1.5$.

Foreign labor input requirements are higher for both products, $a_{LS}^* > a_{LS}$ and $a_{LM}^* > a_{LM}$. The home country has an absolute advantage in both products but it pays to specialize and trade.

The relative autarky price of services is higher in the foreign country. The opportunity cost of service production is higher in the foreign country.

If foreign consumers also spend half their income on each good, the foreign labor force will split equally between sectors. Foreign consumption of services is $120/6 = 20$ and consumption of manufactures $120/4 = 30$.

Consumers in each country are constrained to be on their own PPF with no trade. Each economy values goods according to opportunity costs. If consumers were identical in the two countries, they would consume differently because of the different opportunity costs of production.

Figure 5.2 shows autarky production and consumption. The home produces and consumes at point A, the foreign country at A*. Consumers in both countries spend half of their income on each good. Autarky relative prices of services are 2/3 at home and 3/2 abroad.

EXAMPLE 5.4   *High Tech Comparative Advantage*

The relative price of high tech in terms of manufactured goods is M/H. Mordechai Kreinin (1985) compares these opportunity costs for the US, Japan, and Germany during the 1980s. The US had a slight comparative advantage relative to Japan. Both had a comparative advantage over Germany.

	US	Japan	Germany
M/H	0.90	0.95	1.08

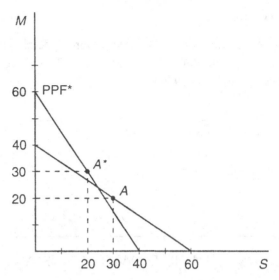

Figure 5.2
Production and Consumption without Trade
Foreign labor inputs are $a_{LS}^* = 6$ and $a_{LM}^* = 4$ with a labor force of 240. Production and consumption in autarky occur at point A in the home country and A^* in the foreign country. Services are cheap in the home country manufactures in the foreign country.

EXAMPLE **5.5**   *International Wage Comparsion*

Countries with low labor costs specialize in labor intensive products with high labor inputs.

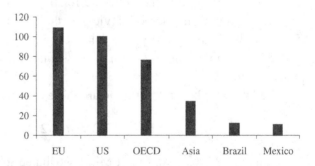

Section A Problems

A1. Draw the PPF for a country with unit labor inputs $a_{LS} = 4$ and $a_{LM} = 5$, and labor force $L = 220$. Find the relative price of S in terms of M.

A2. Draw the PPF with $a_{LS} = 3$, $a_{LM} = 1$, and $L = 60$. Find the relative price of S in terms of M.

EXAMPLE **5.6**   *GDP Shares*

Output in the US has trended toward specialization in services. Services is now the dominant share of the economy. The share of manufacturing in GDP was 20% during the 1980s.

GDP shares

Agriculture, forestry, fishing, mining, utilities, construction	9%
Manufacturing	13%
Services	78%

B.   GAINS FROM TRADE WITH CONSTANT COSTS

Different prices are the stimulus to specialize and trade, leading to efficient global production.

Relative Prices and Specialization

Countries specialize in products with comparative advantage increasing global production. The concepts of lower opportunity cost, relative efficiency, and comparative advantage are equivalent.

With complete specialization in services, the home country moves along its PPF to produce only services. It enjoys gains from trade because services are traded at a price above the domestic relative price of 2/3.

The international price of services is the terms of trade line $tt = 1$ in Figure 5.3. For the home country, the relative price of services must be above 2/3. For the foreign country tt must be less than $M/S = 3/2$ for specialization in manufactures.

The limits to the terms of trade are these minimally acceptable relative prices,

$$3/2 > tt > 2/3.$$

In the late 1700s John Stuart Mill contributed to Ricardo's model by showing how the terms of trade are determined. Mill assumed consumers in both countries spend half their income on each product. The price will be the same in both countries with trade, and trade is balanced.

In Figure 5.3 exports of M from the foreign country are traded for S from the home country at $tt = 1$. The home economy exports 30 units of S and imports 30 units of M. Consumers maximize utility on the terms if trade line tt. The shaded trade triangle in Figure 5.3 shows 30 units of exported S and 30 units of imported M.

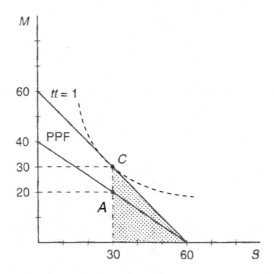

Figure 5.3
The Trade Triangle
Consumers maximize utility on the terms of trade *tt* at $(M,S) = (30,30)$. The shaded trade triangle starts at the point of complete specialization in *S*.

EXAMPLE **5.7**   *Revealed Comparative Advantage*

The US mainly exports high tech manufactures, business services, and some agricultural products. High tech manufactures and business services use relatively high inputs of skilled labor. US import categories are low tech manufactures and some resource products. Input availability explains a good deal of production and trade. David Richardson and Chi Zhang (1999) document the US revealed comparative advantage in high tech products.

More highly valued exports on the world market imply greater gains from trade. Gains from trade are partly due to demand. If home consumers value foreign manufactures more than foreign consumers value home services, the terms of trade would favor the foreign country.

If a large country trades with a small one, trade is thought to benefit the large country. The terms of trade, however, cannot vary much from the large country autarky price. Demand for the small country exports jump substantially.

A small country gains more from trade with terms of trade farther from domestic prices.

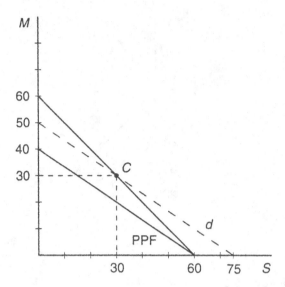

Figure 5.4
Real Gains from Trade
The consumption bundle at C is valued at domestic autarky prices. The domestic price line d is parallel to the PPF. The value of consumption is the endpoint of price line d. Trade creates a gain of 25%.

The Real Gains from Trade

The *real gains from trade* are consumption with trade measured with autarky prices. The real gains from consumption at point C in Figure 5.3 are measured with the domestic autarky price $M/S = 2/3$. This domestic price line d in Figure 5.4 is drawn through C parallel to the PPF.

The value of consumption at C in terms of good M is

$$30M + (2/3 \times 30S) = 30M + 20M = 50M$$

The 30 units of S consumed are worth 20 units of M. Added to the 30 units of M consumed with trade, the real value of consumption is $50M$. The value of autarky consumption in terms of M the endpoint 40 of the M axis on the PPF. The real gain from trade is the difference, $10M$ equal to a 25% increase.

In the foreign country there are also real gains from trade. Specialization pushes it into the production of manufactures. There are only two countries in the world and home imports equal foreign exports.

EXAMPLE **5.8**   *The Capital, Labor, and Land of Ricardo*

Andrea Maneschi (1992) points out that Ricardo relied on models with land and capital along with labor to develop economic concepts. Tariff disputes between workers, landowners, and manufacturing capitalists were a major topic in political economy during the late 1700s when Ricardo wrote economics. Not much has changed since then.

EXAMPLE 5.9   *Iron and Steel Labor Inputs*

During the 1970s Japan switched from a large importer of iron and steel to a large exporter while the US and the UK became net importers. Investment in Japan led to a decrease in unit labor inputs and lower production costs. Mordechai Kreinin (1984) reports these decreases in unit labor inputs between 1964 and 1984 as the US and UK lost their comparative advantages to Japan.

	US	UK	France	Germany	Japan
a_{Li}	−16%	−16%	−55%	−56%	−72%

Section B Problems

B1. Diagram the foreign country in the example of real gains from trade. Show production point P^*, the terms of trade line tt, consumption C^*, and the trade triangle. Find the gains from trade in terms of its export S.

B2. Suppose the home country is characterized by $a_{LM} = 4$ and $a_{LS} = 5$ and the foreign country by $a_{LM}^* = 5$ and $a_{LS}^* = 6$. Which country has the comparative advantage in S? Find autarky relative prices of S in both countries and the limits to the terms of trade.

EXAMPLE 5.10   *Wages and Labor Costs around the Pacific Rim*

Wages and labor inputs determine the labor cost of manufacturing. Susan Hickock and James Orr (1989) report a comparison of manufacturing labor costs around the Pacific Rim. US labor inputs are lower but the US has a difficult time competing due to high wages.

	wages	a_{LM}	unit labor cost
Thailand	$0.86	8.3	$7.14
Taiwan	$2.71	3.8	$10.30
South Korea	$2.65	4.3	$10.84
US	$13.90	1	$13.90

C.   EXTENDING CONSTANT COST TRADE THEORY

For trade to occur, wages and the exchange rate are constrained to limits set by productivities of trading partners. Constant cost trade theory extends to many products and many countries.

Labor Productivity and Wages

Trade changes product prices that influence factor prices. Economic profit in a competitive industry is zero due to free entry and exit of firms. Accounting profit may be positive but there is no excess profit. The price of a good in competition is its average cost, $P = AC$.

With specialization, the price of services is its average cost in the home country,

$$P_S = AC_S = wa_{LS}$$

The dollar price of manufactures produced in the foreign country depends on the foreign wage, foreign unit labor input, and the exchange rate e = \$/peso,

$$P_M = ew^* a_{LM}^*$$

The terms of trade tt is the ratio of the two dollar prices from the countries of origin,

$$tt = P_S/P_M = wa_{LS}/ew^* a_{LM}^*.$$

The relative home wage can be increased through labor productivity or the terms of trade, $w/ew^* = (a_{LM}^*/a_{LS})tt$.

Changing productivity affects relative wages. Suppose home labor becomes more productive with a_{LS} falling. Less home labor is required per unit of service output. For given tt the home relative wage rises. The quality and quantity of other inputs directly affect labor productivity. With better machines and training, labor will be more productive. Investment in physical capital and human capital is required to increase labor productivity. The home wage then increases relative to the foreign wage.

If the terms of trade improve for the home country, services become more valuable and the home relative wage rises. The terms of trade depend partly on demand in the two countries. A country that increases its demand for foreign products will suffer a lower wage. When demand for Japanese manufactures rose in the US during the 1970s and 80s the terms of trade worsened for the US and wages fell.

Higher productivity and better terms of trade increase relative wages.

EXAMPLE 5.11   *Wages, Productivity, and Trade*

Lower relative costs are associated with exports. Countries with low wages also have low labor productivity. Steve Golub (1995) tests the relationship between relative labor costs and bilateral trade flows across pairs of countries. As an example in 1990 wages and labor productivity in Malaysia were both 15% of US levels implying similar labor costs.

Exchange Rates and Wages

For the home economy to export services, the price of services must be lower at home than abroad. The price of services produced at home depends on the home wage and labor productivity, $P_S = wa_{LS}$. The dollar price of foreign labor is ew^*. The dollar price of services produced in the foreign country is $eP_S = ew^*a_{LS}^*$.

For the home country to export services, the dollar price of services produced at home must less than the foreign country, $wa_{LS} < ew^*/a_{LS}^*$. Solving for the exhange rate e,

$$e > wa_{LS}/w^*a_{LS}^*$$

For the foreign country to export manufactures, the dollar price of manufactures produced in the foreign country $ew^*a_{LM}^*$ must be less than the domestic price wa_{LM}, implying

$$wa_{LM}/w^*a_{LM}^* > e$$

The exchange rate is then bounded according to

$$wa_{LM}/w^*a_{LM}^* > e > wa_{LS}/w^*a_{LS}^*.$$

Figure 5.5 illustrates these limits to the exchange rate. For a given exchange rate, the wage can be only so high for the economy to export. If the wage rises too far, the economy loses its cost advantage. The home wage is also limited by labor productivity relative to the foreign country. Given the gains from trade there is little reason to worry about the exchange rate that will find the level where trade is possible.

The wage is constrained by the foreign wage, the exchange rate, and labor productivity.

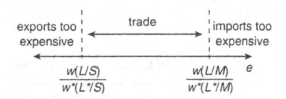

Figure 5.5
Limits to the Exchange Rate
If the exchange rates is too low, exports will cost too much abroad. If e is too high imports will cost too much. This limited range of e is required for trade.

EXAMPLE **5.12**   *Wages and the Exchange Rate*

Dollar appreciation makes US exports more expensive abroad, lowers US exports, and could lower wages as a result. Baekin Cha and Daniel Himarios (1995) find dollar appreciation during the mid-1980s reduced wage growth but the subsequent depreciation had little effect. Between 1971 and 1988, the exchange rate affected wages even for construction and domestic services industries.

Trade with Many Products

The three major categories of output are services S, manufactures M, and agriculture A. Consider the unit labor inputs in Table 5.1. The opportunity cost of one unit of M in the home country is either $3/2$ S or $3/4$ A.

Home services input relative to foreign input is $a_{LS}/a_{LS}^* = 2/3$. It takes $2/3$ of a worker at home to produce as much service output as 1 foreign worker. In manufacturing, it takes $3/4$ of a home worker to match 1 foreign worker, and in agriculture it takes 2.

The home economy has a comparative advantage in services since home labor is relatively efficient in that activity. The foreign country has a comparative advantage in agriculture. Manufactures are between services and agriculture, and could be exported by either country.

Figure 5.6 illustrates the home PPF with labor endowment of 120. In autarky, domestic consumers determine production and consumption at point A. Note 22 units of S and 10 units of A are produced, requiring $2 \times 22 = 44$ workers in and $4 \times 10 = 40$ workers in A. This leaves $120 - 84 = 36$ workers for M to produce $36/3 = 12$ units.

With specialization the home country drops agriculture and moves to point P. Suppose manufactures are not traded and output remains at 12. Service output rises to $84/2 = 42$ with the added 40 workers from agriculture. If the terms of trade are 1 unit of A for each exported unit of S, the economy could trade 15 units of S and consume $(M,S,A) = (12,27,15)$.

With many products, each country exports near the end of its labor productivity ranking.

Table 5.1 Unit Labor Inputs with Three Products

	a_{LS}	a_{LM}	a_{LA}
Home	2	3	4
Foreign	3	4	2

S = services; M = manufactures; A = agriculture.

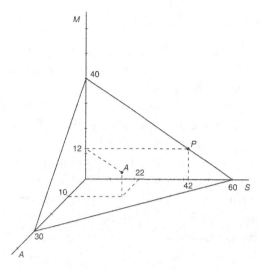

Figure 5.6
The PPF with Three Goods
Labor inputs are in Table 5.1 and L = 120. With three goods, the production frontier
is a triangle. Autarky production and consumption occur at point A where $(M,S,A) =$
(12,22,10). With complete specialization the economy moves to point P where (M,S,A)
= (12,42,0). Trading services for agriculture moves consumption beyond the PPF.

EXAMPLE **5.13**   *US Services Trade*

Major categories of US trade in services are below. Travel is a largest single
category. The US spends more than the rest of the world on freight. Royalties
are important in WTO negotiations. Affiliated services are transactions between
MNF branch firms. Education of foreign students in US universities is growing
as are financial services exports.

	Exports	Imports
Travel	29%	34%
Passenger fares	8%	12%
Freight	4%	12%
Royalties	15%	7%
Affiliated services	11%	12%
Education	4%	1%
Financial services	6%	2%
Insurance	1%	4%
Telecommunications	2%	5%
Construction, engineering	2%	1%

Trade with Many Countries

The constant cost trade model can be applied to many countries. The opportunity cost of a good can be found from labor inputs. Countries with a low opportunity cost export that product.

To illustrate, suppose there are three countries with the labor inputs for M and S in Table 5.2. The relative price of services is $2/3M$ in country 1, $3/4M$ in country 2, and $4/3M$ in country 3.

Country 1 has the lowest opportunity cost and will export services. Country 3 has the lowest opportunity cost and will export M. Country 2 has an intermediate position and the terms of trade will determine trade in country 2. If $tt > 3/4$ country 2 will export services. The limits to the terms of trade come from the extreme countries,

$$4/3 > tt > 2/3.$$

With many goods and many countries, unit labor input rankings can indicate which goods are exported. Table 5.3 illustrates three goods and three countries. The labor input ranking between countries 1 and 2 in each of the goods is

$$(4/2)_A > (3/4)_M > (2/3)_S$$

Country 1 will export S to country 2 in exchange for A. Between countries 2 and 3,

$$(4/2)_M > (3/4)_S > (2/3)_A$$

Country 2 will export A to country 3 in exchange for M. Finally, comparing inputs between countries 1 and 3,

$$(3/2)_M > (4/3)_A > (2/4)_S$$

Table 5.2 Unit Labor Inputs with Three Countries

	a_{LS}	a_{LM}
Country 1	2	3
Country 2	3	4
Country 3	4	3

Table 5.3 Unit Labor Inputs, 3 Countries and 3 Goods

	a_{LS}	a_{LM}	a_{LA}
Country 1	2	3	4
Country 2	3	4	2
Country 3	4	2	3

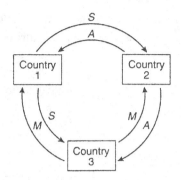

Figure 5.7
Trade with Three Countries and Three Goods
Country 1 has a comparative advantage in S relative to the other countries, country 2 in A, and country 3 in M.

Country 1 will export S to country 3 in exchange for M. Country 1 specializes in S, country 2 specializes in A, and country 3 specializes in M *as* illustrated in Figure 5.7.

There will always be products in which every country has comparative advantage.

EXAMPLE 5.14   *Labor Productivity and R&D*

Research and development R&D can lower unit labor inputs and raise wage. Countries that spend more on R&D enjoy increased labor productivity and higher wages. Almost all R&D takes place in the DCs. Japan's share of world R&D spending has increased while the EU share has remained about constant and the US share has decreased during recent decades.

Section C Problems

C1. Suppose labor inputs are $a_{LM}{}^* = 5$, $a_{LA}{}^* = 3$, $a_{LM} = 2$, and $a_{LA} = 3$. Find the international specialization. Find the relative wage w/ew^* if the terms of trade are 1.
C2. Find the limits to the exchange rate with the labor inputs in the previous problem when $w = \$10$ and $w^* = 1000$ pesos.
C3. If $w = \$16$, $e = \$/\pounds = 1.2$ and $w^* = \pounds 10$ find dollar prices of the three goods using the labor inputs in Table 5.1. Predict the pattern of trade.
C4. Diagram PPF* with the labor inputs in Table 5.1 and $L^* = 228$.

EXAMPLE 5.15   *International Wage Differences*

Assembly line wages vary across countries. Firms considering where to locate production also consider transport costs, local taxes, local work habits, and infrastructure but wage differences can be overwhelming. The three highest and three lowest wage countries during 2000 are listed below.

Norway	$18.90
Switzerland	$18.10
Germany	$18.00
Hungary	$1.20
India	$0.40
Turkey	$0.40

D.   APPLIED CONSTANT COST TRADE THEORY

This section reviews applications and tests of the constant cost model of production and trade.

Improved Technology and Labor Growth

Improved technology is illustrated by decreasing unit labor inputs. When a_{LS} decreases from 2 to 1.5, the PPF in Figure 5.1 expands to PPF′ in Figure 5.8,

$$L = 120 = 1.5S + 3M$$

Total potential output in services is $120/1.5 = 80$. More of both goods can be produced with the improved technology in one sector. The domestic relative price of services falls to $|{-}40/80| = \frac{1}{2}$.

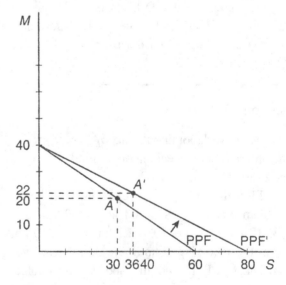

Figure 5.8
Improved Technology in Service Production
If a_{LS} falls from 2 to 1.5 the maximum point along the S axis shifts to $120/1.5 = 80$. The economy is able to produce higher combinations of both goods. Production could jump from point A where $(M,S) = (20,30)$ to point A′ where $(M,S) = (22,36)$.

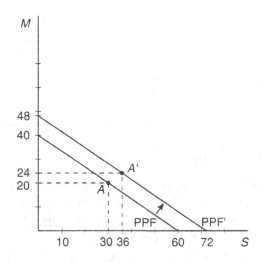

Figure 5.9
Labor Growth
If the labor force grows from $L = 120$ to 144, the economy expands to a higher production frontier. The economy's output could rise from point A where $(M,S) = (20,30)$ to point A′ where $(M,S) = (24,36)$.

Improved technology in one sector expands the PPF in that direction, lowers the relative price of that good, and raises production potential.

Labor growth is pictured by a parallel outward shift of the PPF. In Figure 5.9, the labor force expands from 120 to 144. Input requirements are the original $a_{LS} = 2$ and $a_{LM} = 3$. The equation for PPF′ is

$$L = 144 = 2S + 3M$$

Total $144/2 = 72$ units of S or $144/3 = 48$ units of M can could be produced. The relative price of S in terms of M remains 2/3. With growth, the economy can produce more of both goods.

Labor growth creates is an outward parallel shift of the PPF.

EXAMPLE **5.16**   *Industrial Labor Inputs*

Matthew Shapiro (1987) reports changes in unit labor inputs in US industries between 1974 and 1985. When unit labor inputs decline, the production frontier expands in the direction of those outputs. Where they rise as in mining and construction, the production frontier shrinks.

	$\%\Delta a_{LQ}$
Communications	−2.3%
Agriculture	−1.4%
Manufacturing	−1.4%
Construction	1.1%
Mining	4.3%

Table 5.4 Unit Labor Inputs in High Tech Products

	1963	**1984**
EU	1.25	1.46
US	1.00	1.06
Japan	1.76	0.92

Testing Constant Cost Trade Theory

G.D.A. MacDougall (1951) compared exports from the US and the UK in 1937. Higher labor productivity in an industry implied higher export market share, the prediction of constant cost theory. Other studies confirm the MacDougall test for many countries and products.

Hebert Glesjer, K. Goosens, and Eede Vanden (1982) compare countries in Europe before and after they joined the EU. Countries with lower opportunity costs of goods exported those goods to other member countries.

High tech products have high inputs of R&D. High tech manufactures include electronics, chemicals, aircrafts, computers, and specialized machinery. The unit labor inputs in high tech goods in Table 5.4 explain Japan's export growth. The EU declined in productivity as the US held its position. Japan's improved technology was due to its human capital (education) and physical capital. The Japanese PPF expanded along its high tech product axis.

The 1970s was a decade of decline for the US auto industry. Imports of Japanese cars rose from less than half a million in 1970 to almost 2.5 million by 1980. Japanese autos went from less than 5% to more than 20% of the US market. Labor productivity in Japan increased tremendously. The unit labor input was 1 in the US in 1970 when the Japanese unit input was 1.5. Over the 1970s the US unit labor input rose to 1.15 while the Japanese fell to 0.75. The Japanese automobile industry invested heavily, the stock of capital rising 225%.

EXAMPLE **5.17**   *China/US Trade*

Trade between China and the US has increased dramatically. Major US export categories are aircraft, fertilizer, telecommunications equipment, and cotton. US exports are based on high tech production and agriculture. Import categories were toys & sporting goods, apparel, footwear, and other manufactured goods. US imports are labor intensive manufactured goods.

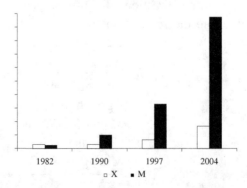

Section D Problems

D1. High tech manufactures require skilled labor. Why might the US be able to produce relatively cheap high tech goods?

D2. Investment spending in the US automobile industry lagged far behind its competitors in the 1970s. How does this account for the high cost of producing autos in the US during the 1980s?

D3. Suppose $a_{LS} = 4$, $a_{LM} = 5$, and $L = 220$ but technology changes in manufacturing from $a_{LM} = 5$ to $a_{LM} = 4.4$. Draw the revised PPF. Explain whether technology improved.

D4. Suppose the economy in Problem D3 grows to labor force $L = 260$. Draw the new PPF.

CONCLUSION

The constant cost theory of international trade makes production simple. While the theory is useful, questions arise. Why does one country have lower labor inputs? What causes labor inputs to change? Do other inputs alter fundamental predictions? Theories in the next two chapters answer these questions with increasing costs of production, various inputs, and different industrial structures.

EXAMPLE **5.18**   *3-Way Trade*

Japan has trade surpluses with NAFTA and the EU while NAFTA has deficits with the other two. The EU has a deficit with NAFTA but a surplus with Japan. This diagram summarizes the net trade flows. Japan exports manufactures, NAFTA foodstuffs and raw materials. Japan and the EU ship more manufactures to NAFTA than to each other.

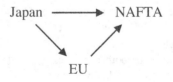

Terms

Absolute advantage	Limits to the exchange rate
Comparative advantage	Limits to the terms of trade
Complete specialization	Mercantilism
Constant costs	Opportunity cost
Unit labor inputs	Relative prices

MAIN POINTS

- A constant cost PPF with constant factor inputs has a slope equal to the relative product price.
- Trade with constant costs involves complete specialization according to comparative advantage.
- The gains from trade are higher utility or the increased value of consumption.
- Constant cost trade theory uncovers the fundamental international links between wages, productivity, and exchange rates.
- Unit labor inputs and comparative advantage contribute to explaining and predicting trade patterns.

REVIEW PROBLEMS

1. In Figures 5.2, which country has a lower opportunity cost of manufactures?
2. Suppose Delta is characterized by a_{LM} = 4 and a_{LS} = 5. Compare Delta with the home country in Figure 5.1 and predict the pattern of trade. Make a similar prediction for Delta and the foreign economy in Figure 5.2.
3. The workforce of the US totals about 150 million, while the workforce of Japan is 60 million. Find the amounts of high tech goods these economies could produce over the years in Table 5.4 if a quarter of each labor force worked in high tech products.
4. Suppose the H country is characterized by a_{LM} = 4, a_{LS} = 5, and L = 260, and F by a_{LM}^* = 6, a_{LS}^* = 5, and L^* = 300. Find comparative advantage. Suppose each country exports half its production to the other. Find the terms of trade. Diagram both trade triangles.
5. Evaluate the gains from trade for both countries in the previous problem in terms of S. Evaluate the gains from trade for both countries in percentage terms. Explain which country enjoys the largest gains from trade.
6. Find the percentage gains from trade in this same example if the terms of trade are M/S = 1 and 30 units of S are exported by F. Explain the difference in the gains from trade compared to the previous problem.
7. If the terms of trade are $tt = M/S$ = 1.4 between the home and foreign countries in Figure 5.2,

find the relative wages w/ew^* implied by free trade. Find the relative wage if tt = 0.7 and explain the effect of trade on the relative wage.
8. Using the information in the previous problem with each terms of trade, find w if w^* = 1100 ¥ and e = $/¥ = 0.008. Compare and explain the limits to the exchange rate under the two terms of trade.
9. In the home country, unit labor inputs are a_{LM} = 2 for manufactures and a_{LA} = 3 for agriculture. In the foreign country, unit labor inputs are a_{LM}^* = 4 and a_{LA}^* = 5. The terms of trade are $tt = A/M$ = 3/4. Find relative wages implied by trade.
10. Find the limits to the exchange rate for the two countries in the previous problem.
11. Find the home wage w if the foreign wage w^* = 10,000 pesos and e = 0.001 in the previous problem. Show what happens to w if
    (a) tt worsens for the home country falling to 7/10
    (b) The home labor input a_{LM} subsequently improves to 1.5.
12. Suppose unit labor inputs for three goods are

	Good 1	Good 2	Good 3
Home	3	5	3
Foreign	2	1	3

Predict the pattern of trade.

13. If the foreign wage is 2250 ¥ and the exchange rate $e = 0.008$ in the previous problem, find the home wage w that makes the price of the middle good the same in both economies. Using this wage, find the prices of the two traded goods in each country. Explain the direction of trade.

14. Find the limits to the exchange rate in the previous problem.

15. Consumer goods such as appliances and apparel require low levels of investment and high levels of unskilled labor. Why does the US have little cost advantage in consumer goods?

READINGS

David Ricardo (1817) *The Principles of Political Economy and Taxation*, New York: Everyman's Library, 1969. Chapter 3 "On Foreign Trade" is Ricardo's own presentation.

Andrea Maneschi (1998) *Comparative Advantage in International Trade: A Historical Perspective*, New York: Edward Elgar. An excellent historical review.

Michio Morishima (1989) *Ricardo's Economics: A General Equilibrium Theory of Distribution and Growth*, Cambridge: Cambridge University Press.

Ron Jones & Peter Kenen (1984) *Handbook of International Economics*, Vol. I, Amsterdam: North Holland. Surveys of international trade.

William Allen (1965) *International Trade Theory: Hume to Ohlin*, New York: Random House. A short paperback with readings from the classics.

CHAPTER 6

Factor Proportions Trade

Preview

This chapter includes capital with labor in production. Trade affects income distribution between the factors. The chapter covers:
- Specific factors of production
- Factor proportions production
- The theorems of general equilibrium trade theory
- Extensions, applications, and tests of factor proportions trade

INTRODUCTION

The economics of production is based on firms maximizing profit. Firms demand inputs in markets for capital, labor, and natural resources. People supply these productive factors to derive income. Product markets and factor markets together reach a general equilibrium. This structure underlies the theory of production and international trade. General equilibrium economics is the study of how all markets adjust together.

A critical issue is the income redistribution due to tariffs. Payments to some productive factors rise while payments to others fall. This chapter develops the tools to find exactly who wins and loses with tariffs.

In the specific factors model each industry uses its own capital and all industries share labor input. In the factor proportions model, capital and labor both move between sectors. Factor abundance and factor intensity lead to the four basic propositions of trade theory. This chapter examines issues of protection, migration, foreign investment, and income redistribution.

A.   SPECIFIC FACTORS AND TRADE

Specific factors of production are inputs only in their industry. The specific factors model is based on its factor markets.

Structure of the Specific Factors Model

Figure 6.1 illustrates the structure of specific factors economy. Labor L is a productive factor shared by manufacturing M and services S. Each sector has its own specific type of capital, K_M to produce M and K_S to produce S.

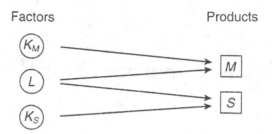

Figure 6.1
Specific Factors Production
Manufacturing M has specific K_M and services S has K_S. Both sectors share labor L.

Factor Demand

Inputs are hired according to the revenue they produce. As the price of an input rises quantity demanded falls. The demand of all firms is factor demand.

Diminishing marginal productivity characterizes production. Marginal product is the added output from an extra unit of input. Diminishing marginal productivity says that marginal product diminishes as the amount of the input increases holding other inputs constant.

A firm will hire a worker only if marginal revenue product is at least as large as the wage. Marginal revenue product is the revenue from the additional worker,

$$MRP = MR \times MP.$$

MR is the marginal revenue of output and MP is marginal product. The MRP slopes downward as in Figure 6.2 due to diminishing marginal productivity. As more L is hired MP diminishes. MR is constant if the firm is a price taker but decreases if the firm has market power.

The demand for labor is its MRP as firms hire according to the revenue labor produces.

The Market for Shared Labor

Figure 6.2 shows the demand for labor in manufacturing. Labor input L_M is measured on the horizontal axis. If the wage w_M is $20 manufacturing hires 30 units of L. Output produced by the 30th worker is worth $20. If w_M = $15 manufacturing hires 40 workers.

The demand for labor in services $D_S = MRP_S$ is in Figure 6.3. Marginal revenue comes from the demand for services. The economy has 100 workers and the length of the axis on the bottom of Figure 6.4 represents the labor endowment. Figure 6.3 combines the two demands for labor. Labor in manufacturing is measured from the left and labor in services L_S is measured from the right.

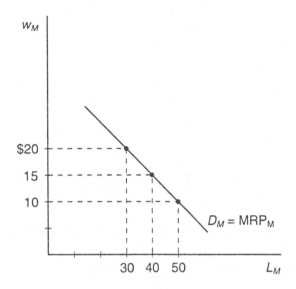

Figure 6.2
Demand for Labor in Manufacturing
The demand for labor is downward sloping due to diminishing marginal productivity. Marginal revenue product MRP_M is MR times MP. Manufacturers would hire 30 L at a wage of $20, and 50 L if w = $10

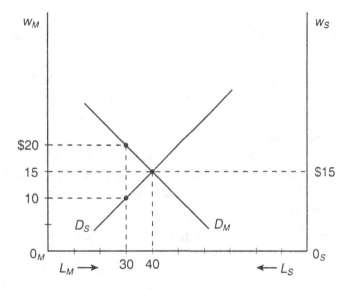

Figure 6.3
The General Equilibrium Labor Market
Labor in services L_S is measured from O_S Demand D_S slopes down to the left. Services would like 70 workers at w = $10. The total L supply is 100. In equilibrium, 40 workers are in M and 60 are in S at the $15 wage.

Where the two demands intersect the wage is $15 with 40 workers in manufacturing and 60 in services. If the wage were higher in manufacturing, workers would move there from services. With 30 workers in M, the wage is $20 in M but only $10 in S. Workers in services would move. Labor moves until wages are equal.

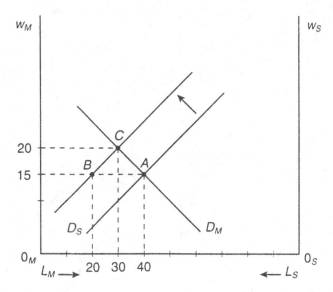

Figure 6.4
Increased Demand for Labor in Services
At $w = \$15$ an increase in labor demand in services creates excess demand of 20. The wage is bid up to $20 as 10 workers move from services. The equilibrium moves from A to C.

> *When a mobile productive input is shared by different industries it moves until its price is equalized.*

An increase in capital input raises labor's MP. A higher demand or price for the output also raises labor demand. A higher price of services increases labor demand in services as in Figure 6.4. A similar shift occurs if capital in services increases.

At $w = \$15$ there is a labor shortage. The original 40 units are demanded in manufacturing and 80 are demanded in services. The wage is bid up to $20 and 10 workers move from manufacturing to services to the equilibrium point C.

> *The economy adjusts to the higher price of services by shifting labor along its PPF.*

EXAMPLE **6.1**   *Predicted Effects of NAFTA*

Henry Thompson (1995a) applies the specific factors model to predict small wage and industrial adjustments in the US with declines in apparel, furniture, and a few labor intensive industries. Changes in industry specific investment, however, will have substantial long run effects. Michael Kouparitsas (1997) predicts the large benefits for Mexico due to incoming investment with Canada hardly affected, as pictured below.

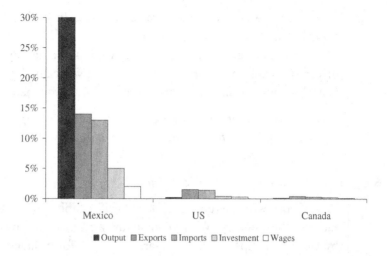

Markets for Specific Capital

When L moves into service production the MP of capital increases because K_S has more labor. Higher productivity leads to a higher capital payment r_S in the service sector. As L leaves M the MP of manufacturing capital falls as does r_M.

Figure 6.5 shows the market for sector specific capital K_S in services. The vertical line is capital supply. Capital remains utilized and its return is determined by demand. Capital may be unique or there might not be enough time to change the supply.

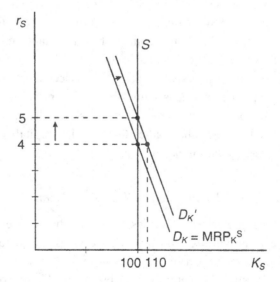

Figure 6.5
Market for Services Capital
The supply of capital in services is inelastic at the endowment of 100. With capital demand D_K the capital payment is 4. When demand increases to D_K' the payment increase to 5.

A higher price of services raises its *MR*. Incoming labor raises the *MP* of capital. The demand for capital and r_S rise.

In the market for manufacturing capital the falling marginal productivity of capital leads to lower demand and a lower capital payment r_K. When labor leaves manufacturing the marginal productivity of manufacturing capital falls.

When output prices change, markets for sector specific capital and shared labor adjust as the economy moves along its PPF.

EXAMPLE **6.2**   *Do Tariffs Protect Specific Factors?*

A tariff raises the return to sector specific capital when there is only one other input in the industry. With other inputs a tariff could lower the return as shown by Henry Thompson (1987). A tariff on steel, for instance, could increase demand for labor and energy in domestic production but lower demand for capital in the industry. Gene Grossman and Jim Levinshon (1989) find evidence, however, that protected industries have higher than normal stock returns.

Trade and Income Distribution with Specific Factors

Income is redistributed by protection, subsidies, and world prices. Protection raises the price of imports causing increased import competing production but falling output in the rest of the economy. A tariff on *M* raises the return to capital specific to *M*.

The wage rises but payment to capital specific to other sector falls. This general result illustrates why stockholders, management, and labor unions in an industry all want their industry protected from foreign competition.

Suppose the home country has abundant and cheap capital in services. The autarky price of services should be low and the home country should export services. With trade, the price of services rises. The wage rises as does the price of capital in services while the capital price in manufacturing falls.

If both sectors share labor and skilled labor, trade could increase demand for shared skilled labor rather than service capital. Demand for service capital falls depressing an already low r_S.

EXAMPLE **6.3**   *Trade and Income Redistribution in Japan*

Three protected industries in Japan that can expect falling prices are iron & steel, agriculture, and business services. Projected impacts on returns to capital and wages in various sectors from 10% decreases in these prices are predicted in the specific factors model by Henry Thompson (1994a). These falling prices lower the return to mobile capital by 5%. Wages in import competing industries fall considerably while labor in other industries enjoy gains indicated below.

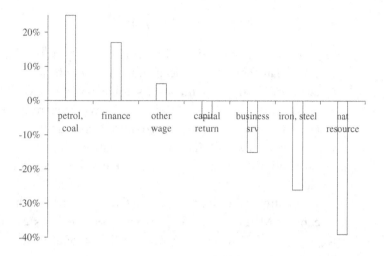

Section A Problems

A1. The price of services is $3 and the capital input 10 units. Draw the *MRP* of *L* if outputs of *S* from *L* are:

L	0	1	2	3	4	5
S	0	2.5	4.5	6	7	7.5

A2. The marginal product of *L* in manufacturers *M* is 3.5 when *L* = 1, then 3 when *L* = 2, 2.5 when *L* = 3, 2 when *L* = 4, and 1.5 when *L* = 5. The price of *M* is $1.50. Draw the demand for *L* in manufacturing.

A3. Combine the labor demands in the two previous problems to determine the equilibrium wage and employment in each sector when the total labor endowment is 5.

B.   TWO FACTOR PRODUCTION AND TRADE

This section introduces the factor proportions model with labor *L* and capital *K* inputs producing manufactures *M* and services *S*. This 2×2 model was developed by Eli Heckscher and Bertil Ohlin who laid its foundations in the 1930s. Abba Lerner and Paul Samuelson developed its structure in the 1950s. The model leads to four fundamental propositions in trade theory.

EXAMPLE **6.4**   *US Output Growth*

Output increases with inputs of capital and labor. In the US between 1940 and 1970 increases in the capital stock were not dramatic but output steadily responded. Since 1970 there has been a structural break with higher capital growth but slower growth in output per worker.

Factor Abundance and Intensity

Exports from a country at low prices are typically based on inputs that are cheaper than those available in importing countries. More abundant supply of a factor of production means its price will be lower. If the foreign country has abundant labor L the foreign wage will generally be lower than the home wage, $ew^* < w$. If the home country has abundant capital, its capital return will typically be less than in the foreign country, $r < r^*$. Abundance of factors of production is a good predictor of exports according to factor intensity in production.

Production of a good is labor intensive if it has a higher input ratio of labor to capital. Manufactures M is labor intensive if its capital/labor ratio is lower, $K_M/L_M < K_s/L_s$. Services production S is capital intensive. Capital may include human capital or skilled labor, widening the application of this ranking.

The capital abundant home country exports capital intensive services S in exchange for labor intensive manufactures M from the labor abundant foreign country. Factor abundance generally explains factor cheapness that lead to cheaper products intensive in those factors. This simple theory of the link between factor abundance and factor intensity is successful explaining up to three-quarters of global trade.

Factor markets and product markets

Figure 6.6 illustrates the labor market in both countries with the marginal revenue product MRP_L or demand D_L for labor in each country. Domestic labor L is measured from the left as usual but foreign labor L^* is measured from the right. The foreign demand for labor D_L^* slopes down as its input increases. The length of the base of the figure is the total labor supply $L + L^*$ in both countries.

Assume labor does not migrate between the two countries. The vertical line line L/L^* indicates labor abundance in the foreign country. Note that $L < L^*$ with 25% of the total labor supply in the home country.

The two labor demands D_L and D_L^* imply the wage in the home country is higher than in the foreign country, $w > ew^*$. In Figure 6.6 w = $20 and $ew^* = \$5$. The labor abundant foreign country has lower wages. Workers in the labor scarce home country enjoy higher wages.

Figure 6.7 illustrates the related markets for labor intensive manufactures in the two countries. The demand for manufactures $D_M = D_M^*$ is the same in both countries. The two supply curves, however, are much different. The labor abundant foreign country has lower wages leading to its higher supply of manufactures S_M^*. The labor scarce home country has higher wages w resulting in lower supply S_M. In autarky the price of manufactures is lower in the foreign country, $ePM^* < P_M$ In the example $P_M = \$100$ and $ePM^* = \$60$.

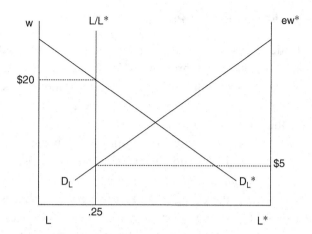

Figure 6.6
The International Labor Market
The demands for labor are similar in the home and foreign countries. Labor supply L in the home country is only 25% of the total L + L*. The labor abundant foreign country has lower wages, ew* < w. If e = $/peso = ½ then w* = 10 pesos.

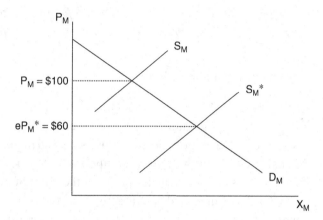

Figure 6.7
Labor Intensive Manufactures and a Labor Abundant Foreign Country
With the same demand for manufactures, the labor abundant foreign country has a lower price, eP$_M$* < P$_M$. If e = ½ then P$_M$* = 120 pesos. The higher foreign supply is based on the lower foreign wages ew* < w as in Figure 6.6.

Similarly the capital abundant home country has a lower autarky price of services Ps < eP$_s$* based on its lower return to capital r < r*. When trade opens between the two countries, the home country exports services and imports manufactures.

The fundamental prediction of factor proportions trade theory is that countries export products intensive in their abundant factors.

Trade and Factor Prices

Trade raises prices of cheap exported products and lowers prices of expensive import competing products. Consumers enjoy the falling price of imported products while the import competing industry suffers the falling price and lowers output. Home export producers enjoy the rising price in their industry as their output expands.

In the home country the falling P_M lowers home demand for intensive labor in Figure 6.6. This downward shift in labor demand lowers the home wage w. Labor demand depends on manufactures where it is the intensive input. Meanwhile, the rising price Ps of exported services raises demand for intensive capital. This increase in demand for capital raises the low capital return r.

In the foreign country the effects on factor demands are the opposite. Increased demand for cheap labor L^* to produce manufactures M^* increases the demand and the low ew^*. In Figure 6.6 the two demand shifts lower the home wage below $20 and raise the foreign wage above $5. Production of import competing services S^* falls in the foreign country as does its capital demand and r^*.

Trade raises prices of the cheaper factors of production in each country, leading to factor price convergence across countries.

Tariffs and Factor Prices

Tariffs move factor prices in opposite directions. Tariffs raise the price for the import competing industry, creating deadweight loss and shifting production away from the export sector. Tariffs redistribute income toward the scarce intensive factor in the import competing industry. Tariffs raise the price of the factor that is higher than its price in the foreign country.

A tariff on imported manufactures in the home country raises the price of manufactures to $p_M = (1 + t)eP_M^*$. The higher price increases the demand for intensive labor raising labor demand D_L in Figure 6.6. The increased labor demand raises the home wage w that is already higher than the foreign wage ew^*.

Tariffs polarize factor prices between trading partners making the distribution of factor income more uneven across countries.

Section B Problems

B1. Diagram the international market for capital similar to Figure 6.6. Explain which country is capital abundant. Explain the international difference between the two capital returns, r and r^*.

B2. Diagram the international market for services similar to Figure 6.7 for manufactures. Explain differences in supplies S_s and S_s^*. Predict the direction of trade based on P_s and eP_s^*.

B3. Create the example of trade between a resource abundant foreign country and a labor abundant home country. Assume their capital endowments are similar. Show the factor markets in each country and explain the differences in factor prices. Explain the supplies of each product in each country.

C.   TWO FACTORS AND TWO GOODS

The 2×2 production model has four fundamental theorems that describe the effects of protection, a move to free trade, migration, and international capital movements on factor income distribution, production, and trade.

Competitive Pricing

Figure 6.8 shows a competitive price taking firm. A competitive industry has many such firms each taking the market price $p = \$1$ as given. A competitive firm can sell any amount it wants at this market price. Marginal revenue MR is the extra revenue from selling output. For a competitive firm $MR = P$. Marginal cost MC is the additional cost for a unit of output. Profit is maximized where MC equals MR.

Entry and exit of firms drives price to average cost AC in a competitive industry. If profits are positive, firms enter the industry, supply increases, price falls, and costs rise. If there are losses, the opposite occurs. At the profit

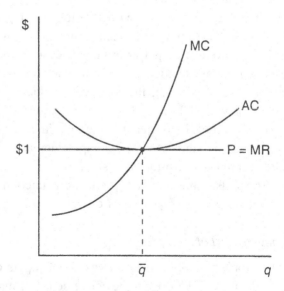

Figure 6.8
Price Taking Competition
This competitive firm takes the market price of $1. Marginal revenue MR equals price for a competitive firm. Marginal cost MC is the additional cost of each unit of output. Where $MR = MC$ profit is maximized at output $\bar{q}$.

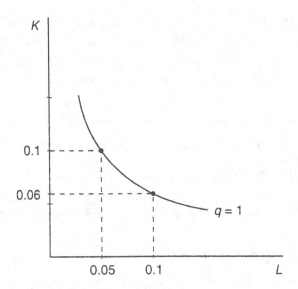

Figure 6.9
Unit Isoquant
Capital and labor are substituted along this unit isoquant. Two possible input combinations
are $(K,L) = (.1,.05)$ and $(.06,.1)$.

maximizing output $\bar{q}$ average cost is minimized for a competitive firm.

Input Substitution

A ditch can be dug with a tractor and a bit of labor or with shovels and a lot
of labor. The price of labor relative to capital (tractors and shovels) determines
which combination is more economical. The firm chooses how to combine L
and K to produce output at minimum cost.

The isoquant in Figure 6.9 slopes downward as one input is substituted for
the other. For instance, the firm can produce 1 unit of output with 0.1 K and
0.05 L or with 0.06 K and 0.1 L.

The slope of the isoquant is the marginal rate of technical substitution $MRTS$
of capital for labor. As capital input increases, the increase MRTS implies it
takes capital to substitute for labor.

Isoquants come from the production function $q = q\,(K,L)$ relating inputs to
output. Along an isoquant q is constant.

EXAMPLE **6.5**   *Converging Labor Inputs*

When trade equalizes factor prices, labor inputs convergence. David Dollar and
Edward Wolff (1988) examine convergence of manufacturing labor inputs across
industrial countries between 1963 and 1982. The chart shows converging unit
labor inputs relative to US manufacturing. Italy used more than twice as much
labor in 1963 but only 10% more by 1982.

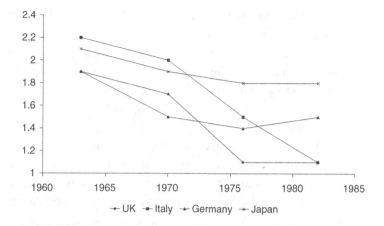

— UK — Italy — Germany — Japan

Cost Minimization

Suppose the capital rent is $r = \$5$ and wage $w = \$10$. Let a_{Kj} be the capital input and a_{Lj} the labor input per unit of output. The cost c of producing one unit of output is

$$c = ra_{Kj} + wa_{Lj} = \$5a_{Kj} + \$10a_{Lj}$$

Competitive firms have zero profit implying price equals average cost,

$$P = \$1 = AC.$$

The isocost line in Figure 6.10 shows combinations of inputs that cost \$1. The labor that would cost \$1 if no capital is hired is $c/w = \$1/\$10 = 0.1$. The

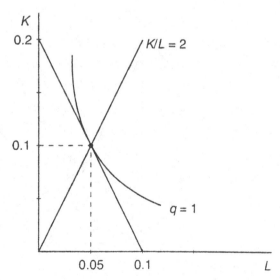

Figure 6.10
Cost Minimization
The firm wants to produce 1 unit of output at minimum cost. Wages are \$10 and the return to capital is \$5. The firm looks for the isocost line with this slope that just touches the unit isoquant. At this cost minimization point, the K/L ratio is 2.

endpoint along the capital axis is $1/$5 = 0.2$. The isocost line connects these endpoints. The slope of the isocost line is $-(c/r)/(c/w) = -w/r = -2$.

The firm looks for the lowest isocost line to produce a unit of output. The unit isoquant and the $1 isocost are tangent at the cost minimization. At this point the isoquant and isocost lines are tangent, and MRTS $= w/r$.

Cost minimization leads to inputs $L = 0.05$ and $K = 0.1$. The expansion path shows the optimal capital/labor ratio. Along the expansion path, inputs proportionally increase and output expands.

If the wage w increases the slope of the isocost line is steeper and the firm substitutes toward capital. The expansion path shifts toward a higher K/L. If the capital rent r increases, the isocost line becomes flatter and K/L falls.

Firms minimize cost to maximize profit, substituting away from a factor when its price increases.

2 × 2 Production

The 2 × 2 production diagram in Figure 6.11 was developed by Abba Lerner and Ivor Pearce. Unit value isoquants are $M = 1$ and $S = 1$ are scaled to $1. The two sectors share the same isocost line since wages and rents are equalized by competition. Cost minimization leads to inputs of $(a_{KS}, a_{LS}) = (.1, .05)$ in services and $(a_{KM}, a_{LM}) = (.04, .08)$ in manufacturing.

Expansion paths have ratios $k_S = 1/.05 = 2 k_M = .04/.08 = 1/2$ where k is the capital/labor ratio K/L. Manufacturing uses a lot of labor and has a lower k.

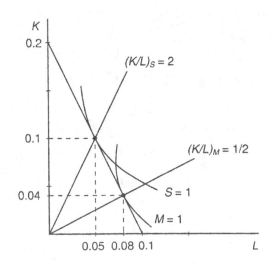

Figure 6.11
2 × 2 Production
Both industries face the same isocost line. Cost minization leads to different K/L ratios. Manufacturing is labor intensive and services capital intensive.

EXAMPLE **6.6**   *Competitiveness and Growth*

The 1999 *Global Competitiveness Report* surveyed 4,000 business leaders and constructed an index of competitiveness. The top and bottom three countries are listed along with major US trading partners. More competitive economies have higher per capita incomes (in $000).

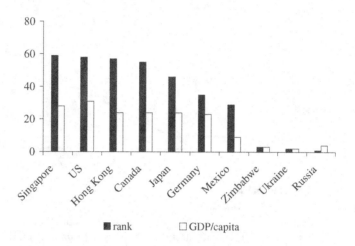

In Figure 6.10 the input ratio K/L in services equals 2 and in manufacturing 1/2. Manufacturing is labor intensive, and services is capital intensive.

The country has endowments of capital and labor $(K,L) = (100,110)$ at point E. Outputs of M and S are consistent with full employment of labor and capital. To find output levels complete the parallelogram. Outputs m and s are unique and consistent with cost minimization and full employment.

Investment and Labor Growth

Increased capital shifts endowment point E as in Figure 6.12. The parallelogram becomes taller and thinner. Output of services rises to s' and output of manufactures falls to m'. Both capital and labor leave manufacturing. If K increases to 112 all of the new capital and 4 more units from manufacturing move to the expanding capital intensive services sector.

When the endowment of a factor increases and prices are constant, output of the product using it intensively increases and output of the other good falls. This result was proven by T.M. Rybczynski in the early 1950s.

In Figure 6.13 the international relative price line p begins with production at point P. Outputs m and s correspond to points m and s in Figure 6.14. When capital increases, the PPF shifts out with a bias toward capital intensive services. The new production point P$'$ is where the new PPF is tangent to the

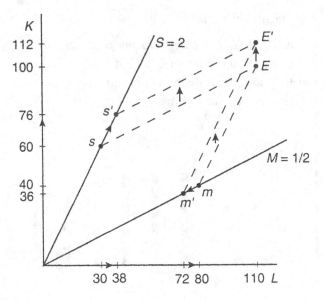

Figure 6.12
Increased Capital
When K/L rises the economy moves toward capital intensive production. The K endowment rises from 100 to 112, and the service sector gains 16 units of K and 8 units of L. Output of manufactures falls to m' and output of services rises to s'.

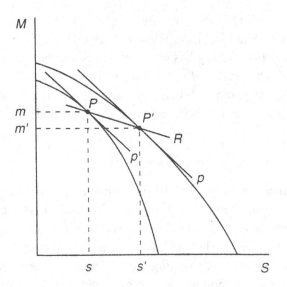

Figure 6.13
Rybczynski Line
An increase in the capital endowment shifts the PPF out with a bias toward capital intensive services. Production moves from P to P'. The line connecting outputs for different capital endowments is the Rybczynski line R for capital.

price line *p* at output levels *m'* and *s'*. The *Rybczynski line* R connects these production points.

EXAMPLE **6.7**   *Skilled Labor Content*

The US has historically exported agricultural products. Bob Baldwin (1971) estimates that farm labor was 1.4 times more involved in export than in import competing activity. Estimates of relative export involvement for skill types are below. Professionals are more involved in exports, operatives and laborers in import competition. Skills decline moving down the list of export activity.

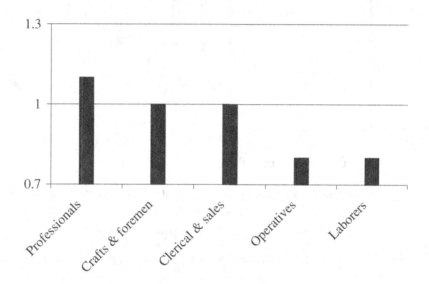

Factor Abundance and Exports

The home country is capital abundant if it has a higher capital/labor ratio,

$$k > k^*.$$

The foreign country is then labor abundant. The capital abundant home country has a higher ratio of capital intensive services.

If consumers in the two countries have similar preferences, they will want to consume the same ratio of outputs with free trade and equal prices. The capital abundant home country exports capital intensive services in exchange for labor intensive manufacture.

This proposition developed by Eli Heckscher and Bertil Ohlin in the 1930s is part of the fundamental intuition in international trade:

Countries export products that use their abundant factors intensively.

EXAMPLE **6.8**   *Skilled Labor Intensity*

Ed Leamer (1984) constructs industry rankings with inputs of capital K, labor L, and skilled labor S. Skilled labor includes professional, technical, and scientific workers. US industries are ranked according to S/L and S/K. The US has abundant skilled labor and comparative advantage in products with high S/L and S/K ratios. US industries toward the top of the list prosper and export, while those toward the bottom face import competition.

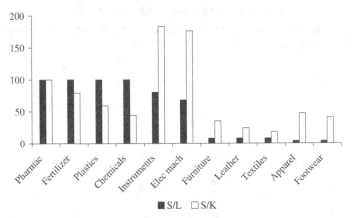

Factor Price Equalization

Isoquants in Figure 6.14 represent $1 of outputs S and M. When trade equalizes prices, the unit value isoquants are the same in both countries. The isocost line and factor prices must then also be the same in the 2×2 model.

Free trade between two factor proportions economies leads to equal prices for each factor between then.

Factor price equalization continues to cause disagreement among economists. Some claim factor proportions theory is useless since observed wages vary so much. Others use the potential to equalize factor prices as an argument for free trade. There is evidence that trade brings prices for similar productive factors closer together across countries.

A labor abundant country will typically have low wages and cheap labor intensive products. Trade increases for these products and for labor. If $ew^* < w$ due to abundant foreign labor, tarde increases the demand D_L^* for labor in the foreign country raising w^*. Meanwhile labor demand D_L in the home country falls. Wages ew^* converge with trade.

EXAMPLE **6.9**   *Trade and Convergence*

Increased trade causes both convergence of wages and per capita income as shown by Farhad Rassekh and Henry Thompson (1998). David Dollar and Edward Wolff (1993) find evidence of wage convergence. Jeffrey Williamson

(1996) find evidence of wage convergence in the 1800s. David Ben-David (1993) shows convergence of per capita income has occured with trade in Europe. Ben-David and Alok Bohara (1997) find per capita income convergence is stimulated by free trade agreements. Farhad Rassekh (1992) shows there has been convergence of per capita income among the OECD countries. For LDCs the recommendation is free trade. Meanwhile unskilled labor in the DCs can expect falling wages and should invest in becoming skilled.

Protection and Factor Prices

Trade equalizes prices of factors across countries but protection drives factor prices apart. The following property was proven by Wolfgang Stolper and Paul Samuelson in the early 1950s:

A tariff raises the price of the factor used intensively in the import competing industry and lowers the other factor price.

If a tariff raises the home price of manufactures, the physical amount of the good worth $1 falls. The inputs required to make $1 of the manufactured good falls.

In Figure 6.14 the original cost minimization is pictured. A tariff pushes the manufacturing unit isoquant toward the origin. The new equilibrium occurs at with a higher wage w and lower capital return r. The price of expensive labor

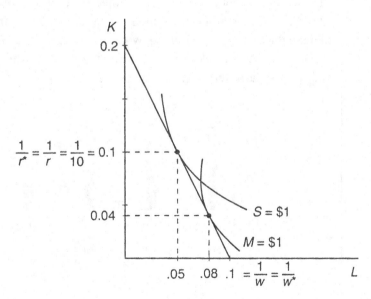

Figure 6.14
Factor Price Equalization
With free trade unit isoquants are the same in each country, the unit isocost line is $c = 10L + 5K$. Wages are the same in both countries, $w = w^* = \$10$. Capital rents are also the same, $r = r^* = \$5$.

increases and the price of cheap capital falls with the tariff that creates a more uneven distribution of income across countries.

The increase in the relative price of labor causes both industries to become more capital intensive. The ratio of capital to labor rises from M to M' in manufacturing and from S to S' in services. Protected labor intensive manufacturing increases output while capital intensive services declines.

The wage rises with the tariff but workers must pay higher prices for manufactures. It turns out that the percentage wage increase is greater than the percentage increase in the price of manufactures. With a tariff, one productive factor always enjoys an increase in real income but the other loses due to the magnification effect of Ron Jones.

EXAMPLE 6.10   *Factor Price Convergence*

Science progresses through theory with testable propositions. Farhad Rassekh and Henry Thompson (1993) review the status of factor price equalization. FPE has been pronounced dead since wages differ so greatly around the world, but survives as part of the foundation of trade theory. FPE is the conclusion of a process wage convergence. There is wide empirical support for wage convergence.

EXAMPLE 6.11   *LDC Trade and Income Redistribution in LDCs*

Trade will raise prices of manufactures but lower prices of business services in LDCs. Henry Thompson (1995b) projects the effects of changing prices across LDCs in a factor proportions model. The effects of a 10% increase in the price of manufactures are combined with a 10% decrease in the price of business services. Wages of unkilled labor rise considerably while wages of skilled labor and the capital return fall.

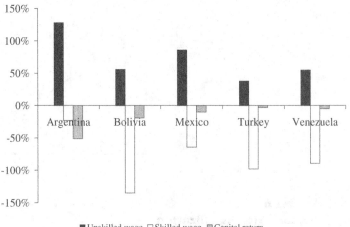

Section C Problems

C1. Diagram a competitive manufacturing unit value isocost line if $w = \$2$, $r = \$3$, and $c = \$1$. Find capital input with 0.2 units of labor.

C2. Sketch the manufacturing unit value isoquant in the previous problem and show the cost minimization. Draw the expansion path. What is k in manufacturing?

C3. Let point E in Figure 6.10 represent the home country. The foreign country has less capital and more labor. The two countries trade freely. Compare the different employments of K and L across sectors.

C4. Compare ratios of foreign outputs in the previous problem with home outputs. Which country produces a higher ratio M/S? Which will export M if consumers in both countries have the same preferences?

C5. How would the switch from autarky to free trade affect payments to K and L for each country in the previous problem?

EXAMPLE **6.12**   *3 Way Trade*

With 3 factors, 3 goods, and 3 countries Henry Thompson (2001) shows trade between any two countries does not have to be balanced. Each country exports at least one product. All three may export two products. Tariffs help at least one factor in each country. It is impossible to predict which factor price will rise with a tariff based on factor intensity since substitution can play a critical role.

D. APPLYING FACTOR PROPORTIONS TRADE THEORY

Factor proportions trade theory is tested like all scientific theories. This section covers tests and extensions of factor proportions theory.

EXAMPLE **6.13**   *NAFTA and Elastic Labor Supply*

International trade between Mexico and the US might lower unskilled wages in the US but Kenneth Reinert and David Roland-Holst (1998) predict wages of different labor groups may rise in all three countries. With elastic labor supply, there are potential wage increases for all labor skills. Free trade raises average wages 1% in the US, 3% in Canada, and 3% in Mexico with elastic labor supply.

Testing Factor Proportions Trade Theory

Wassily Leontief (1953) examines the capital and labor content of US trade and finds labor intensive exports. The K/L ratio was 1.41 for export production and 1.82 for import competing goods. Capital abundant US importing capital intensive goods is called the Leontief paradox.

Robert Baldwin (1971) finds the K/L ratio of US imports and exports were virtually identical excluding natural resource products. Baldwin also finds US exports were intensive in skilled labor.

Robert Stern and Keith Maskus (1981) find the Leontief paradox had disappeared. Keith Maskus (1985) subsequently reports the paradox is common with the US frequently a net exporter of labor intensive products.

Ed Leamer (1980) makes the point that products consumed in the US are much more labor intensive than exports, but it seems odd that imports could be capital intensive. Francisco Casas and Kwan Choi (1985) calculate what factor content would have been had trade been balanced and find no Leontief paradox. William Branson and Nikolaos Monoyios (1977) show that the US exported goods intensive in skilled labor and imported goods intensive in unskilled labor. Capital holds an intermediate position in this intensity ranking.

Ed Leamer (1984) finds the US exports products intensive in a scientists, engineers, technicians, and draftsmen. Robert Stern and Keith Maskus (1981) come to the similar conclusion that US reveals abundance in skilled labor as well as physical capital.

Tests of factor proportions theory are challenging because data are lacking from different countries on inputs, factor abundance, prices, outputs, and trade. Data on service production is rare Industries within manufacturing vary from very capital intensive to very labor intensive, and skilled labor can be critical. Capital is difficult to measure. Land, and natural resources are important in production and very different across countries.

EXAMPLE **6.14**   *Industrial Factors Proportions Theory*

Links between prices of products and factors depend on factor intensity. Farhad Rassekh and Henry Thompson (1997) examine factor intensity of 9 industries across 12 DCs between 1970 and 1985. A higher price for a labor intensive product increases its share of output, raises the wage, and raises the capital to labor ratio. A higher price for a capital intensive product should lower the capital to labor ratio but only for 5 industries. Predictions of the specific factors model hold for 7 industries. The ranking below compares capital intensity in thousands of dollars per worker in the US, Canada, Germany, and Japan. Canada has the most capital intensive minerals industry. Canada and Japan have capital intensive paper industries. US textile production is the most labor intensive. Germany has low capital intensities in chemicals and basic metals.

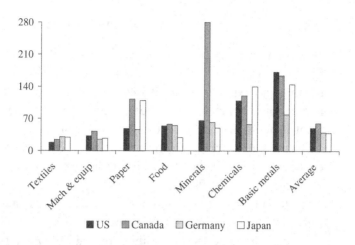

Applications of Factor Proportions Trade Theory

Hundreds of economies trade tens of thousands of goods and services. Production involve various types of skilled labor different vintages of capital inputs, and numerous sorts of natural resources. Factor intensity and factor abundance are a challenge in such applications.

Trade in business services is growing quickly. Skilled labor is used intensively to produces business services and developed countries have an abundance of skilled labor. The evolving pattern of specialization in services and imported manufactures is predicted by factor proportions theory for the DCs.

Computable general equilibrium CGE models of production and trade are based on factor proportions theory. CGE models predict the effects of protection, export subsidies, oil price shocks, exchange rate changes, and more across many products and inputs.

EXAMPLE 6.15   *Evidence on Factor Abundance and Exports*

Ed Leamer (1984) examines links between endowments and exports in 47 countries producing 10 outputs with the 11 inputs capital, professionals, unskilled labor, skilled labor, coal, minerals, oil, and 4 types of land. Outputs are petroleum, raw materials, forest products, tropical agriculture, animal products, cereals, L intensive manufactures, K intensive manufactures, machinery, and chemicals. Belgium, France, Germany, Italy, Japan, the Netherlands, Sweden, Switzerland, UK, and the US are abundant in capital and skilled labor, and export chemicals (capital and skilled labor intensive) and machinery (skilled labor intensive). Austria, India, Korea, and Spain export capital intensive manufactures. Brazil, Colombia, Cyprus, Egypt, Finland, Greece, Malta, Sri Lanka, Thailand, and Turkey are labor abundant and export labor intensive manufactures. LDCs are capital scarce and export tropical agricultural goods, raw materials, cereals, and animal products. Trade in agriculture, minerals, and oil is explained by the locations of land and natural resources.

Production and Trade with Unemployment

Unemployment arises for various reasons. It takes time and resources to match firms and workers. Searching for a job is costly. Some labor markets require training and experience. Industries expand and contract with business cycles and international competition. Labor contracts create wage inflexibility. Unemployment benefits provide incentive to remain unemployed.

Firms hire labor according to marginal revenue product. If the minimum or contract wage is higher than the market wage, unemployment occurs with the economy below its PPF.

In the probability wage model of James Harris and Michael Todaro (1970) rural wages w_R are low but everyone has a job in the rural area. Urban wages w_U are higher but there is only a probability P of finding a job. Workers in rural areas discount the high urban wage. If $P = 80\% = 0.8$ and $w_U = \$70$, the discounted urban wage is $0.80 \times \$70 = \$16$. If $w_R < \$16$, rural workers move to the urban area. Other considerations such as moving costs and tastes for urban versus rural life also influence the decision.

LDCs report high rates of unemployment but everyone is constantly working. In the DCs workers draw unemployment benefits and work in the "underground", economy. Underground economies are very active, producing valuable goods and services.

Minimum wage legislation and labor contracts create unemployment. A fall in the demand for labor results in either lower wages or unemployment. Neither is desirable but lower wages are less of a burden. Support of unskilled workers lessens their incentive to upgrade skills. Flexibility in wages and hours worked would lead to more efficient labor markets.

Properties of trade theory are not much affected by unemployment. Certainly unemployment is no motivation for protectionism.

EXAMPLE **6.16**   *Free Trade in Bolivia*

Free trade will impact production and factor prices in Bolivia as examined Hugo Toledo and Henry Thompson (2001) in an applied factor proportions model. Natural gas and manufacturing exports will expand while agriculture and services suffer import competition. Bolivian farmers will lose their protection in Mercosur. Bolivian business service industries are skilled labor intensive, government owned or subsidized, and inefficient. Skilled and unskilled labor will lose with free trade in Bolivia. Outputs in services and agriculture will fall. Capital in services and agriculture will suffer losses while capital owners in natural gas, manufacturing, and mining enjoy gains as gauged below.

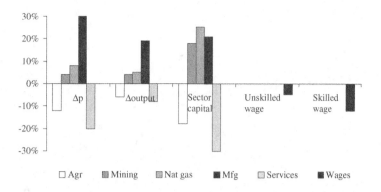

Factor Proportions with Constant Costs

The factor proportions model and the constant cost model are integrated by Roy Ruffin (1988) in the constant cost endowment CCE model. Trade occurs between different skills of labor residing in different countries. Services S and manufactures M are produced by labor L or skilled labor H.

The constant cost unit labor inputs are $a_{LM} = 1$, $a_{HM} = 2$, $a_{LS} = 2$ and $a_{HS} = 1$. The home country has an abundance of skilled labor where $(L,H) = (100,400)$ and $(L^*,H^*) = (500,50)$.

Skilled labor at home can produce $400/2 = 200$ M as shown in Figure 6.16. Home unskilled labor can produce an additional $100/1 = 100$ units of M. Alternatively the H at home could produce $400/1 = 400$ S and the L another $100/2 = 50$ S. The endpoints on the home PPF are $300M$ and $450S$.

Starting at $M = 300$ in Figure 6.15, skilled labor would begin producing S according to comparative advantage. If all available skilled labor produces S and only unskilled labor produces M output is at the pivot point $(M,S) = (100,400)$.

In antarky, consumers pick a point along the PPF. In Figure 6.15 home consumers maximize utility at point A with some skilled labor in manufacturing.

The foreign PPF* connects endpoints $M = 525$ and $S = 300$ with pivot point $(M,S) = (500,50)$. Foreign consumers are constrained to their PPF in autarky, maximizing welfare at point A^*. Some foreign unskilled labor produces services.

Trade moves production to the pivot points according to P and P^*. The terms of trade are the dotted line connecting pivot points. Abundant factors specialize according to comparative advantage. All of the skilled labor at home produces S and all of the unskilled labor in the foreign country produces M. The home country exports 175 units of S in exchange for 200 units of M from the foreign country. Both countries consume $300M$ and $225S$ at point $T = T^*$ with higher utility.

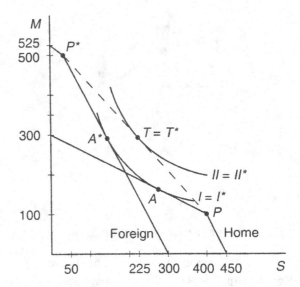

Figure 6.15
Constant cost factor proportions
Each country specializes by producing the good with low input of its abundant factor, skilled labor in the home service sector and unskilled labor in foregn manufacturing. The terms of trade are $tt = M/S = 200/175 = 8/7$. Each country consumes $(M, S) = (300, 225)$ beyond its PPF with higher utility.

Income is more evenly distributed with trade. The home country has a relative abundance of skilled labor. Trade increases the price of cheap services and skilled labor is pulled into services by a higher skilled wage. In the foreign country, trade increases the price of manufactures and the wage.

This constant cost endowment trade model shows the gains from trade based on specialization in a simple model. Constant cost models are simple to apply. Production and trade can readily be explained by the constant cost factor proportions model.

EXAMPLE **6.17**   *Trade and Labor Skills*

Trade leads to gains but redistributes income. William Cline (1997) presents evidence that unskilled US manufacturing wages have fallen and suggests they will continue to fall. Skilled labor enjoys benefits due to increased trade as the US specializes in production intensive in skilled labor. The endowment ratio of skilled to unskilled labor has increased over decades as workers respond to market incentives by increasing education and training.

EXAMPLE **6.18**   *Trade & the Wage Gap*

> Skilled wages have increased relative to unskilled wages in the US with imports
> of unskilled intensive products. Improved technology may also favor skilled labor
> study. Robert Baldwin and Glen Cain (2000) find the US wage gap declined due
> to a net increase in the supply of skilled labor. Eli Berman, John Bound and
> Stephen Machin (1998) find evidence of skill biased technical change during
> the 1980s but suggest trade contributes. Robert Feenstra and Gordon Hanson
> (1999) find that 35% of the wage gap is explained by computers and 15% by
> outsourcing. Jonathan Haskel and Matthew Slaughter (2002) find evidence that
> sector biased technical change in the skilled intensive industries best explains the
> wage gap. John Francis and Henry Thompson (2009) simulate a specific factors
> model and find free trade lowers both skilled and unskilled and unskilled wages
> but widens the wage gap.

Section D Problems

> **D1.** What is one explanation other than those in the text for the Leontief paradox?
> **D2.** Use a 2×2 production diagram to illustrate the effects of increased
> unemployment benefits on outputs.

EXAMPLE **6.19**   *Labor Moving along the PPF*

> Trade moves the economy along its production frontier with labor and other
> factors of production moving to export industries. Romain Wacziarg and
> Jessica Wallan (2004) examine trade liberalization from the 1970s to the
> 1990s across 25 LDCs and NICs. Labor market reactions vary. There was
> no movement between manufacturing, services, and agriculture but there
> was movement between industries and firms in manufacturing. Labor market
> adjustments were more dramatic following the privatization of socialized
> industries.

CONCLUSION

> The factor proportions model of production and trade is the foundation of
> trade theory, neoclassical production frontiers, and offer curves. Its basic
> assumption is that markets are competitive. The next chapter examines trade
> with noncompetitive pricing due to monopoly, monopolistic competition, and
> oligopoly. Each industrial structure has its own implications for trade and
> trade policy.

Terms

Computable general equilibrium	Isocost line
Constant cost	Isoquant
Cost minimization	Leontief paradox
Diminishing marginal productivity	Marginal cost (MC)
Exit and entry	Marginal product (MP)
Expansion paths	Marginal revenue (MR)
Factor abundance and scarcity	Marginal revenue product (MRP)
Factor demand	Price-taking firm
Factor intensity	Probability wage unemployment
Factor price equalization	Specific factors
Factor substitution	

MAIN POINTS

- Tariffs protect factors of production specific to an industry but hurt factors specific to other industries. Shared factors may win or lose.
- Factor intensity and factor abundance are key concepts in production and trade with a positive link between abundance, intensity, and exports.
- Free trade equalizes factors prices between countries raising demand for abundant cheap factor to produce exports.
- Factor proportions theory does a reasonable job of explaining and prediction international trade and the effects of trade policy.

REVIEW PROBLEMS

1. In the specific factors economy from the problems in Section A suppose the price of imported M rises to $2.40 with a tariff. Show what happens in the labor market.

2. Diagram what happens in the previous problem to markets for sector specific capital inputs. Explain adjustments in outputs?

3. Suppose country A imposes a tariff on imported manufactures and its terms of trade with country B improve. Predict what happens to income distribution in country B with the specific factors model.

4. Diagram the international capital market with a capital abundand country. Figure 6.6 is a guide.

5. Diagram the international productional production of services with a capital abundant home country siminar to Figure 6.7.

6. Sketch the cost minimization with w = $2, r = $3, c = $1, and 0.2 unit of L input. Find the capital input and sketch the unit value isoquant. Describe what happens if r falls to $2.

7. Describe what happens to the cost minimization in the previous problem if w rises to $3.

8. Given factor prices $w = \$2$ and $r = \$3$ suppose 0.35 units of labor are employed in manufacturing to produce $1 of output. Sketch the manufacturing cost minimization and the expansion path. Find K/L in manufacturing.

9. Draw the production diagram of the economy with the service sector in problem 6 and the manufacturing sector in problem 8.

10. Two economies have endowments $(K,L) = (100,200)$ and $(K^*,L^*) = (110,190)$. With the technology in Problem 9 predict the pattern of trade. Explain which country is labor cheap.

11. If the foreign country described in the previous problem 8 imposes a tariff what happens to w^* and r^*? Illustrate with a diagram. What happens to the K/L ratios in manufacturing and services?

12. Illustrate factor price equalization using a production diagram when the home country has twice as much capital and half as much labor as the foreign country.

13. Draw the home PPF in the constant cost endowment model with endowment $(L,H) = (400,500)$ and unit inputs in the text. Draw the foreign PPF* with endowment $(L^*,H^*) = (300,600)$.

14. Find the terms of trade and consumption for the two economies in the previous problem. Explain the pattern of trade.

15. With three factors (capital, labor, natural resources) and two goods (manufactures, services) define factor intensity.

16. If agricultural output is added to the previous problem, define factor intensity and factor abundance.

READINGS

William Baumol, Richard Nelson, and Edward Wolff (1994) *Convergence of Productivity*, Oxford: Oxford University Press. History of convergence across countries.

Brian Berry, Edgar Conkling, and Michael Ray (1997) *The Global Economy in Transition*, New Jersey: Prentice-Hall. Graphical blend of geography, energy analysis, population dynamics, and economics.

David Richardson (1993) *Sizing Up US Export Disincentives*, Washington: Institute for International Economics. Policies leading to lower exports.

John Pool and Stephen Stamos (1994) *Exploring the Global Economy*, Shenandoah University: Durell Institute of Monetary Science. Short excursion into importance of international commerce.

A.G. Kenwood and A.L. Lougheed (1992) *The Growth of the International Economy, 1820–1990*, London: Routledge. A nice economic history.

Alan Deardorff and Robert Stern (1986) *The Michigan Model of World Production and Trade: Theory and Applications*, Cambridge: MIT Press. CGE model of production and trade.

Edward Leamer (1984) *Sources of International Comparative Advantage*, Cambridge: MIT Press, 1984. Quantitative basis of factor abundance and trade.

Ron Findlay (1988) *Factor Proportions, Trade, and Growth*, Cambridge: MIT Press. Clearly written short book.

CHAPTER 7

Industrial Organization and Trade

Preview

Industrial organization describes how firms form an industry. The four types of industrial organization are competition, monopolistic competition, oligopoly, and monopoly. These are important examples of each in international trade. Competitive industries have many firms producing a homogeneous product with free entry and exit of firms driving economic profit to zero. Monopolies are a single firm searching for price to maximize profit. Oligopolies have a few firms. Monopolistic competition involves differentiated products. Topics include:

- Price searching firms in international markets
- Intraindustry trade and product differentiation
- Oligopolies and trade
- Technology, product cycles, and increasing returns in trade

INTRODUCTION

The simplest industry is a monopoly, a single firm. An international monopoly is a single foreign firm as the only supplier. An exporting monopolist restricts output, sells at a high price, and enjoys positive profit. There is monopoly power in international markets for some primary commodities.

International monopoly price searchers can discriminate by setting price according to demands of different countries. Buyers with higher or more inelastic demand will pay a higher price.

In an international oligopoly, a firm in one country competes with a few firms in other countries. Decisions made by a foreign firm affect the home firm. An oligopoly can be nearly as competitive as a market with many firms Firms may be able to collude and share monopoly profit.

Monopolistic competition has firms with some monopoly power setting their own price. Foreign firms or foreign demand for home products lead to trade. Free entry and exit of firms drive profit to zero under monopolistic competition.

If two countries have different production technologies, trade benefits both. Some countries have a comparative advantage in new products, leading to trade in a product cycle. Different income levels across countries affect demand and trade. Increasing returns to scale lead to specialization and trade as unit costs decline with increased output.

A.   PRICE SEARCHING FIRMS AND TRADE

A firm that faces downward sloping demand can search for the price that maximizes profit. There are unique principles of production and trade for monopolistic price searchers.

Price Searching Firms

A single firm in an industry is a monopoly. Natural monopolies occur when average cost declines for the firm all the way to the output that meets market demand. Average cost declines due to economies of scale. One large firm is more efficient than a number of smaller firms. Small firms are driven out of business.

Legal monopolies arise from property rights that exclude potential competitors. Profits may be high but entry is illegal. Patents, franchises, licensing, and resource ownership are property rights that lead to legal monopolies. A production process may be patented ensuring other firms cannot copy a product or process. Copyright law ensures the property rights of authors, musicians, and movie producers. International patent and copyright agreements are a focus of trade negotiations.

Utility companies have the sole right to sell their services in their franchised area. Licensing restricts competition. Foreign telecommunication firms and doctors are prohibited from entry. OPEC and other resource cartels have international monopoly power based on property rights.

With a single firm in an industry, the monopolist searches for the price and quantity combination that maximizes profit. The monopolist chooses a supply point on the demand curve. The profit maximizing price and quantity are found comparing marginal revenue MR and marginal cost MC of an additional unit of output. If MR is greater than MC the monopolist produces the additional unit. If MC is greater than MR profit rises if the monopolist reduces output.

Suppose all the world's gold is owned by a single mining firm. In Figure 7.1 world demand for gold is D. The single firm is constrained by demand. There are substitutes for gold: silver in jewelry, titanium in industrial uses, and real estate as an asset. If the monopolist sets the price of gold at $3000 none is bought. Marginal revenue MR is below demand D since the monopolist must lower price to sell more.

With linear demand the *inverse demand function* is $P = a - bQ$ where a and b are positive numbers. Total revenue TR is price P times quantity Q, $TR = aQ - bQ^2$. MR is the change in TR for a one unit change in Q: $MR = a - 2bQ$. Students with calculus recognize MR as the derivative of TR. Work through the example of the inverse demand function $P = 1000 - .5Q$ to derive marginal revenue $MR = 1000 - 10Q$. Note that MR is twice as steep as linear demand.

Another constraint on monopoly pricing and output is the cost of production. The monopoly has a certain amount of machinery and equipment to go along with labor. To produce more gold requires more labor, more wear and tear on machinery and equipment, and more energy input.

Marginal cost generally increases with output. The marginal cost curve *MC* is a short run marginal cost curve that holds capital input constant. *MC* slopes upward due to diminishing marginal productivity. Additional workers add to total output but beyond some point these increments shrink. Increasing output also raises demand for inputs and their prices may rise.

At outputs below 2000 tons, the marginal revenue from selling an extra unit of output is larger than the marginal cost of producing it. The monopolist raises profit by increasing output and continues until $MR = MC = \$1200$.

After finding output that maximizes profit, the monopolist sets the price of gold according to demand. All 2000 tons can be sold at a price of $1600 where the output of 2000 meets demand *D*.

Price searching firms maximize profit at the output where MR = MC and set price according to demand to clear the market.

EXAMPLE **7.1**   *A Snapshot of Exporting Firms*

Manufacturing firms account for about 70% of US export revenue followed by wholesalers, freight forwarders, transportation, services, business services, engineering, management, gas and oil extraction, coal mining, and communications. Large firms with 500 or more employees account for most of export revenue.

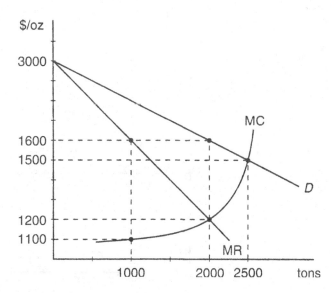

Figure 7.1
A Price Searching Monopoly Exporter
For a monopolist, marginal revenue (*MR*) is below demand *D*. This monopolist produces where *MR* equals marginal cost (*MC*) at 2000 tons. Output is sold according to demand at $1600.

Intrafirm trade is almost half of total merchandise export revenue. Most firms trade with only one foreign country. The few firms that trade with 50 or more countries account for about half of all merchandise export revenue.

A Price Taking Firm

An industry can be made up of many small competitive firms. Each firm is a competitive price taker. A price taking firm in the competitive international corn market is pictured in Figure 7.2. Each price taking firm has no power to vary the international price of $5 where demand equals supply for the industry. MR equals $5 for each firm because every bushel is sold for the same price. For competitive firms D and MR are horizontal lines at the market price. Profit is maximized where $MR = MC$ at a quantity of 2500.

Imagine marginal revenue MR were equal to demand D for the price searcher in Figure 7.1. The monopolist would then maximize profit where $MR = MC$ by setting the price at $1500 and selling output Q of 2500 similar to the outcome in Figure 7.2. A monopoly prices higher and produces less output than a competitive firm.

EXAMPLE **7.2**   *Steel Trigger Prices*

During the 1960s the US steel industry faced increased competition from Japan and Europe after they had rebuilt following World War II. Their wages were about half those in the US. Ingo Walter (1983) estimates their production costs were

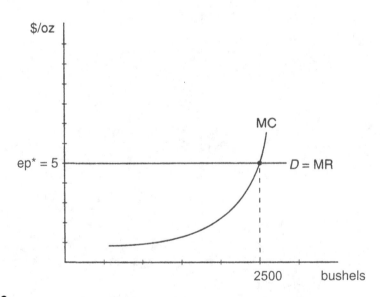

Figure 7.2
A Price Taking Exporting Firm
The international price of corn is $5. This price taker can sell any quantity at this international price. This firm maximizes profit where $MR = MC$ at 2500 bushels.

about 40% of US costs. The share of imports in steel consumption rose from 5% in 1960 to 18% in 1980. US steel firms pressured the government which pressured foreign governments which pressured foreign steel firms to agree to "voluntary" export restraints. Repeated cases resulted in the trigger price mechanism in 1978. If the price of steel imports fell below cost plus shipping, imports are stopped. Trigger prices proved impossible to administer. Since the 1980s competition in the international steel market has increased from NICs such as South Korea, Taiwan, Spain, and Latin America as well as some LDCs. Rather than depending on protection, the US steel industry has become internationally competitive by specializing in high tech specialty alloys.

Monopoly Profit

If firms in a competitive industry make a profit, other firms enter, supply increases, and price falls. *Free entry* implies competition and zero profit. Entry is ruled out by law for a legal monopoly.

Monopoly profit is the difference between price P and average cost AC at the optimal output. In Figure 7.3 profit is maximized where $MR = MC$ at $Q = 100$. Output is sold according to demand at $90.

For the lowest cost at AC_1 with the optimal output 100, $AC_1 = \$70$ and total cost $TC = AC \times Q = \$70 \times 100 = \$7000$. With $P = \$90$ and $Q = 100$ total

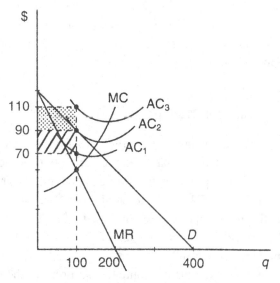

Figure 7.3
Profit for a Monopolistic Firm
Profit is maximized where $MR = MC$ at $q = 100$. Price is set according to demand at $15. Profit depends on average cost AC at the profit maximizing output. With AC_1, profit is $\$3 \times 100 = \$300$. With AC_3 total loss is $-\$300$. At AC_2 profit is zero.

revenue is $TR = \$9000$. Profit π is the difference between total revenue and total cost: $\pi = TR - TC = \$9000 - \$7000 = \$2000$, the lined area. Profit is positive since average revenue (price) is greater than average cost.

At the highest average cost AC_3 total cost $TC = \$110 \times 100 = \$11,000$ is greater than $TR = \$9000$. With AC_3 there is a loss, $\pi = \$9000 - \$11,000 = -\$2000$, the dotted area. A monopoly may operate for a time with a loss if future profit is expected.

A monopolist would *shut down* if fixed costs were less than losses. When a firm shuts down it lays off labor and ceases operation but fixed costs including utilities and rent have to be paid. A monopolist may sell out its capital if it does not expect improved market conditions.

With costs AC_2 profit is zero where $P = AC$. A price searcher has no guarantee of positive profit. Demand for the product and cost of production determine profit.

EXAMPLE **7.3**   *Trade Agreements*

The WTO continues to provide a hearing for trade disputes. OECD discussions on investment and legal coordination continue. NAFTA is evolving according to schedule. Negotiations for Free Trade Area of the Americas FTAA continue. Asia-Pacific Economic Cooperation APEC is involved in talks over product standards. The Transatlantic Economic Partnership TEP coordinates legal issues between the US and the EU. China and the US have a working trade agreement. Taiwan and the US have problems over pirating of US software. The US Generalized System of Preferences GSP defines which tariff schedules apply to which countries. Textile market sharing quotas attempt to govern textile imports. The International Trade Commission ITC is the main administrator of all US trade agreements.

International Monopolies

A tariff may be optimal with imports from an international monopolist, . Domestic consumers have to pay a higher price but the domestic government taxes away some of the profit of the foreign monopoly. Tariff revenue is also generated.

In Figure 7.4 domestic demand is D. Costs for the foreign monopolist to sell in the home market are MC^* and AC^*. The monopolist would produce where $MR = MC^*$ at $Q = 100$ and $P = \$15$. With AC at $\$12$ profit of the foreign monopolist is $\$300$.

A $\$2$ tariff transfers some of that profit to the home government. The effective demand curve falls by $\$2$ to D' and marginal revenue falls to MR'. Output falls to 90 where MR' equals MC^*. Price in the domestic market rises to $\$15.50$ but the foreign monopolist receives only $\$13.50$.

The home government collects tariff revenue in the shaded area $\$2 \times 90 = \$180$. This tariff revenue can compensate consumers. The size of the tariff revenue and

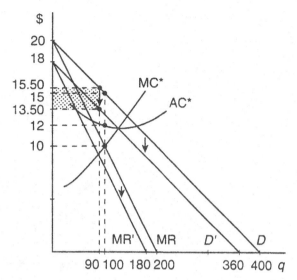

Figure 7.4
Taxing a Foreign Monopolist
A tariff on a foreign monopolist lowers demand from D to D'. Profit maximizing output falls from 100 to 90 and price from $15 to $13.50. The $2 per unit tax is collected by the government. Tariff revenue is $2 \times 90 = $180. Profit falls. Domestic consumers pay a higher price and reduce consumption. The lost consumer surplus of $47.50 is less than the tariff revenue.

the lost consumer surplus depend on demand and costs. In Figure 7.4 the transfer to the government is larger than the lost consumer surplus making the tariff optimal.

International Price Discrimination

An international price searcher that can distinguish among groups of buyers will increase profit by pricing to the demand of each group. With price discrimination consumers in countries with higher or more inelastic demand pay higher prices.

The international monopolist in Figure 7.5 faces domestic and foreign demand D and D^* with marginal revenues MR and MR^*. For simplicity MC is constant. Each additional unit of output costs the same to produce making AC constant. A price discriminating monopolist produces where marginal cost MC equals MR for each group.

Profit maximization is 37.5 units of output for the home market and 32 for the foreign market. Foreign buyers have higher and more inelastic demand and pay $6 while domestic buyers pay only $5. Profit is higher than if the two demands are summed. Selling in the home market, the monopolist makes a profit of $3 per unit for a total of $3 \times 37.5 = $112.50. Foreign profit is $4 \times 32 = $128. Resale of products from home country to the foreign country must be ruled out.

International dumping is predatory pricing, a foreign firm temporarily selling below average cost to eliminate domestic competition. The foreign firm

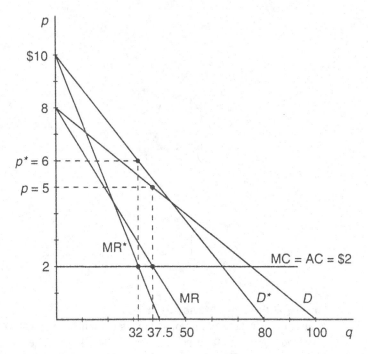

Figure 7.5
Price Discrimination by an Exporting Monopolist
This monopolist can discriminate between home demand curve D and foreign demand curve D^*. MC is constant at $2, and making average cost (AC) is $2. The monopolist equates MC with MR and MR^*, 32 units selling abroad for $6 with and 37.5 units sold at home for $5.

plans to enjoy monopoly profit later. The International Trade Commission ITC hears dumping complaints and can award damages and import quotas. Other countries have similar restrictive measures.

Japanese computer chip firms were found guilty of dumping. The US steel industry has repeatedly charged European firms with dumping. Vietnamese firms were found guilty of dumping catfish. China is accused of dumping. Without cost information it is impossible to determine whether a foreign firm is dumping. Determinations by the ITC are based on politics.

Trying to police dumping is not worthwhile. Dumping is not a long run problem. International price competition is too sophisticated for government officials to control. Protection from alleged dumping offers industry another nontariff barrier with large payoffs. The "unholy alliance" between industry and government promotes corruption.

EXAMPLE **7.4**   *ITC Protectionism*

The International Trade Commission ITC hears cases and awards protection if foreign industry competes unfairly. Antidumping duties are awarded if foreign firms appear to be dumping. Countervailing duties are awarded if there appear to be foreign subsidies. Wendy Hansen and Thomas Prusa (1997) examine 744 dumping cases filed between 1980 and 1988. The steel industry has the highest probability of a favorable ruling. Industries with more Congressional representatives on the House Ways and Means Committee are more likely to receive protection. Political Action Committee donations increase the probability of a favorable ruling, Foreign countries with growing market shares are more likely guilty, as are nonmarket economies. Western Europe was 17% less likely due to the threat of retaliation. Political considerations dominate decisions.

Dominant Firm Imports

Some industries have a dominant firm that sets price plus a number of competitive fringe firms that follow. Suppose there is a dominant foreign exporter with a number of fringe domestic firms. Fringe domestic firms supply according to the price set by the dominant foreign firm, a higher price leading to more output by the domestic fringe.

Domestic demand D in Figure 7.6 is the sum of demand for the product of the foreign dominant firm DF^* and the residual domestic fringe supply FS. If the foreign dominant firm sets price below $80 it captures demand and the

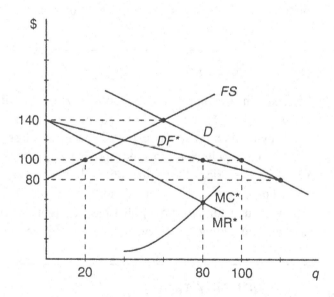

Figure 7.6
A Dominant Fringe Import Market
Domestic demand D is composed of the foreign dominant firm demand DF^* and domestic fringe supply FS. The dominant foreign firm produces where $MC^* = MR^*$ and prices output at $100. Domestic fringe suppliers produce residual output of 20. A tariff taxes the dominant foreign firm and stimulates domestic fringe firms, but creates losses for domestic consumers. The tariff generates tariff revenue and may be optimal.

domestic competitive fringe supplies nothing. Domestic fringe suppliers cannot produce for less than $80.

The domestic fringe would completely take over the market at $140. The dominant foreign firm sets price and the domestic competitive fringe responds with output. For any price between $80 and $140 the domestic fringe shares the market.

Marginal revenue MR^* for the foreign dominant firm is derived from demand DF^*. The dominant foreign firm maximizes profit by producing where MR^* equals marginal cost MC^* at $Q = 80$ and $P = \$100$ leaving a residual of 20 units for the domestic fringe on FS.

A tariff reduces output of the dominant foreign firm and increases the market share of the domestic fringe. Domestic consumers would pay a higher price. The tariff produces revenue for the government. The tariff takes away some of the foreign dominant firm market power and profit. Net gains depend on demand and costs.

EXAMPLE **7.5**   *Import Quality Competition*

US imports have become more differentiated since the 1970s with lower quality products coming from low wage countries as shown by Peter Schott (2004). About 3/4 of all products come from low wage countries with more expensive varieties from high wage countries. Shirts imported in 1994 from Japan were 30 times more expensive than from the Philippines. The factor content theorem is supported when products are aggregated by quality.

Section A Problems

A1. Explain whether legal monopolies are more likely within a country or internationally. Do the same for natural monopolies.

A2. Why might a monopoly exporter operate at a loss? Should we be concerned if a foreign monopoly wants to export products for less than their cost of production?

A3. Illustrate price discrimination with home consumers paying more. How might home consumers react? Would claims of dumping be heard?

A4. Assume a foreign monopolist has constant marginal cost. Show the effects of a tariff including tariff revenue, lost profit, and consumer surplus.

B.   INTRAINDUSTRY TRADE

Exports and imports of the same product are called intraindustry trade. Theories up to this point suggest countries specialize and export some products and import others. This section looks into intraindustry trade, exporting and importing the same category of products.

Product Differentiation

Basic commodities such as grains and metals are graded and standard. At the other extreme, the computer market has a wide variety of products. Most products have product differentiation.

Grains are different from fruits although they are both food. Rice is different from barley, although they are both grains. Long grain rice is different from short grain rice although they are both rice. Regardless of how fine the category, there is some product differentiation.

Buyers and sellers in a market are familiar with their product. Firms competing internationally know the products better than anybody else. Economists work with categories of products designed by governments interested in applying tariffs. Categories such as yarn, glass, medical products, alcoholic beverages, and telecommunications apparatus are very coarse. When goods are disaggregated into a finer classification, product differentiation falls.

EXAMPLE **7.6**   *Intraindustry Trade Index*

Trade within an industry decreases when there are more categories of products. The index of intraindustry trade is

$$I = (X - M)/(X + M)$$

If a product is only exported $I = 1$ and if only imported $I = -1$. If export revenue and import spending are identical $I = 0$. As an example $I = 0.21$ for harvest machines. For harvest machine parts $I = 0.47$ with more intraindustry trade in the broader category. Herbert Grubel and Peter Lloyd (1975) show intraindustry trade in Australia varies from 43% to 6% of total trade depending on aggregation.

Intraindustry Trade

Intraindustry trade occurs if products in the same category are imported and exported. Cost differences in producing different qualities lead to intraindustry trade. A consumer buying a shirt is interested in shirts service including days of dress, warmth, and style. Higher quality means more shirt service but has higher marginal cost.

Figure 7.7 illustrates marginal costs of two qualities along with demand D for services. Profit is maximized for each quality by producing where MR equals MC. The firm would sell 10 units of the high quality shirt for $20 or 20 units of the low quality shirt at $15.

If production of the high quality shirt is capital intensive, a capital abundant country would specialize and export it. A labor abundant country would specialize

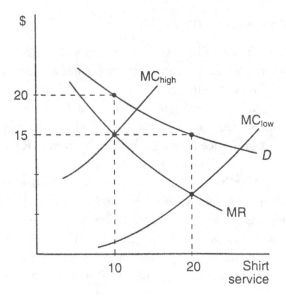

Figure 7.7
Quality Differentiation and Price
When quality varies, consumers demand the services the product provides. A high quality shirt has a higher cost of production than a low quality version. This firm would produce a lower quantity and charge a higher price for the high quality shirt.

in the labor intensive low quality shirt. Consumers in each country want both types of shirts leading to *intraindustry trade*.

> *Intraindustry trade with the same product category imported and exported can occur due to quality differences.*

Another cause of intraindustry trade is transport cost, both international and domestic. International sea shipping may be cheaper than crossing land. In large countries border regions can be closer to other countries than to domestic regions on another border.

For instance, Texas is closer to Central America than to New York. The US exports chemicals from California and imports them from the EU. Location and transport costs explain some intraindustry trade.

Products with high intraindustry trade include envelopes, transformers, plumbing fixtures, machine tool accessories, synthetic rubber, fans, and sheet metal. Goods more narrowly defined have less price dispersion and less intraindustry trade: women's handbags, soap, radios, TV sets, leather gloves, costume jewelry, refrigerators, and vacuum cleaners.

Manufactured goods are more differentiated than primary products and agricultural goods. As countries develop they produce more manufactured goods. DCs have more intraindustry trade than LDCs.

EXAMPLE **7.7**   *Intraindustry Price Dispersion*

Intraindustry trade depends on national and industrial characteristics as well as aggregation. Elizabeth Wickham and Henry Thompson (1989) show more capital abundant countries have more intraindustry trade. Smaller labor abundant countries produce more homogeneous products, raw materials, and basic manufactures. Price dispersion increases with intraindustry trade.

Monopolistic Competition and Trade

Firms selling differentiated products have price searching power. Positive profit, however, attracts other firms. Entry reduces the demand for each firm and may raise input prices. Entry leads to zero profit. Such an industry with price searching firms but zero profit is monopolistic competition. Firms face downward sloping demand because consumers recognize brand names.

Figure 7.8 illustrates a firm with monopolistic competition and zero profit. The firm maximizes profit where $MC = MR$ by producing 100 units of output and price $10 equal to average cost AC.

When such firms are located in different countries, there is intraindustry trade. If domestic firms enjoy positive profit, entry by foreign firms can lower demand for domestic firms. A tariff raises demand for domestic firms but the foreign government can retaliate.

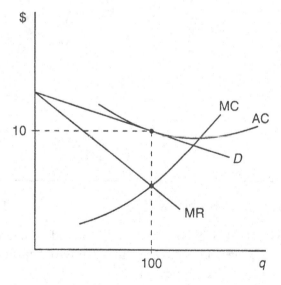

Figure 7.8
A Typical Firm in Monopolistic Competition
The firm faces downward sloping demand and marginal revenue. It maximizes profit where $MR = MC$ with output $q = 100$ and price = $10. Competition pushes cost to zero economic profit where $P = AC$.

When a country opens to trade, domestic firms have to compete with foreign ones. Suppose a protected domestic industry is making a positive profit but the country moves to free trade. Foreign firms enter the industry and drive domestic firms toward zero profit. Foreign firms make the domestic industry more competitive. Trade limits market power and encourages more efficient production.

EXAMPLE **7.8**   *Intraindustry Beer Trade*

The level of international competition and intraindustry trade in beer is increasing as shown by Jeffrey Karrenbrock (1990) with the index of intraindustry trade I. France has the most intraindustry trade but exports only a small share X/Q of its output. The US and France consume the highest ratio of imports M/C. Ireland and the Netherlands are the most involved exporters. Consumers in Denmark and Czechoslovakia had no imports due to protection.

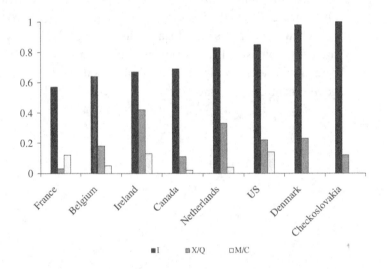

Section B Problems

B1. The US imports cars across a wide range of quality. How would a VER on Japanese imports affect the quality of Japanese imported cars? Explain what happens to domestic quality.

B2. With three products (food, clothing, household goods) what are the advantages of aggregating clothing and household goods into manufactured goods? What happens to the level of intraindustry trade?

B3. With monopolistic competition in an export industry and negative profit, describe what will happen to the number of firms and profit of the typical firm.

EXAMPLE **7.9**   *Beer and Wine Trade*

> Beer is locally produced and consumed everywhere. Wine is produced where grapes are grown, and has been rising in global popularity. Joshua Aizenman and Eileen Brooks (2005, *NBER Working Paper*) examine consumption across 38 countries and find wine consumption catching up with beer. Local tastes matter, however, with Latin Americans for instance strongly preferring beer.

C.   OLIGOPOLY TRADE

An industry with only a few firms is an oligopoly. In an international oligopoly has firms in different countries. An oligopoly can exhibit the full range of competition from monopoly to perfect competition.

Oligopoly Collusion

Firms in an oligopoly have the incentive to collude and share monopoly profit. Collusion raises price and reduces output, but firms in the cartel face the problem of how to share the profit.

Collusion across international borders is legal. There are a number of international cartels mainly in primary products such as oil, rubber, coffee, tea, and bananas. *Antitrust laws* in the US are designed to limit monopoly power and collusion. There are no international antitrust laws.

EXAMPLE **7.10**   *Bananas, Airplanes, and Export Taxes*

> Export taxes are unconstitutional in the US because the colonists were tired of sending export tax revenue to the King of England. All other countries tax exports. Jessica Bailey and James Sood (1987) propose a banana export tax to maximize revenue in Latin America. The tax would raise price to the monopoly level. Fewer bananas would be sold but export revenue would increase. The problem is how to split the profit. The US has some market power in aircraft and could tax aircraft exports if it were constitutional.

Oligopoly Demand

The dilemma of an oligopoly firm is illustrated in Figure 7.9. The price is $100 and the firm has the option of raising or lowering price to increase profit. If it raises price, consumers buy cheaper substitutes. Other firms in the industry enjoy increased demand. Revenue falls with the price increase. Demand facing the firm is elastic for prices above $100. If the firm lowers price, other firms do the same to keep from losing customers. Revenue falls with the price reduction. Demand is inelastic for prices below $100.

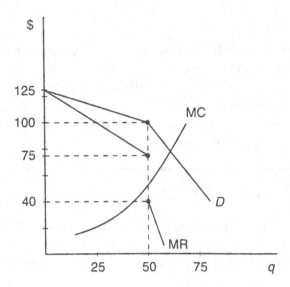

Figure 7.9
Kinked Oligopoly Demand
Suppose the current price is $100 and quantity 50. If the firm raises price, competing firms will not follow suit. Demand is elastic. If the oligopolist lowers price, the competition also does. Demand is inelastic. Revenue falls whether the firm lowers or raises price.

The demand curve facing this firm is kinked. Revenue falls for the firm whether price is raised or lowered. Kinked demand implies a broken marginal revenue curve.

Each firm in an oligopoly faces the same dilemma. All firms tend to keep price and output constant. This can occur with an explicit cartel agreement or through informal monitoring of prices.

EXAMPLE 7.11   *Quotas and Domestic Downgrading*

Quotas can cause import quality upgrading as foreign exporters aim to increase revenue per unit sold. Examples include imports of compact pickup trucks and cheese. Randy Beard and Henry Thompson (2003) show domestic quality downgrading can also occur. The domestic producer raises output and reduces quality to the monopoly level. While foreign quality upgrading is likely, domestic quality downgrading is necessary.

An International Duopoly

A duopoly is an oligopoly with two firms. A duopoly with a home and foreign firm is an international duopoly. Suppose each firm has the option of high or low output. The profit of each firm depends on its choice and the choice of the other firm. In such a setting, game theory can predict how the two firms behave.

Table 7.1 presents the outcomes. Home profit first in parentheses. If the home firm produces high output and the foreign firm low output, profit for the home firm is $2 million while the foreign firm loses $1 million. If both firms produce

Table 7.1 An International Duopoly Game
(Home Profit, Foreign Profit)

		Foreign Output	
		Low	High
Home Output	Low	($1 mil, $1 mil)	(−$1 mil, $2 mil)
	High	($2 mil, −$1 mil)	($0, $0)

high output, they break even with zero profit. If the two firms collude and restrict output by producing low levels, they split monopoly profit of $2 million.

Collusion is preferred to the competitive outcome but the dilemma is the temptation to cheat on the cartel. If the foreign firm cheats by producing high output, it takes $2 million profit and the home firm suffers a loss of $1 million.

If this game is repeated yearly, the firms have the incentive to collude and restrict output. An international cartel between the two firms restricts output resulting in profit for both.

Regardless of the choice of the foreign firm, the home firm benefits by producing high output. The game is symmetric with the same true for the foreign firm. Given a correct guess about opponent behavior, each firm will produce high output. If both firms produce high output, however, they make zero profit.

Both firms will do better by producing high output regardless of the opponent's choice. Competition is a stable equilibrium. The home firm could restrict its own output one year suffer and a loss. The foreign firm notices the home firm credibility as a cartel partner. The foreign firm may restrict output as well. If the home firm continues to restrict output, the cartel has been established.

EXAMPLE **7.12**   *International Aircraft Oligopoly*

The US remains the world leader in the aircraft industry. The EU and UK are also major producers. Producers compete to design and sell new and more efficient aircraft. The firms may price according to cartel behavior. They sell military aircraft as part of the military industrial complex described by President Eisenhower in the 1950s.

International Cartels

Payoffs for collusion can be large but cartels typically break apart during periods of falling demand and prices. OPEC has enjoyed more success and lasted longer than predicted when it formed in the 1970s. The problem for OPEC is keeping its members from selling more than their alloted cartel quota.

OPEC produces about 1/3 of world oil output and faces competition from other sources. Oil prices fell during the 1990s. In 1999 OPEC countries agreed to quotas and prices rebounded. Prices since 2000 have been much more erratic due to refining problems, wars, and growing demand in China and India. Prospects are that oil prices will rise due to increasing scarcity although supply technology continues to improve. The 2015 price collapse was due to improved extraction technology.

International cartels easily break down into competition. Members often have too much to gain by breaking the agreement and selling at the high price. Consumers benefit from the competitive prices of a cartel collapse.

> *Strategies determine the outcome of international oligopolies. There are various possible strategies and no general conclusions.*

Oligopolies are made competitive by the threat of entry. Profits encourage entry. Existing firms may behave more competitively to discourage entry. Existing firms can discourage potential entrants by making a credible threat to lower price. Oligopoly firms may try to keep price near the competitive level to discourage entry. Other sorts of nonprice competition such as advertising can discourage entry. In a contestable market the threat of entry is as forceful as competition.

EXAMPLE 7.13   *Pricing to Market*

When a currency appreciates, prices of exports for buyers in foreign countries rise. For an exporting firm appreciation decreases demand. The monopolist has the option of lowering price to keep the foreign currency price of its product constant and protect its market share. Michael Knetter (1989) finds German exporters price to the US market but US exporters do not price to foreign markets. The dollar depreciation of the late 1980s did not raise the US trade deficit because prices of imports were kept low as foreign exporters priced to market.

International Duopoly Subsidies

Suppose the US firm Boeing and the EU firm Airbus face the decision of whether to produce and export a new type of passenger jet. Paul Krugman (1987) examines such an international duopoly and suggests a government subsidy to raise profit.

Table 7.2 presents profits with and without production in a one time game. If Boeing correctly guesses that Airbus will produce, Boeing will not produce because zero is more than minus 5. If Boeing correctly guesses that Airbus will not produce, Boeing will make profit of 100. If Boeing produces and Airbus does not Airbus is trapped. If Boeing is established, entry by Airbus is deterred.

The US government may want to subsidize Boeing to encourage production. The cost of the subsidy may be less than the profit enjoyed by Boeing. Such strategic trade policy may seem like a good idea.

Governments, however, cannot recognize and react to such situations. Subsidized industries typically fail. Economists know the theory but typically little about industries. All industries lobby for subsidies. It is wise to leave important

Table 7.2 A Duopoly Dilemma
(Boeing Profit, Airbus Profit)

| | | Airbus | |
		Produce	Don't Produce
Boeing	Produce	(−5, 5)	(100, 0)
	Don't Produce	(0, 100)	(0, 0)

business decisions to the experts in the industry. Subsidies as strategic trade policy are understandably popular but ill advised.

EXAMPLE 7.14   *Japanese, German, Canadian Pricing to Market*

Japanese transport and electrical equipment producers price to market according to Richard Marston (1998). These firms maintain foreign currency prices with a wedge between prices in Japan and export prices. Japanese, Canadian, and German exporters to the US are more inclined to price to market than are US exporters according to Michael Knetter (1989). Exporters to the US must sell in competitive markets while US exporters maintain their dollar prices with less worry about foreign competition.

Section C Problems

C1. Suppose cost rises for the firm in Figure 7.9 so *MC* intersects *MR* at $100 and $q = 25$. Find the price. Explain how other firms in the industry would react. Find and explain the change in revenue.

C2. When OPEC income increased dramatically during the 1970s the OPEC countries did not spend it all. Explain what had to happen.

C3. If the oil import elasticity is −0.6 and price increases from $20 to $22, find the percentage change in the level of imports. What are the two sources of this decrease? If OPEC raises price to $40 find the reduction in imports. Explain what happens to OPEC revenue with these price increases.

D.   OTHER THEORIES OF TRADE

Other causes of trade are technology differences, the product cycle, increasing returns, and income differences.

Technology and Trade

Production depends on the technology to combine inputs into outputs. Estimated production functions describe relationships between inputs and outputs. Firms

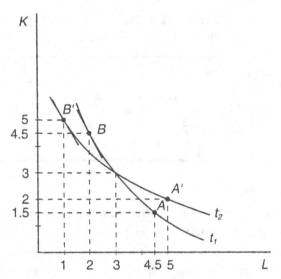

Figure 7.10
Production with Different Technologies
Isoquants t_1 and t_2 represent different ways to produce the same amount of output with different technologies. Less of both inputs may result in the same output, illustrated by A and A'. Cost minimizing inputs will vary, illustrated by B and B'. Different technologies can result in international trade.

in different countries employing capital, labor, and natural resources may get different outputs due to different production functions.

Figure 7.10 shows unit isoquants of two production functions. The same amount of output is produced along isoquant t_1 or t_2. At point A, there is 1.5 capital and 4.5 labor resulting in 1 unit of output with technology t_1. With technology t_2 two K and five L produce the same output at A'. Points B and B' illustrate different cost minimizing inputs for the same input prices.

Suppose two countries have identical factor endowments, the same number of consumers, and identical preferences. Different technologies would provide incentive to trade. If the home country has better technology for producing services and the foreign country better technology for producing manufactures, both benefit from specialization and trade.

Technology differences across countries can lead to international specialization and trade.

Different input ratios do not indicate different technologies. To minimize cost a firm picks the optimal input mix depending on input prices. Firms produce with the same production functions but mix inputs according to local input prices. Labor abundant LDCs economize with labor intensive production. Multinational firms provide the same technology available around the world. LDCs send students to the DCs to become familiar with the latest technology. Technology is widely available suggesting technology differences do not explain much trade.

EXAMPLE **7.15**   *Unexposed Manufactures*

Average tariffs for the US, EU, and Japan are fairly low with the EU the highest at 8%. NTB is the percentage of products subject to nontariff barriers. Import spending M relative to consumption C indicates the US is most involved. Exposure E includes both imports and exports and ranges from 0% with $X = M = 0$ to 100% with $M = C$ and $X = 0$. Japanese manufacturing is the least exposed due to the *kerietsu* system of trade associations.

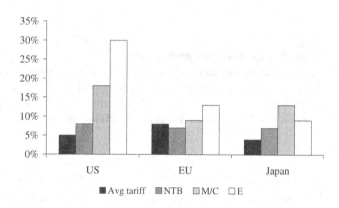

Product Cycle Trade

Table 7.3 shows shares of worldwide spending on research and development R&D. Developed countries do almost all R&D. Exports from DCs have a high intensity of R&D. DCs have comparative advantage in high tech products. Exports with high levels of R&D relate to the product cycle.

Table 7.3 Shares of World R&D Spending

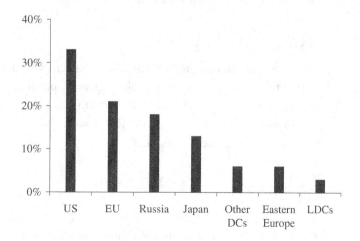

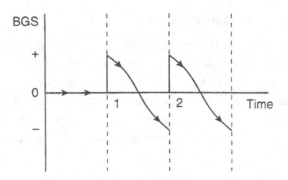

Figure 7.11
The Product Cycle and Trade
The research and development (R&D) country creates innovations at times 1 and 2 resulting in trade surpluses as the new product is exported. Over time, other nations copy the technology and the R&D country loses market power and slips into deficit. Innovations lead to new products that jump the R&D country back to a surplus.

The product cycle predicts export of new high tech products from DCs in exchange for low tech products from LDCs. Over time, new products are produced by LDCs. Products cycle from new to old, and from DCs to LDCs.

In Figure 7.11 new products are unveiled at times 1 and 2. The R&D country exports new products with a monopoly position in the new product. As time passes LDCs learn to make the new product and begin low cost manufacturing. Soon the DC becomes a net importer of the good and moves to a trade deficit in that product.

Products cycle from new to old as production shifts from innovative to copying countries. R&D countries are net exporters of new products.

Product cycle trade would be more prevalent if DCs did not protect their domestic labor intensive industries. Protection discourages LDCs from adapting routine manufacturing processes.

EXAMPLE **7.16**   *R&D and High Tech Exports*

The US has almost half of the R&D scientists in the world. The US has a comparative advantage in developing new products and leads other countries in the product cycle. The EU and Japan have increased R&D. The rest of the world has less than 10% of all R&D scientists. The US has consistent export surpluses in high tech products.

Returns to Scale and Trade

Returns to scale refer to how inputs affect firm output. Constant returns to scale CRS occur when a proportional changes in all inputs result in the same proportional

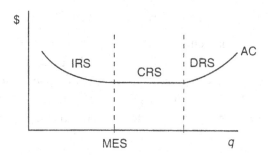

Figure 7.12
Returns to Scale in the Firm
Average cost AC is decreasing with increasing returns to scale IRS up to the minimum efficient scale MES. AC is constant with constant returns to scale CRS. Then AC rises with decreasing returns to scale DRS.

change in output. Output doubles if all inputs double. With increasing returns to scale IRS, output more than doubles. With decreasing returns to scale DRS output rises but by less than 100%.

Returns to scale can be external or internal to the firm. External influences include transportation, communication, utility infrastructure, local suppliers, and trained workers. Internal returns to scale occur inside the firm with better utilized machinery and other resources.

Average cost decreases up to the minimum efficient scale MES of the firm. Figure 7.12 illustrates a long run average cost curve. With IRS the *AC* declines. In the region of CRS the *AC* is constant. With DRS the *AC* curve rises. As the firm expands DRS might occur due to problems of organization or communication inside the firm.

With IRS the firm operates at an output below its *MES*. A firm producing output less than *MES* could not compete with other firms at *MES*. Firms are typically observed operating in the region of CRS.

Two countries with IRS have an incentive to specialize and trade in different products to increase export production. With specialization, world output would be higher and both countries would enjoy higher income.

Increasing returns to scale may play a role in some specialization and trade but firms generally operate with constant returns.

EXAMPLE **7.17**   *International IPRs*

International intellectual property rights IPRs of patent protection would raise the level of trade. Keith Maskus and Mohan Penubarti (1995) find evidence across LDCs that increased patent protection increases trade. Foreign firms with patents do not want to sell to countries where their product could be copied and produced locally.

EXAMPLE **7.18**   *Factor Endowments versus Returns to Scale*

> Two fundamental causes of trade are availability of factors and increasing returns to scale. Donald Davis and David Weinstein (1995, 1998) find that factor endowments explain a good deal of trade with the cost minimizing factor mix of each country. Increasing returns are not critical. Geography is important with transport costs and borders contributing to trade.

Income Effects and Trade

Countries with higher income consume more services and luxury goods while in low income countries spend on basic food, shelter, and clothing. Comparative advantage determines the pattern of production but income contributes to the pattern of consumption and trade.

Income elasticity is the percentage change in quantity demanded for a one percent increase in income,

$$E_1 = \%\Delta Q/\%\Delta Y$$

Goods with positive income elasticities are normal goods. As income rises, the quantity demanded of a normal good rises. With a positive income elasticity less than one, the good is a necessity such as food, transportation, housing, and clothing. A good with income elasticity greater than one is a luxury good such as steak, foreign travel, imported cheese, and restaurant meals. Goods with negative income elasticities are inferior goods such as public transport, used clothing, economy cars, and red beans.

Figure 7.13 illustrates such a pattern of trade between DCs and LDCs. If production is uniform across countries LDCs would be importers of necessities and inferior goods, and DCs would be importers of luxury goods.

> *High income countries import luxury goods while low income countries import necessities and inferior goods.*

Linda Hunter and James Markusen (1988) study income in 34 countries and trade in 10 commodities and report income elasticities. Food, furniture, fuel, and education are necessities. A 10% increase in income would raise the quantity of food consumed by 5%, furniture 8%, fuel and power 8%, and education 9%. The rest of the goods are luxuries. A 10% increase in income brings about a 19% increase in medical services. Recreation is a luxury good. The influence of income on consumption patterns is significant but there is little influence of income on trade.

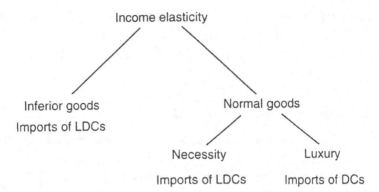

Figure 7.13
Income Elasticity and Trade
LDCs tend to import inferior goods and necessities. Developed countries DCs tend to import luxury goods.

The Bottom Line on Other Trade Theories

The supplemental theories in this section contribute to an overall understanding of trade and can be applied to particular cases. Factor proportions theory remains the fundamental tool for explaining international production and trade. The relative abundance of different skills of labor, productive capital, and natural resources is the fundamental explanation of international trade.

EXAMPLE **7.19**   *Coca Leaf Production and Trade*

The tropical Chapare region in Bolivia specializes in producing coca leaf for cocaine as well as traditional and commercial products. Hugo Toledo (2005) estimates how much it would cost to eliminate illegal coca production. Small competitive farmers earn $3000 per acre selling coca leaves and only $1000 under government programs to substitute pineapples, bananas, and peppers. Workers face income decreases of 25% with coca elimination. Countries wanting to control drug imports could directly subsidize landowners in Chapare.

Section D Problems

D1. Draw the PPFs of a home country with better technology for producing food and a foreign country with better technology for producing clothing. Show the pattern of specialization and trade.

D2. Explain whether it would be wise for a DC to spend resources protecting its steel industry or developing new steel products.

D3. What do income elasticities predict regarding international trade in inferior goods?

EXAMPLE **7.20**   *Regional Competition in Mexico*

Large countries are made up of economic regions that adjust differently to trade. Mexico opened to trade in 1985 after decades of misguided import substitution and subsidized nationalized industry as described by Gordon Hanson (1998). With trade, industry became competitive and moved north toward the US border due to transport costs. Northern Mexico is an economic region that includes the southwestern US and has little in common with central or southern Mexico, or for that matter with the rest of the US.

CONCLUSION

Industrial organization including monopoly and oligopoly characterizes a number of international markets. International economics includes theory that helps explain at least some trade. The next chapter turns to international movements of labor and capital.

Terms

Cartel quota	Luxury good
Collusion	Minimum efficient scale (MES)
Contestable market	Monopolistic competition
Credible threat	Necessity
Dominant and fringe firms	Oligopoly
Income elasticity	Price discrimination and dumping
Inferior good	Price taker versus price searcher
International duopoly	Product cycle
International monopoly	Product differentiation
Intraindustry trade	Returns to scale
Kinked oligopoly demand curve	Technology and trade
Legal versus natural monopoly	Trigger prices

MAIN POINTS

- A price searching monopoly restricts output and raises price relative to a competitive firm. A tariff on imports from a foreign monopolist takes some of its profit and may generate net gains.

- Product differentiation can lead to intraindustry trade in monopolistically competitive industries. Product differentiation and intraindustry trade increase as products are aggregated.
- Firms in an international oligopoly have incentive to collude and form a cartel for monopoly profit. Depending on the structure of payoffs and strategic behavior, oligopolies can be almost as competitive as industries with many firms.
- Other theories that apply to at least some international trade include different technologies, product cycles, increasing returns to scale, and differences in income elasticities of demand.

REVIEW PROBLEMS

1. Complete Figure 7.1 with an average cost curve for a domestic firm with profit of $300,000. Illustrate zero profit for a foreign firm. Which firm has higher costs?
2. Suppose higher energy costs raise the home firm's cost in Figure 7.1 dropping output to 1000. Find the price. Is demand elastic? If all output is exported what happens to export revenue?
3. Suppose a monopolist has two plants, one in the US and one in Mexico. The Mexican plant has lower unit costs. Which plant will produce more? How does the monopolist determine the price of its export to the EU?
4. Find monopoly profit in the example of price discrimination in Figure 7.5 separating domestic and foreign profit.
5. The following costs were estimated from steel production in the US and Japan by Peter Marcus in *Comparative Circumstances of Major Steel Mills in the US, European Community, and Japan* (1982). Numbers represent costs per ton for labor, capital machinery, and material inputs:

	Labor	Capital	Inputs
US	$209	$134	$330
Japan	$97	$171	$291

Which country spent more on labor input? What are two possible reasons? If it costs $100 per ton to ship steel to the US find the cost of Japanese steel in the US assuming Japanese profit is zero. If Japanese producers make 2% profit, find the price. Where will US producers want the trigger price?

6. With the cost data in the previous problem suppose the ratio of wages to capital rent (w/r) is 1 in Japan and 1.4 in the US. Explain labor intensive production.
7. Explain which categories of goods are likely to have more intraindustry trade: yarn or medical products; computers or laptop computers.
8. In an international industry, suppose there is a dominant domestic firm and a competitive foreign fringe. At a price below $3 the foreign fringe cannot compete. At prices above $10 the fringe will take over the market. Diagram this market with an international price of $7. Show the effects of an increase in domestic costs.
9. Find the index I of intraindustry trade in Example 7.3 for the following product categories. Figures are millions of dollars for the US in 1985. Explain the likely cause of the different levels of intraindustry trade:

	Exports	Imports
Footwear	$128	$354
Cotton	$1671	$258
Leather	$287	$425
Leather goods	$121	$374
Toys and games	$271	$2968
Automotive electric equipment	$443	$568

10. This is hypothetical duopoly between Saudi Arabia and Russia in the international oil market. Figures are economic profit in millions of dollars. The first figure in parentheses is Saudi Arabia. Find the equilibrium. Is it stable? Who has the greater incentive to cheat on a cartel

agreement? How can the other discourage cartel cheating?

(Saudi Arabia, Russia)

		Russia	
		Low	High
Saudi Arabian	Low	(30, 10)	(−20, 40)
	High	(40, −30)	(0, 0)

11. Classify the following as internal or external returns to scale:
    (a) Workers in the firm become more experienced
    (b) A better port is built near the factory
    (c) New imported machines lower unit costs
    (d) Local schools improve
    (e) Internet service improves

12. Show what happens over time to the PPF as a country specializes in manufactures when there are external IRS. Explain the change in level of trade.

READINGS

Gerald Meier (1988) *The International Environment of Business*, Oxford: Oxford University Press. International political and business institutions.

Roger Blair and David Kaserman (1985) *Antitrust Economics*, Chicago: Irwin. Tools of industrial organization and regulation.

P.K.M. Tharakan and Jacob Kol, eds. (1987) *Intra-industry Trade: Theory, Evidence, and Extensions*, New York: Macmillan. Articles on intraindustry trade.

Stefan Linder (1961) *An Essay on Trade and Transformation*, New York: Wiley. Linder's original.

Paul Krugman, ed. (1986) *Strategic Trade Policy and the New International Economics*, Cambridge: MIT Press. Some "new" trade theory.

Ryuzo Sato and Paul Wachtel, eds. (1987) *Trade Friction and Prospects for Japan and the United States*, Cambridge: Cambridge University Press. Collection of articles.

Yves Bourdet (1988) *International Integration, Market Structure and Prices*, London: Routledge. Range of issues on international industrial integration and market structures.

INTERNATIONAL ECONOMIC INTEGRATION

CHAPTER 8

Migration and International Capital

Preview

International movements of labor and capital pursue higher income and redistribute income. Immigration is the main source of population growth for many countries. International investment remains an important economic stimulus for developing as well as developed countries.

The main points of this chapter are:

- International migration is due primarily to wage differences
- International investment results from differences on capital returns
- Income redistribution occurs due to international migration and investment
- Production and trade adjust to international factor movements

INTRODUCTION

People leaving their homes to emigrate to other countries are typically looking for higher wages or income. The difference has to be large enough to offset costs of relocating.

International capital movement, vital for most countries, is created by differences in capital returns. As with labor, the incentive to relocate is based on differences in income.

Governments control international migration and investment. Incentives to control the international movement of labor and capital include income redistribution and production adjustments.

When unskilled labor immigrates, unskilled wages fall due to increased supply. Skilled labor and capital, however, enjoy higher productivity and income. When capital leaves a country, the capital return rises because of its lower supply but labor productivity falls. International factor movements influence prices of productive factors in both source and host countries.

These effects involve interactions across markets for factors of production and products. A model of the economy including factor markets is critical to examine the causes and effects of international factor movements.

A.   INTERNATIONAL MIGRATION

A comparison of labor markets across countries explains the fundamental cause of migration. Prices for labor and capital are determined in factor markets.

EXAMPLE **8.1**   *Land of Immigrants*

The US is populated by relatively recent immigrants. There have been periods of massive immigration. From 1850 until World War I, the annual immigration averaged 1% of the population. If such immigration occurred this year, a city as large as Minneapolis would be filled. In the first part of this century one million people immigrated per year, about the current level. San Antonio will soon become the second largest US city due to immigration.

Marginal Revenue Product and Marginal Factor Cost

A firm makes revenue selling output produced by the factors it hires. Demand for a factor is the value of what it produces. The marginal revenue product MRP of a factor is marginal revenue MR times marginal product MP,

$$MRP = MR \times MP$$

MRP is the value of the last unit of the input. Suppose price P and MR are constant at the competitive market price $2. If the MP of an extra worker is 5 units of output then MRP = $2 \times 5 = $10.

A firm will hire an input if the value of what it produces is greater than its cost. The marginal factor cost MFC the cost to hire an extra unit of input. MRP must be greater than MFC to be hired, MRP > MFC.

In a competitive labor market the firm can hire all the workers it wants at the market wage. The wage then equals MFC. If the MFC of an extra worker is $18 per hour and the MRF is $20, the firm increases profit by $2 per hour by hiring the worker.

Labor Demand and Supply

Figure 8.1 illustrates the labor market. According to MRP firms will hire between 30 million workers with MFC = $5 and no workers if MFC = $20. Labor demand slopes downward due to diminishing marginal productivity.

Assume labor supply is perfectly inelastic. Workers then accept any wage. Labor supply slopes upward at low wages and may bend backward at high wages as workers choose to enjoy more leisure.

The labor market clears where demand equals supply at a wage of $15. If the wage is over $15 there is a surplus and workers would offer to work for a

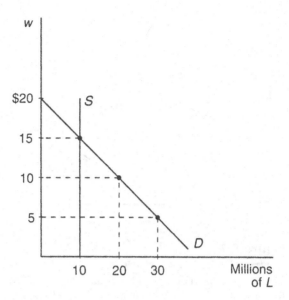

Figure 8.1
The Labor Market
With inelastic labor supply S this labor market clears at the market wage $w = \$15$.

lower wage. At a wage below \$15 there is a labor shortage and firms compete for available workers by offering a higher wage.

   Labor markets clear at the market wage where demand equals supply.

EXAMPLE **8.2**   *International Labor Growth*

Labor growth rates are highest among the LDCs, labor abundant countries evidently trying to maintain their comparative advantage. Free trade would raise wages in the LDCs but there will be continued migration pressure. LDC exporters of manufactures have lower labor growth. Labor growth rates in DCs are declining. All US labor force growth is due to immigration.

International Labor Market

Figure 8.2 presents the international wage model developed by economist Stanley Jevons in the late 1800s. The vertical axis w measures domestic wages and relates to domestic demand D. Foreign labor demand D^* is measured from the vertical axis. The foreign wage in terms of the domestic currency is ew^*.

   The length of the bottom axis represents total labor in both countries, 40 million workers. Home labor L is measured from the left and foreign labor L^* from the right.

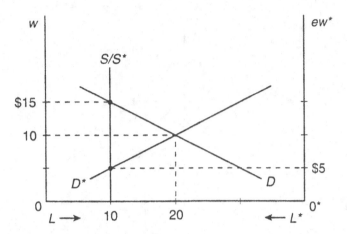

Figure 8.2
International Labor Market
The home labor market with demand D and wage w is measured from origin 0. The foreign labor market with demand D^* and wage ew^* is measured from 0^*. There are 10 million workers in the home country and 30 million in the foreign country as indicated by supply line S/S^*. The home wage is $15 and the foreign wage $5.

The vertical supply line indicates 10 million workers are in the home country. Demand for labor in the two countries is the same in this example but home has less labor supply. The home wage is found where home labor demand intersects supply at $15. Foreign labor supply is 30 and the foreign wage $5.

With free migration and no relocation costs, foreign workers would migrate to the home country for the higher wage. The foreign migration decreases the foreign labor supply. Immigration increases the scarce home supply. The supply line in Figure 8.2 shifts to the right with the migration.

Migration could continue until wages are equal at $10 with 20 million workers in each country. World output increases because labor is moving to a capital abundant country where its marginal product is higher.

With migration the host country enjoys expanding resources. In terms of production possibilities and national income, the host gains and the source country loses. Migrating workers gain and typically repatriate part of their earnings, partially compensating the source country.

EXAMPLE **8.3**   *Recent US Immigration*

Immigration increased since 1970 and is now about 1 million per year, the level of the early 1900s before disruptions of two World Wars and the Great Depression. Since 1950 immigration has grown steadily to account for the yearly population increase. There will be a much different population after another century.

Trade versus Migration

Trade leads to international wage equalization or convergence. Trade increases demands for cheap products and associated cheap inputs. Free trade is a substitute for migration. Protectionism increases the incentive for migration.

In the international labor market of Figure 8.3, the foreign country is labor cheap. Autarky labor demands are D_A and D_A^* and supplies of labor are $L = 10$ and $L^* = 30$.

With trade the foreign country exports labor intensive products. The price of labor intensive products increases as does the demand for labor from D_A^* to D_T^*.

The price of labor intensive products in the home country decrease, as does demand for labor from D_A to D_T. The equilibrium with free trade occurs where D_T intersects D_T^* at $w = ew^* = \$10$.

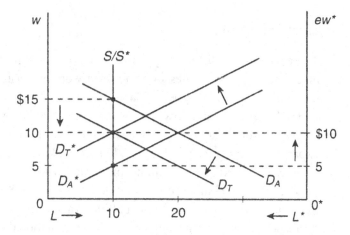

Figure 8.3
Trade and Wages
With trade the labor cheap foreign country increases labor intensive production and D_A^* rises to D_T^*. Home production of the labor intensive good falls as does labor demand, from D_A to D_T. Trade equalizes wages at $10.

Free trade raises the wage in the labor cheap country and lowers the wage in the labor expensive country by shifting demands. Labor migration shifts supplies.

International trade is a substitute for labor migration as both lead toward equal wages across countries. Wages rise in low income countries due to increased production of labor intensive products reducing the incentive for emigration.

Trade may be preferred politically to migration. The choice faced by DCs may be whether to import manufactured products or perhaps labor from LDCs. Illegal immigration remains a problem. Trade decreases the incentive for migration, both legal and illegal.

Migration raises international efficiency as labor moves to where it is more productive. Free trade creates similar efficiency gains through specialization. Labor scarce countries can discourage immigration with trade. Migration is a more costly since it is easier to move products than people.

EXAMPLE **8.4**   *Early US Immigrants*

Immigration to the American colonies was open to Europeans. The population in 1790 was close to 4 million including about 700,000 African slaves. English, Irish, and Germans immigrated as indentured servants serving up to 14 years. When the slave trade ended in 1808, African and Asians were excluded from immigration. Up to 1850 immigrants were English, Scotch-Irish, Dutch, German, and north Europeans. Between 1850 and the early 1900s, immigrants tended to be central or southern Europeans including nearly one million French Canadians fleeing religious persecution in Canada.

Legal Immigration

There are many different types of labor ranging from physicians to butchers, machinists, college professors, and farm workers. Insight comes from examining markets for different types of labor.

High demand and low supply are the two basic influences creating high wages. People making the highest wage are the most productive and work in expanding high priced industries. People making the lowest wage are the least productive working in declining industries with low prices.

The various skill groups of labor are in Table 8.1. Groups are listed from the highest to the lowest paid. Falling wages might be due to immigration or decreased demand in an industry facing international competition.

The lowest paid labor in Table 8.1 have most immigrants in the DCs. Immigration keeps wages of unskilled workers low. Unions favor strict enforcement of tight immigration laws. Business people who hire immigrants benefit from the cheap labor. Wages of other groups of labor increase with unskilled immigration as production changes.

Table 8.1 US Census Skilled Labor Groups

L1 = professionals
L2 = craft, repair
L3 = transportation
L4 = machine operators
L5 = administrative, sales
L6 = handlers, laborers
L7 = agricultural, forestry, fishing
L8 = janitors, restaurant workers

Wages for immigrating unskilled workers are higher than in their source nations. DCs have a scarcity of labor and large amounts of cooperating capital, skilled labor, and natural resources. High levels of cooperating inputs imply higher productivity and wages compared to source countries.

The wage in a skill group is lowered by its own immigration. When the US cut off immigration of foreign trained doctors in the 1970s the main beneficiaries were domestic doctors. The American Medical Association lobbied for the cutoff arguing that foreign doctors are unreliable.

The DCs attract some skilled workers from around the world. The brain drain refers to emigration of skilled workers from LDCs. Resources are spent by LDCs to train engineers, scientists, doctors, and other skilled workers who then emigrate to a DC for higher wages. Students from LDCs sent to study in the DCs often stay to work. The brain drain hinders growth in source nations. Skilled labor is scarce in the LDCs but there is not enough capital for skilled workers to be highly paid. In many LDCs skilled workers are underemployed by unproductive governments.

In the 1970s there was an influx of Vietnamese political refugees to the US. As they entered wages in their line of work shrimping were depressed along the Texas Gulf Coast. The price of shrimp fell also.

When workers immigrate payments to capital and natural resources are also affected. Groups hurt by immigration want stricter quotas while groups helped favor immigration.

Income redistribution caused by migration is key to understanding why some groups favor but others oppose immigration.

EXAMPLE **8.5**   *US Immigrants and Population*

Before the 1940s most immigrants were economic but many have been political refugees since the 1960s. The chart shows how large immigrants of each period would have become with a conservative 1% growth rate. The sum nearly equals the US population. About 40% of the total has immigrated since 1900, the largest group between 1900 and 1920.

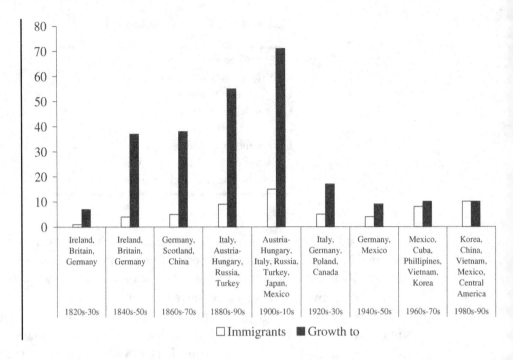

Ireland, Britain, Germany	Ireland, Britain, Germany	Germany, Scotland, China	Italy, Austria-Hungary, Russia, Turkey	Austria-Hungary, Italy, Russia, Turkey, Japan, Mexico	Italy, Germany, Poland, Canada	Germany, Mexico	Mexico, Cuba, Phillipines, Vietnam, Korea	Korea, China, Vietnam, Mexico, Central America
1820s-30s	1840s-50s	1860s-70s	1880s-90s	1900s-10s	1920s-30s	1940s-50s	1960s-70s	1980s-90s

□ Immigrants   ■ Growth to

Illegal Immigration

Many workers enter DCs from bordering countries as illegal immigrants. The risk of being detained enters into the migration decision. For illegal migrants benefits must outweigh costs. Part of the cost is the probability of a penalty if caught. Laws penalize firms that hire illegal immigrants but enforcement is difficult. There is too much to gain through immigration for the migrants and their employers.

Illegal immigration can be reduced by lowering marginal benefits or raising marginal costs. The marginal benefit *MB* curve in Figure 8.4 illustrates the difference between wages in the host and source countries. As illegal workers enter, wages fall in the host country. *MB* slopes downward. The marginal cost *MC* schedule reflects the cost of relocation and the discounted cost of penalties. As the number of illegal immigrants rises so does *MC*.

Making it more difficult to hire illegal workers would reduce *MB*. Trade reduces *MB* by lowering the international wage difference. International investment attracts capital to low wage countries and lowers *MB*. Increased patrolling of the border and stiffer penalties for illegal labor raise *MC*.

The main cause of illegal immigration is a large wage difference between the source and host countries. Trade and international investment reduce the incentive for illegal migration.

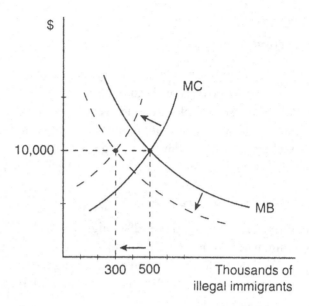

Figure 8.4
Decreasing Illegal Immigration
MB represents the marginal benefit from migration for the migrant, and *MC* the marginal cost. Illegal immigration can be controlled by lowering *MB* or raising *MC*.

EXAMPLE **8.6**   *Sources of Illegal Immigration*

Almost all immigration to the US from Europe is legal while more than half from Mexico is illegal. The largest group of foreign born FB are from Europe at 5 million. Asia counts for just over half as many FB residents as Europe and now has more immigration. FB immigrants from Mexico, Central America, and the Caribbean are about half illegal.

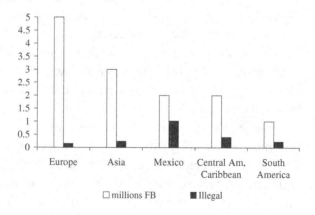

Section A Problems

A1. Find the wage in each country that would result from migration of 5 million to the home country in Figure 8.2.

A2. Suppose the relocation and readjustment cost is $2/hour in Figure 8.2. Find the equilibrium distribution of labor between the two countries. How many workers emigrate from the foreign country?

A3. Name one other way to reduce illegal immigration in Figure 8.4.

EXAMPLE **8.7**   *Migrants Worldwide*

The world population is 3% migrants with 0.2% of world income paid as remittances. Immigration to the DCs occurs at a rate of 0.2% of population. In the US 12% of the population is migrant, 5% of GDP is remitted, and the immigration rate is 0.5%. Australia has the largest stock of immigrants at 23% of the population.

B.   INTERNATIONAL CAPITAL

Capital owners seek the highest international return. Capital is more mobile internationally than labor because people do not have to move with their capital. International movement of capital is critical for world production and trade.

International Capital Markets

Capital machinery and equipment combine with labor and energy to produce goods and services. Most LDCs rely heavily on DCs for productive capital. Capital also flows between DCs. For example, foreign capital accounts for growth of the US automobile industry since the 1980s. Paul Romer (1994) shows protection on capital good imports decreases production.

International capital is reflected by stock markets that represent ownership of capital. International capital earnings are repatriated to the source country. In the host country, incoming capital raises labor productivity as the production frontier expands. When foreign capital but the capital enters the wage rises but the capital return falls.

Incoming capital contributes to economic growth. Jong-Wha Lee (1994) finds that imported capital goods are more of a growth stimulus than domestic capital. Countries should not restrict foreign investment.

Figure 8.5 presents the fundamental theory of international capital movements. The principles that explain international capital movements are the same as those that explain migration.

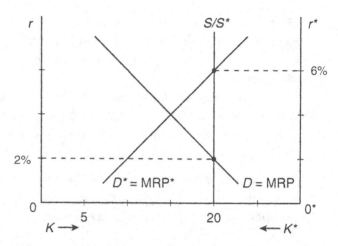

Figure 8.5
The International Capital Market
The domestic capital market with demand D and return r originates from origin 0. The foreign capital market with demand D^* and return r^* is measured from origin 0^*. The relative supply line S/S^* shows 20 units of capital at home and 10 in the foreign country. Return to capital are 4% at home and 12% in the foreign country.

The domestic capital market is plotted from the left. The marginal product of capital diminishes given other home inputs. Foreign capital demand is plotted from the right.

The return to capital is expressed as a percentage, the expected return on capital netting out inflation and depreciation wear and tear on the capital equipment. If inflation is 3% and depreciation 2% a nominal return of 7% implies a 2% real return to capital.

The rate of return is the return divided by the capital stock. With a 2% rate of return the $100,000 of machinery, equipment, and structures produces a net $2000 of output during the year. This 2% rate of return is the rental rate of capital.

In Figure 8.5 there are 20 units of capital at home and 10 abroad. The return to capital is 2% at home where capital is abundant and 6% in the foreign country where capital is scarce.

The difference in the return to capital lessens with capital movement between the countries. Policy may limit foreign investment. In the DCs there are appeals to keep foreigners from buying farmland and skyscrapers. LDCs limit foreign investment by requiring majority domestic ownership.

When capital moves to the foreign economy in Figure 8.5 the supply line shifts left. The rate of return to capital r^* in the foreign country declines. In the home country the supply of capital falls and the rate of return r rises. Capital returns converge with international capital movement.

Restrictions on foreign capital in the host are due to the desire of capital owners to keep their input scarce and return high. In the source country, labor groups want to keep capital from leaving to maintain labor's marginal productivity.

Owners of home capital in Figure 8.6 will want to move their capital to the foreign country. International capital market equilibrium is attained when 5 units of capital move from the home to the foreign country. Each country then has a stock of 15 at the international rate of return of 4%.

International differences in the capital return arise due to differences in capital demands or supplies. If free to move, capital moves toward an international equilibrium with equal returns across countries.

EXAMPLE **8.8**   *Foreign Capital in the US*

The US owns more than twice as much capital abroad as foreigners own in the US. The US holds net credit positions with Canada and Latin America but net debit positions with Europe and Japan. Foreign firms invest in the US to jump protection or locate close to US consumers or producers of intermediate products. Foreign capital increases labor productivity and wages.

Trade Substitutes for International Capital

Trade substitutes for capital movement. DCs export capital intensive business services and high tech manufactures. Trade increases the price of these exports and raises demand for capital. Trade lowers the capital return in countries that import capital intensive goods. In the limiting case, trade leads to equal capital returns across countries.

International capital movements equalize capital returns across countries. Trade substitutes for capital movement as it equalizes the returns to capital across countries.

EXAMPLE **8.9**   *Foreign Capital and Trade*

Foreign capital has been growing faster than trade. Linda Goldberg and Michael Klein (1999) investigate whether foreign capital serves as a complement or substitute for trade in Latin America. US capital shifts Latin American manufacturing, increasing capital intensive production and exports.

Table 8.2 Distribution of US FDI

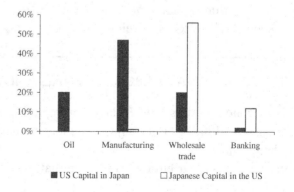

US and Foreign Capital

US foreign direct investment (FDI) in subsidiaries is mostly totally owned. The largest shares of FDI is distributed across industries in Table 8.2.

Mexico is relaxing its restrictions on foreign capital. Each country presents a unique legal and policy environment. Some countries are much more open to foreign capital than others.

The largest owners of foreign capital inside the US are Canada, the Netherlands, UK, Japan, Germany, France, and Switzerland. Many well known companies are foreign owned including Budweiser, Shell Oil, A&P, Mack Trucks, Carnation, and Nestle. About 20% of all foreign assets in the US are direct investment.

EXAMPLE **8.10**   *Foreign Capital Movement between the US and Japan*

Foreign capital between the US and Japan is the result of protectionism, investment incentives, trade, and local practices. The US has capital in the oil industry and manufacturing, while Japan focuses on business services. The largest US manufacturing investment is in chemicals. The US has a net negative capital position with Japan.

International Loans and Capital

Productive capital includes equipment, machinery, and structures. In application to a particular industry, it makes sense to look at the market for its particular capital. Firms may borrow to acquire capital input. International credit markets work alongside markets for capital inputs. In the popular press and journalism "capital markets" refers to credit markets but the two senses of "capital" are separate.

There are links between international capital movements and the international credit market. If a US real estate company wants to establish a branch operation in England it can take funds out of the US or it can borrow. The borrowing can take place in the US or the UK credit market.

When a multinational firm sets up a foreign branch plant, it may attract local or international investment. International capital and credit markets are closely linked.

EXAMPLE **8.11**   *Foreign Capital from DCs to LDCs*

Capital moving from DCs to LDCs has increased since the 1980s. Firms in the DCs prefer to operate branch plants in the LDCs. Most of the foreign capital in the LDCs is in foreign direct investment FDI

Section B Problems

B1. Illustrate and explain the effects of trade in Figure 8.5 with an international capital return of 4% brought about by free trade.

B2. Show and explain what would happen to the international pattern of capital returns in Figure 8.5 with labor emigration from the foreign country.

EXAMPLE **8.12**   *Foreign versus Home Capital*

The stock of US owned capital in foreign countries remains ahead of the stock of foreign owned capital in the US but foreign capital is gaining. Prices of tangible assets (machinery, equipment, structures, land, inventories) and intangible assets (patents, trademarks) are their discounted streams of expected profit in the future.

C.   INTERNATIONAL LABOR, CAPITAL, AND INCOME DISTRIBUTION

The economy adjusts when labor or capital enter or leave. Outputs, exports, imports, and factor prices adjust. The income redistribution typically determines whether migration and capital movements are favored. This section examines the income redistribution due to international migration and capital.

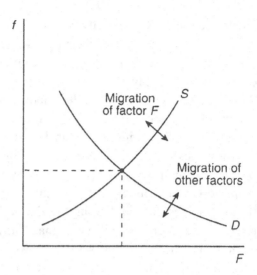

Figure 8.6
Factor Market Shifts
The domestic market for factor F is influenced by international factor movements. When the factor migrates, supply shifts. When other factors migrate, productivity and demand shift.

Factor Market Effects of Migration and Foreign Capital

An increase in a factor supply reduces its return but raises national income. Prices of other factors of production adjust. If increased supply of one factor causes payment of another to rise, the two are *factor friends*. If payment to another factor falls, those two are *factor enemies*.

Figure 8.6 shows the market for factor F with price f. Migration of F changes its supply. International movements of other factors change its marginal productivity of F.

If F is a friend of immigrating labor the marginal product and demand for F rise and f increases. The market for F adjusts in the general equilibrium along with outputs. If F is an enemy of skilled labor, demand for F falls with immigrating skilled workers.

International factor inflow raises prices of its factor friends but lowers prices of its factor enemies.

Labor Skills and Migration

The lowest paid groups of labor are unskilled handlers, laborers, agricultural workers, janitors, and restaurant workers. Higher paid groups including professionals, craft workers, transport workers, operators, and managers are skilled labor. The effects of labor migration on income distribution between capital owners and these skill groups depend on the substitution and output adjustments.

Unskilled labor is generally a friend of skilled labor and capital. When unskilled workers immigrate, the marginal productivity of skilled workers and capital increase. The skilled wage and capital return rise. Unskilled wages fall due to increased supply.

Labor unions represent unskilled labor and have long opposed immigration. Many people, however, benefit from immigration of unskilled labor.

Local effects of immigration can be large. Construction wages in Houston and farm wages in California are kept low by the supply of immigrant workers. Wages of restaurant workers are kept low by the supply of immigrants. The Sun Belt in the US benefits from immigration.

Demographics of the US in the 2050s will be much different. Various "minority" racial groups will soon make up most of the US population. The population is shifting to the south and west. Migration plays a role as labor moves into and around the country changing production and trade.

Migration and investment result in higher world output and more equitable income distribution. Free trade and factor mobility lead toward similar incomes for similar productive factors regardless of location.

A trading country effectively exports its cheap factors. With international factor movement, the cheap factors are exported.

EXAMPLE 8.13   *Immigrants and Skills*

Asian immigrant households do better financially than other immigrant groups, and better than US natives as well. Immigrants from Mexico have the highest poverty rate with about 1/3 on government benefits, double the rate of the native population. Median income below depends on labor skills.

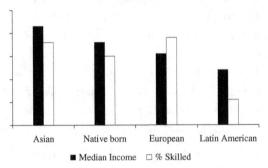

■ Median Income   □ % Skilled

Foreign Capital as a Specific Factor

International capital is often in particular industries such as Korean car plants in the US, or Dutch oil refineries in the Middle East.

Figure 8.7 shows the market for sector specific manufacturing capital. At supply *S* of 10 the capital return is 4%. The corresponding market for shared labor is in Figure 8.8. The original equilibrium wage is $10 with 20 million workers in manufacturing and 30 million in services on supply line *S*.

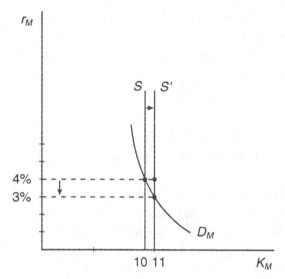

Figure 8.7
Foreign Capital in Manufacturing
When the supply of manufacturing capital K_M rises from S to S' due to foreign capital, the equilibrium return r_M falls from 4% to 3% along demand D_M.

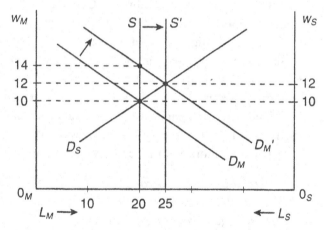

Figure 8.8
Foreign Capital and Labor
Labor productivity rises in manufacturing with foreign capital. Demand for labor in manufacturing rises from D_M to $D_{M'}$. Wages increase from \$10 to \$12 across the economy as 5 million workers move to manufacturing.

Foreign capital increases the supply of manufacturing capital to S' in Figure 8.7 lowering the rate of return. In Figure 8.8 labor demand rises in manufacturing due to the increased capital. The wage in manufacturing w_M jumps to \$14. Workers move to manufacturing causing w_S to rise and w_M to fall. Labor supply shifts to S' as 5 million workers move and the wage settles at \$12.

In the market for service capital, demand falls as labor leaves and the capital return falls. Foreign capital lowers the return to that capital and other sector capital. Capital owners oppose foreign capital. Labor favors foreign capital due to higher wages.

EXAMPLE **8.14**   *Mariel Immigration*

The labor force in Miami increased by 7% in 1980 when 62,000 workers fled Cuba from the port of Mariel. David Card (1989) shows this immigration had little effect on wages in Miami. Even among unskilled workers competing directly with the immigrants, there was no wages decline and no increased unemployment. Production of goods intensive in unskilled labor, especially textiles and apparel, increased. Ethan Lewis (2004) finds evidence that the immigration of unskilled Cubans slowed adoption of computer technology. The Mariel immigration shows that changes in the labor force have little impact on wages but affect the pattern of production.

Income Redistribution in CGE Models

Computable general equilibrium CGE models provide forecasts to shape economic policy. CGE models can simulate adjustments in income distribution to international migration and capital.

Simulations indicate migration and foreign capital have small long run effects on income distribution. Skilled labor and capital benefit when unskilled labor immigrates, explaining the lack of persistent opposition.

Skilled labor and capital are weak enemies. Capital outflow raises the skilled wage as well as the capital return. Unskilled labor is hurt by capital out-flow since it works more with machinery and equipment.

Unskilled immigration raises the income of skilled labor and capital owners but the effects are small due to output adjustments. International capital affects wages according to skills.

EXAMPLE **8.15**   *Immigration Winners and Losers*

Wages for unskilled workers are lower in Mexico than in the US. Clark Reynolds and Robert McClery (1988) calculate the gains and losses from the Mexican immigration. US unskilled workers lose but skilled workers and especially capital gain. In Mexico the emigrating labor wins as do remaining unskilled workers. Skilled workers and capital in Mexico lose. The effects in the US are stronger especially for capital that includes land. The US is a net winner due to immigration.

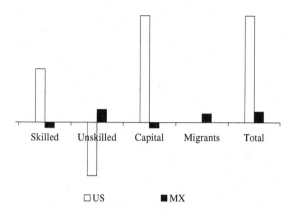

Section C Problems

C1. Illustrate the effects of unskilled immigration on markets for unskilled labor, skilled labor, and capital with factor markets similar to Figure 8.6.

C2. Use the estimated factor friendship elasticities in Example 8.7 to predict the effects on unskilled and skilled wages of a 5% increase in the supply of skilled workers. Assume the skilled wage starts at $80,000 and the unskilled wage at $40,000.

EXAMPLE **8.16**   *Foreign Capital and Wages*

Foreign capital raises labor productivity but the effects are uneven across labor skill groups and regions. Robert Feenstra and Gordon Hanson (1997) find evidence that foreign capital in Mexico from 1975 to 1988 raised skilled wages in northern Mexico with the maquiladora factories. Foreign capital outsourcing by multinationals shifted production toward products intensive in skilled labor. Foreign capital accounts for over half the increased skilled labor income. Anna Falzoni, Giovanni Brunno, and Rosario Crino (2004) find an increase in all wages due to foreign capital in Poland, Hungary, and the Czech Republic during the 1990s.

D.   MIGRATION, INTERNATIONAL CAPITAL, AND TRADE

International movements of labor and capital change the pattern of production and trade.

Output Adjustments in the Factor Proportions Model

An increased factor supply raises output intensive in that factor. If domestic production of an import rises due to international factor movement, imports fall. If export production rises, so do exports.

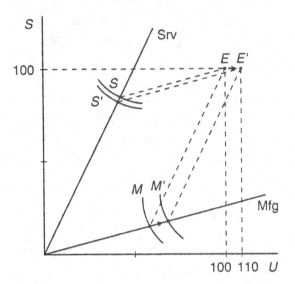

Figure 8.9
Unskilled Labor Immigration and Outputs
Unskilled immigration shifts the endowment point from point E to E'. Production using the immigrating workers intensively rises but other production falls. If services are exported, exports and imports fall. If manufactures are exported, exports and imports rise.

Figure 8.9 shows expansion paths for business services and manufactures for inputs of skilled labor S and unskilled labor U. Services use skilled labor and manufacturing unskilled labor intensively. Point E is the endowment of 100 units of each labor. Outputs isoquants are S and M.

Unskilled labor immigration moves endowment point E to E' with a 10% increase. Output of manufactures rises to M' as services falls to S'.

Production shifts toward labor intensive manufactures as both types of labor leave services. All of the immigrating unskilled workers plus some unskilled workers in services move to manufacturing. Skilled labor also leaves services.

Immigration of unskilled labor lowers its wage but raises the skilled wage. These changes in factor prices are small and adjustment in input ratios would be small.

Assume prices of traded services and manufactures do not change in the small open economy. If services are exported, the level of trade falls. The country becomes less abundant in skilled labor, the input used intensively in exports. Factor mobility substitutes for trade.

If manufactures are exported, immigration raises the level of trade. The country becomes more abundant in unskilled labor, the input used intensively in exports.

The effect of migration on the pattern of trade depends on factor intensity.

EXAMPLE **8.17**   *Immigration, Foreign Capital, and Trade*

Kar-Yui Wong (1995) estimates the effects of US labor and capital in production of traded goods. Immigration increases exports of nondurable goods and services. A 1% increase in the labor force increases those exports 2.2% and durable goods exports by 1.5%. Imports rise because of increased consumption. Foreign capital has smaller export and import elasticities.

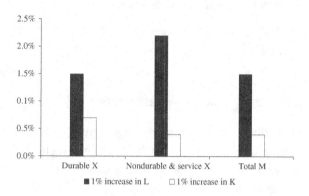

Output Adjustments with Specific Factors

In the specific factors model, capital in each sector combines with shared labor. Figure 8.10 shows the expansion paths for each industry. Supplies of capital in sectors M and S are the vertical lines at $K_M = 10$ and $K_S = 10$. In sector M, 20 million workers are employed with a K/L ratio of 1/2. With 50 million workers in the economy, the other 30 million are employed in services at the K/L ratio 1/3.

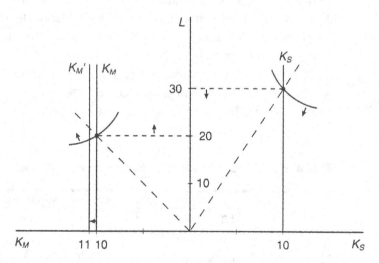

Figure 8.10
Foreign Manufacturing Capital and Outputs
Foreign investment in manufacturing draws labor from services. Output in manufacturing rises but falls in services.

If foreign capital increases supply in manufacturing from 10 to 11 output of *M* rises. Labor is attracted to sector *M* because of increased productivity and a higher wage. Labor leaves sector *S* and its output falls. Output of the sector receiving the capital rises but other output falls. In services the decreased labor input lowers capital productivity and its return.

International sector specific capital raises sector output but draws labor away from the rest of the economy.

Immigration increases all outputs since the incoming labor is shared. Wages fall but capital returns rise in every sector.

Simulated Output Adjustments

The three major industrial aggregates are services S, manufacturing M, and agriculture A. Labor can be split into eight skill types. Table 8.3 presents US elasticities of outputs with respect to changing supplies of capital and the eight types of labor in Table 8.1.

Changes in supplies have largest impact on industries where they are used intensively. Agriculture is very capital intensive with capital owners receiving 58% of income. A 1% increase in the capital stock resulting from incoming foreign investment results in a 2.7% increase in agricultural output.

Immigration of 1% of agricultural workers L7 raises agricultural output by 0.9%. The US is a net exporter of agriculture. Immigration of agricultural labor increases exports.

Operators L4 receive 29% of manufacturing income. Immigration of L4 workers would cause manufacturing output to rise but services and agriculture drop. Manufacturing output is elastic with respect to the supply of operators. Immigration amounting to a 1% increase in operators supply would spur manufacturing output by 1.8%.

Majorities of professionals L1, craft L3, and sales L5 are employed in services. Professionals and sales receive 27% and 21% of services income. The largest output effects on the service sector come from immigration of these two

Table 8.3 Output Elasticities of Migration and Investment

	1% Increase in Supply of								
	L1	L2	L3	L4	L5	L6	L7	L8	K
A	1.4	0	0	−0.2	−1.0	0	0.9	−0.2	2.7
M	−0.5	0.7	0.1	1.8	−0.5	0	0	−0.1	−0.4
S	0.5	0	0	−0.3	0.5	0	0	0.1	0.3

Source: Henry Thompson (1991).

skilled groups. The US is a net exporter of services. Immigration of skilled labor increases comparative advantage, specialization, and exports.

Output adjustments to international factor movements are tied to factor intensity.

EXAMPLE **8.18**   *Foreign Capital by State*

The foreign capital stock in the US increased from under $200 billion in 1980 to over four times that by 2000 when foreign firms employed about 5% of the workforce. This ranking shows states with higher than average percentages of workers employed by foreign multinationals.

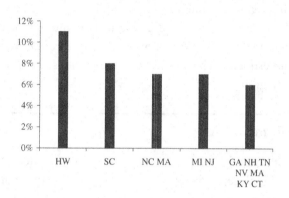

Section D Problems

D1. Show what happens in Figure 8.10 with emigration of skilled labor. If services are exported, predict what will happen to exports and imports.
D2. Predict what happens to production and trade with outflows of skilled labor from a DC. Compare with an LDC.

EXAMPLE **8.19**   *Global Foreign Capital: Up, Down, Up Again?*

Global foreign capital flows increased through the 1990s but tailed off during the 2000s. The recent decline is due to investor concerns about recession, protectionism, and terrorism. Only about 30% of global capital flows go to LDCs. By region the largest recipients are the US, China, the EU, and Asia-Pacific. Foreign capital will increase over the coming decades unless there is increased protectionism. Weak government policy and property rights keep global capital flows below potential.

EXAMPLE **8.20**   *US Immigrant Remittances to Mexico*

Mexican born immigrants are about 1/3 of foreign born workers in the US. Their remittance payments are an important source of income for Mexico. Catalina Amuedo-Dorantes, Cynthia Bansak, and Susan Pozo (2005) review the evidence from a survey of Mexican workers and find the motivations for remittances are to support families, meet a goal for savings, and pay debts. Remittances have been declining due to improved living standards in Mexico. Mexicans are staying longer and becoming permanent residents. Undocumented workers with low education and family members in Mexico remit a larger share of income.

CONCLUSION

International migration and capital movements are vital to the global economy. Outputs and factor prices adjust to international factor movements. Countries can integrate their economic activity through trade, migration, and foreign direct investment. The next chapter examines the process of international economic integration.

Terms

Brain drain	International capital mobility
Capital depreciation	International factor markets
Emigration, immigration	Legal and illegal migration
Factor friends, enemies	Labor skills migration
Foreign capital	Marginal factor cost (MFC)
Host and source countries	Marginal revenue product (MRP)
	Remittances

MAIN POINTS

- Workers respond to international wage differences by migrating to higher wages. Migration leads to converging wages across countries. International trade substitutes for migration and leads toward wage equalization.
- Capital moves between countries seeking a higher return. Free international capital movement leads to the same result as free trade, international convergence or equalization of capital returns.
- When labor or capital enter a country, national income rises but the price of that factor falls. Factor friends gain while factor enemies lose income. International factor movements redistribute income.
- International factor movements affect the pattern of production and trade. Migration and capital movement may substitute for or stimulate trade.

REVIEW PROBLEMS

1. Illustrate adjustment to trade with wages equalizing at $10 in Figure 8.2.
2. What else could wages of the various labor groups in Table 8.1 reflect besides the skills and training to enter each group?
3. Predict how foreign capital in the auto industry would affect wages of the labor groups in Table 8.1.
4. Given trends in US immigration, predict the pattern of production and trade.
5. If capital owners in the US traded evenly their capital with owners in the EU, what would be the effect?
6. Explain how the industries in Table 8.2 in which the US has substantial foreign investments compare with comparative advantage.
7. Explain which groups in an economy most favor restricting foreign investment. Which groups most oppose restrictions?
8. Services includes categories such as wholesale trade and banking as in Example 8.10. What have been the effects on income redistribution and outputs of this foreign capital?
9. Predict what will happen to wages of the various types of labor in Table 8.1 with emigration of professionals.
10. Explain what happens to the income of the various types of labor and capital when a foreign firm opens a new factory in the US.
11. What happens to the long run distribution of income when US firms decide to open factories in Mexico? What would be the difference if the plant opened on the US side of the border but Mexicans were allowed to cross over for work?
12. Explain whether it is more likely that the US would join a common market with free trade and free movements of labor and capital with Canada or Mexico.
13. With higher birth rates among unskilled immigrants in the West and South, predict what will happen to the pattern of trade inside the US.
14. Free trade zones attract foreign firms by eliminating customs procedures. Explain whether they promote or inhibit trade
15. Describe the output effects of the three sectors when there is a 10% immigration of machine operators L4 in Table 8.3. Predict the effects on imports and exports.

READINGS

Edward Graham and Paul Krugman (1991) *Foreign Direct Investment in the United States*, Washington: Institute for International Economics. Loads of information and detail on FDI.

Aad van Mourik (1994) *Wages and European Integration*, Maastricht: BIV Publications. Detailed analysis of integration.

Kaz Miyagiwa (1990) *International Capital Mobility and National Welfare*, New York: Garland. Review of theory.

Barry Chaswick, ed. (1982) *The Gateway: US Immigration Issues and Policies*, Washington: American Policy Institute. Studies on immigration.

International Migration Review, New York: Center for Migration Studies. Journal on migration.

"The New Refugee," *US News and World Report*, October 23, 1989. A startling look at migration.

John Shoven and John Whalley (1984) Applied general equilibrium models of taxation and international trade, *Journal of Economic Literature*. Survey of CGE models.

Julian Simon (1999) *The Economic Consequences of Immigration*, London: Blackwell. Economic analysis of immigration.

CHAPTER 9

International Economic Integration

Preview

International economic integration has accelerated with increased trade and investment and numerous agreements around the world. Economic integration involves steps to lower the economic barriers of national borders. This chapter covers:

- Multinational firms
- International externalities
- International political economy of free trade agreements
- Stages of economic integration

INTRODUCTION

Multinational firms MNFs have increasing in importance in world trade. Direct investment by firms in foreign branch operations is a rising share of foreign investment. International franchising is critical for the global economy.

There are thousands of MNFs. One-fifth of US multinational branches are in business services followed closely by energy. Foreign MNFs employ over 5% of the US workforce.

Some countries restrict MNFs motivated by mistrust of foreign motives or national pride. MNFs bring skilled labor and capital that lower the return to the host skilled labor and capital. MNFs increase the demand for local labor and raise wages.

International pollution presents another avenue to integrate economies. There are no international pollution taxes or liability laws to address international pollution externalities.

The world is shrinking due to improved transportation and communication. Economies are becoming more specialized and dependent. International trade and foreign capital lead to gains all around. International economic integration facilitates international commerce and raises income.

Governments enjoy autonomy and may want to impede economic integration. Governments want to enhance their own power and protect supportive industries. Economic integration progresses through steps as governments give up this local power in favor of raising income and development.

A.   MULTINATIONAL FIRMS

A multinational firm MNF has headquarters in one country and branch operations in others. MNFs are critical to trade and investment.

International Marketing

A firm selling in another country has four options that require increasing familiarity with the foreign market:

- Produce at home and export.
- License agreement with a foreign firm.
- Joint venture with a foreign firm.
- Invest in a branch plant as an MNF.

The choice is based on familiarity with the foreign legal system, transport costs, contacts among foreign firms, levels of protection, local economies of scale, fixed costs of a branch plant, relative cost of foreign labor, home and foreign skilled labor, and the level and elasticity of foreign demand.

Licensing with a foreign firm is an easy way for a domestic firm to begin production in a foreign country. If the source firm has a special production process, licensing allows technology transfer. The branch firm attaches its label to the product and receives a royalty.

Joint ventures are another way to enter foreign markets. Agreements are made between firms to share management, production processes, market information, and raw materials. By specializing in R&D, management, or marketing, firms lower costs.

If a firm wants to protect a process, it will export or set up a branch plant. The firm specific input or production process might have a patent. International patent protection is improving under the WTO.

The four basic options of a firm wanting to sell its product in foreign markets are export, licensing, joint venture, and branch plant.

EXAMPLE 9.1   *MNFs in Business Services*

Over recent decades a large part of MNF growth has occurred in business services. About half of outward investment in the US is in business services. For other DCs the percentage is about one third. Most investment coming into the US is also in business services.

International Entrepreneurs

DCs have an abundance of entrepreneurs who organize firms and manage economic decisions. This comparative advantage is revealed by the net export of business services.

An increase in MNF activity lowers the return to entrepreneurs inside the host. Other productive factors generally benefit from MNFs and become more productive.

Firms in an industry have to compete with new MNF branch plants. There is political pressure to keep out MNFs competition.

The US automobile industry provides an example of how MNFs increase productivity of the domestic industry. Foreign MNFs since the 1980s have forced domestic car makers to become more competitive. There is little difference in domestic value added between domestic and foreign models produced in the US. The quality of cars has increased dramatically over the past 30 years due to competition from the MNFs.

EXAMPLE **9.2**   *MNFs in the US*

There are more Japanese MNF branch operations in the US than from any other country. The UK has about half as many branch operations, Canada and the EU about a third each.

MNF Horizontal Integration

Horizontal integration occurs when a firm produces the same product at different locations. A horizontally integrated MNF decides how much to produce in each branch plant. The MNF in Figure 9.1 wants to produce where marginal revenue

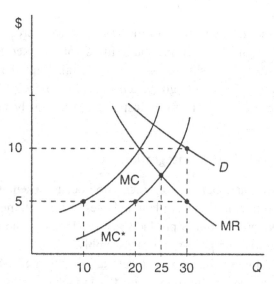

Figure 9.1
Horizontal MNF Integration
This MNF produces the same product in two countries and equates *MR* and *MC* across plants setting price according to demand. The foreign plant has lower costs and produces 20 units while the higher cost home plant produces 10 units. At the total output of 30, $MR = \$5 = MC$ in both plants and price = $10.

MR equals marginal cost *MC* to maximize profit. It considers *MC* in its domestic and branch plants. Both plants make the same product and the foreign branch has lower marginal cost, *MC**.

Optimal outputs involve equating each *MC* with *MR* and summing outputs to match MR. Profit is maximized where $MR = MC = MC^* = \$5$. Domestic output of 10 plus foreign output of 20 adds to total output of 30. At any price above $5 the two quantities from the *MC* and *MC** add to more than the quantity on the *MR* curve. The output of 30 is sold according to demand at $10. Output is higher at the lower cost plant.

> *With horizontal integration, an MNF produces more output at a lower cost plant.*

One question is why the firm would continue to operate the higher cost plant. All production could be shifted to the foreign plant where $MC^* = MR$ at $Q = 25$. The profit of each location depends on each plant's average cost. Profit may be higher from operating both plants. Transport costs may be an incentive to keep plants operating since buyers may be closer to the home plant. One plant may be located closer to a natural resource. There might be costs of shutting down the domestic plant. Domestic production might train foreign managers. If the firm expects costs to change at home or abroad, it may operate branch plants as a hedge.

EXAMPLE **9.3**   *Foreign MNFs in the US*

Foreign investment in the US is spread across industries. Ed Ray (1991) finds foreign MNFs go into large firms with market power in large growing industries intensive in skilled labor and capital. Capital inflow increases when the dollar depreciates. Foreign capital avoids unionized labor, does not seek protection, is spread across many industries, and is mostly in business services.

MNF Vertical Integration

Multinational vertical integration occurs when an MNF produces an intermediate product in the host plant and uses it in the home plant to produce a final product. Natural resource products are produced in the host country and shipped to the source for processing or assembly.

Figure 9.2 shows a vertically integrated MNF with demand and marginal revenue for furniture F on the left. Part of the marginal cost MC of producing furniture is the lumber L produced in the foreign branch on the right side of the diagram. The demand for lumber L is marginal revenue product, the marginal revenue of furniture times the marginal product of lumber.

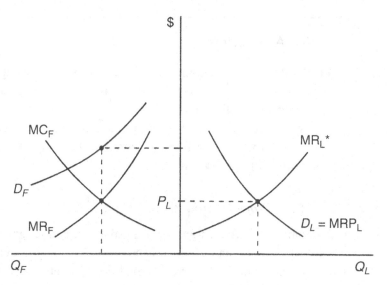

Figure 9.2
Vertical MNF Integration
This MNF producing furniture F is vertically integrated producing lumber L in the foreign country. Lumber demand is derived from the upstream furniture demand. An increase in furniture demand would raise their price as well as the MRP and price of lumber.

The demand for lumber is derived from the demand for furniture since the MR of the lumber depends on the price of furniture. The firm ships the lumber from its foreign branch operation to the home assembly plant.

An MNF avoids the market through vertical integration by producing its own raw materials or components in foreign branch plants.

The MNF can transfer price when it buys components from its own foreign branch operations. The foreign branch firm will appear less profitable and less tariff will be paid on the imported intermediate product if the price of the import is understated. The transfer price of the lumber in Figure 9.2 would be less than its price. If the transfer price of the components is overstated the foreign branch firm will appear more profitable. The MNF can transfer price to shift profit to the country with lower taxes.

Transfer pricing is an incentive for a foreign branch in a low tax country.

EXAMPLE **9.4**   *Obstacles to MNFs*

A survey by the World Bank indicates a ranking of obstacles to international commerce. Taxes top the list. Corruption involving paying government officials or local thugs for "protection" is next. Financing ranks third, more difficult in some countries. Poor infrastructure resulting from inefficient government is next on the list. Last is crime and theft.

Section A Problems

A1. Explain why the domestic automobile industry disagrees with the domestic electronic industry on foreign MNF car factories. Predict how domestic consumers feel about the MNF plants.

A2. Speculate on whether a textile factory or an insurance company would be more likely to license a foreign operation. Explain which would be more likely to set up a foreign branch.

EXAMPLE **9.5**   *Do MNFs Promote Growth?*

Economic research shows MNFs spur economic growth. Theodore Moran, Edward Graham, and Magnus Blomström (2005) find evidence of more benefits in countries with high human capital, sophisticated private sectors, competition, and free trade and investment. Mandatory joint ventures with domestic firms are a hindrance. Tax incentives also hinder foreign capital.

B.   INTERNATIONAL EXTERNALITIES

Externalities occur when some of the costs (or benefits) of a decision are paid (enjoyed) by others. International externalities cross borders.

Negative Production Externalities

A negative production externality occurs when a firm does not pay some of its production cost. Pollution is a negative externality. People near a polluting firm pay part of the production costs suffering dirty air, diminished health, frequently painted houses, and rusting cars.

The economic solution to pollution is in Figure 9.3. Demand facing the firm is D and marginal revenue MR. Marginal private cost MPC is the explicit costs of labor, capital, energy, intermediate inputs, and raw materials. The implicit costs of pollution is the $6 distance between MPC and marginal social cost MSC. A firm insensitive to the external pollution costs produces where $MR = MPC$, 12 units of output at a price of $20.

Firms wanting goodwill choose to operate on the MSC schedule, restricting output to 10 and raising price to $22. The $6 difference could be spent on R&D to lower pollution. A firm that ignores its pollution may make higher temporary profit but bad publicity ultimately lowers profit.

Negative externalities are costs of production not explicitly paid by the producer. Firms interested only in short run profit ignore implicit external costs.

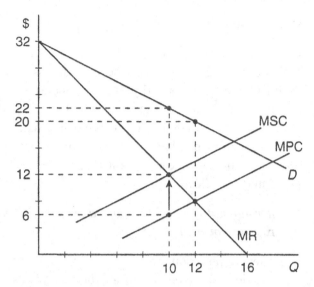

Figure 9.3
Negative Production Externality
The difference between marginal social costs *MSC* and marginal private costs *MPC* is external pollution cost of $6 per unit. A myopic profit maximizer disregards external cost and produces where *MPC* = *MR* at *Q* = 10 and *P* = $20. A pollution tax of $6 per unit of output raises *MPC* to *MSC* restricting output to 10 and raising *P* $22.

If the firm is responsible or liable for the costs it imposes on others, it will cut output to the social optimum. With civil liability, property rights govern pollution.

Residents could pay the firm to produce the optional amount of pollution by negotiating. According to the Coase theorem, the socially optimal output is reached given costless negotiation. Those paying the external costs may not be aware of the costs. Negotiations are costlier for international externalities.

The government can tax a firm into internalizing its external costs. The tax equals the difference between *MPC* and *MSC*. In Figure 9.3 a tax of $6 per unit of output forces the *MPC* up to *MSC*. The pollution tax forces the firm to explicitly consider the cost of pollution and restricts output to 10 at a price of $22. Tax revenue is $6 × 10 = $60. Revenue of the firm with the pollution tax is $160 = $220 − $60. The tax is an economical solution to pollution.

The US Environmental Protection Agency EPA uses command and control to limit pollution with little regard to costs. Firms in the US face fines when sampling turns up pollution outside arbitrary limits. Firms need only install what EPA determines the Best Available Technology BAT. Needless to say BAT introduces potential conflicts of interest for EPA administratiors.

Civil liability would lead to efficient pollution levels. Pollution taxes are an economic solution to pollution. Command and control policy is the least efficient method of pollution control.

International Externalities

International externalities occur across borders. Pollution externalities are more difficult when external costs are paid across boundaries. Countries may have different legal systems and pollution policies.

There are few international legal precedents that offer remedies for international externalities. There is no international civil liability. Cooperation among governments, industries, and citizens groups across countries is difficult. Awareness of negative externalities and the desire for goodwill and long term profit may be effective.

International externalities pose a problem in that civil liability and pollution taxes do not apply.

Different pollution control standards have been cited as an influence on the decision of where to locate branch plants. DCs typically have stricter environmental enforcement than LDCs. Relaxed standards may attract industry. One goal of the WTO is consistent international pollution standards.

Pollution can be eliminated but the cost has to be weighed against the benefit. Pollution control adds to the cost of production. For LDCs the cost of pollution control may outweigh the benefits of income. As incomes rise, the demand for clean air and water increases.

EXAMPLE **9.6**   *International Environmental Agreements*

Various international treaties address environmental issues. The *Basel Convention* controls the movement of industrial wastes across borders. The *Biodiversity Convention* is an agreement to preserve wildlife diversity. The *Convention on International Trade in Endangered Species of World Fauna and Flora* requires permits on trade in some species. The *Climate Change Convention* encourages countries to stabilize greenhouse emissions. The *London Convention* regulates dumping of hazardous waste at sea. The *Montreal Protocol on Substances that Deplete the Ozone Layer* phases out trade in some chemicals. The *Nuclear Test Ban Treaty* aims to control production of nuclear waste. The *International Whaling Agreement* has the goal of preserving whale species. The US has signed all but the Basel Convention and the Biodiversity Convention, making the rest the law of the land. Austria, Brazil, Canada, Denmark, Finland, Italy, Netherlands, Norway, Poland, South Africa, Spain, Switzerland, and the UK have signed all agreements. Japan has signed all but the whaling agreement.

Positive International Externalities

Positive externalities are benefits enjoyed by someone other than the decision maker. Positive international externalities are enjoyed across borders. Education has positive externalities. LDCs send their brightest students abroad to study. International trade in education services has positive externalities.

Another example of an international positive externality occurs around ocean oil rigs that supply breeding grounds for fish. Other examples of products with positive international externalities are electricity, roads, water, sewer, radio, television, telecommunication, and the internet.

With a positive externality, *MSC* is below *MPC*. Spillover benefits of production make social costs less than private costs. A firm that does not consider the positive spillover produces too little. Those enjoying the external benefits would compensate the firm to increase output. The government can subsidize the firm to increase production. The aim of policy is to match *MPC* and *MSC*.

Positive international externalities require policy coordination between partner governments.

International Public Goods

Public goods such as police, national defense, public health, parks, roads, highways, docks, and safe air travel create positive externalities. Public goods suffer the free rider problem of people who enjoy the product without paying. Markets fail to provide public goods because those enjoying the product do not pay. Nonexclusion is a characteristic of public goods.

Governments provide public goods that may be undersupplied close to borders. Parks close to a border might be used heavily by foreign citizens. Governments not wanting to subsidize foreign citizens reduce the supply of public goods close to the border.

Some public goods cross national borders. Police, military, public health, ports, and airports benefit citizens of neighboring countries. International externalities and public goods raise political issues. There are efforts to integrate international electricity systems. International telecommunication and internet face local protection. Highways that span borders require international coordination. Defense spending in one country affects its neighbors.

The solution to an international externality or public good requires international political cooperation.

EXAMPLE **9.7**   *TRIPs and IPRs*

The WTO oversees Trade Related Intellectual Property Rights (TRIPs) to oversee international disputes on Intellectual Property Rights IPRs. International trade and investment would increase with an international IPR system. The TRIPs agreement sets minimum standards and settles disputes.

Section B Problems

B1. Find the revenue of the firm in Figure 9.3 without the pollution tax. Find the tax revenue and revenue of the firm with the tax.

B2. Suppose pollution standards limit output of the firm in Figure 9.3 to 10 units. Contrast this outcome with the pollution tax.

B3. Comment on "International pollution is harmful to the environment and should be eliminated".

C.   INTERNATIONAL POLITICAL ECONOMY

Political decisions that affect economies are made by international organizations such as the IMF, GATT, WTO, and World Bank. Political agreements and treaties are also made between trading partners. Income redistribution is the connecting thread in international political economy.

EXAMPLE **9.8**   *Unfair Competition?*

US trade law can counter subsidized imports with countervailing duties. The sale of imports at prices below fair value is countered with antidumping duties. If imports cause material damage duties can be imposed regardless of trade agreements. Kenneth Kelly and Morris Morkre (1998) find small impacts of unfairly traded imports on the revenue of competing domestic industries between 1980 and 1988. Out of 174 cases of unfair trade 117 resulted in loss of less than 5% of revenue.

International Political Economy and Income

International political economy attempts to influence international income distribution. DCs support the status quo and are politically conservative. LDCs use politics to redistribute income, some calling for a new international economic order.

Laws and customs inside a country are typically well defined. Ownership of goods and resources is settled through the legal system. Damages are awarded if a firm or individual is negligent. Such everyday legal affairs are more difficult to settle internationally due to the inability to collect judgment across borders. The laws and practices of international law are developing as international trade and investment increase.

> *International political economy is concerned with laws and practices between countries that affect international income redistribution.*

One example of an international political agreement is the Bretton Woods fixed exchange rate system of the 1950s and 1960s. Stable exchange rates allowed international trade and finance to grow steadily. There was little or no risk from fluctuating exchange rates. The US dollar was undervalued, US products were cheap abroad and foreign products expensive in the US. The US had chronic trade surpluses during the 1950s.

Another international political institution is the International Monetary Fund IMF that manages exchange rates and overseeing finances. The IMF is a bank for government central banks, imposing constraints on government deficit spending.

Another example of an active international political agreement is the General Agreement on Tariffs and Trade GATT and its World Trade Organization WTO. Member countries agree to lower protection. Governments would not weather constant protectionism without the international GATT treaty. Negotiations are organized by the WTO to hear complaints on trade disputes and hand out settlements. Decisions of the WTO have the status of international law.

Protectionism, foreign exchange controls, limits on international investment, and migration laws are tools of international political economy. Every government would like to use policy to distribute more income its own way.

EXAMPLE **9.9**   *Regional versus Global Free Trade*

Regional free trade agreements may divert trade from the rest of the world. Kym Anderson and Hege Norheim (1993) show that trade is increasing both within and between regional blocs. Trade is returning to its high levels of the late 1920s before the protectionist Great Depression and World War II. There is no evidence regional trade agreements impede the growth of trade.

International Public Choice

Governments may act on the principle of majority rule with policy based on approval by a majority of voters. Given a choice of policies on protection, foreign investment, and migration, voters choose policies that distribute the most income their way.

Voters may be inconsistent in their choices due to the paradox of voting. Suppose there is a choice between three restrictive policies,

- protect industry that competes with imports
- restrict foreign investment
- restrict immigration

Three groups of voters rank their preferences as in Table 9.1. Each group knows how the policies will redistribute income. Each ranks policies according to their own advantage.

If there is a vote between protection and restricting foreign investment, group B restricts foreign investment while A and C choose protection. If there is a

Table 9.1 Policy Preferences

| | **Voting Groups** | | |
	A	**B**	**C**
Protection	1	3	2
Restrict foreign investment	2	1	3
Restrict immigration	3	2	1

vote between restricting foreign investment or immigration C restricts immigration but both A and B would restrict foreign investment. Protection is preferred to restricting foreign investment which is preferred to restricting immigration.

With a vote between protection and restricting immigration, group A chooses protection while B and C choose to restrict immigration.

The paradox of voting in public choice explains why politics seems irrational.

Voters seem apathetic but could be politically inactive because of rational ignorance. Becoming familiar with issues such as protection takes a good deal of effort. Benefits that would come from an informed vote may be outweighed by the costs of becoming informed. With trade policies, benefits are concentrated but costs are dispersed. The average voter may be rational to remain ignorant on particular issues. Rational ignorance is tied to the free rider problem since the average voter may assume that well informed voters are likely to determine the outcome.

Principles of public choice are crucial for understanding political economy. International economic policy is open to inequities created by special interest groups and logrolling. Lawmakers logroll by trading votes on issues. A representative from Iowa, for instance, may agree to vote for a new highway in California if the California representative votes for new post offices in Iowa. Neither keeps the interests of the entire country nor economic efficiency in mind. International negotiators enter into similar deals.

EXAMPLE **9.10**   *The Houdini Clause*

The US government is committed to reduce protectionism in the WTO but industries can apply for temporary protection. The US International Trade Commission ITC has the authority to award "escape clause" protection. Appeals may examine available evidence on costs. Foreign firms found to be dumping face tariffs or quotas. Gary Hufbauer, Diane Berliner, and Kimberly Elliott (1986) summarize the history of the escape clause. The value is the estimated producer surplus in millions due to escape clause protection.

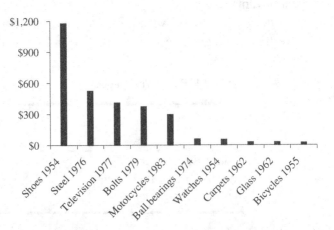

International Political Economy and Growth

The developed North is abundant in capital and skilled labor; and the less developed South in labor and natural resources. For global efficiency the North would specialize in services and high tech manufactures and the South in labor intensive manufacturing and resource products. There are gains in both regions with increased specialization and trade.

This international specialization is painful for the North's manufacturing. Imagine how protection looks to the LDCs as they try to specialize and export labor intensive manufactures in the face of protection.

The opening of trade in manufactures remains a central issue in international political economy. Adjustment in the North may be less painful with gradual reduction of protection. Workers can receive trade adjustment assistance to retrain and relocate.

The WTO has fundamental effects on international political economy. Countries are committed to systematic reduction in trade barriers. The WTO has been successful in lowering tariffs.

The International Monetary Fund IMF is as a bank for national central banks. The IMF makes loans to governments that have foreign exchange shortages. The IMF has its own currency, the Special Drawing Right SDR, accepted by central banks. The SDR is part of the monetary base of every country.

The IMF was formed at the end of World War II for stability in international monetary policy. Prior to World War I countries were on the gold standard. Exchange rates were stable. The 1920s and 1930s were different with each country pursuing its own monetary policy. Exchange rates fluctuated hurting international commerce.

After World War II, countries met in Bretton Woods, New Hampshire to promote cooperative monetary policy. Until 1958 the dollar was the stable international currency. The US government traded gold for dollars. The system began to unravel in the 1960s as countries pursued independent monetary policies. Germany revalued the mark while the UK and France devalued the pound and franc. Money supply growth in the US rose to finance the Vietnam War. In 1973 Nixon ended the fixed exchange rate system by pulling the dollar off the gold exchange standard.

The IMF has since been a lender of last resort for central banks. The insurance provided by the IMF creates a moral hazard problem. If bailouts are readily available, central banks can afford to be more careless. The IMF has become heavily involved in loans to LDCs imposing policy on borrowers. The IMF provides a forum for international bankruptcy. The IMF can provide a stable anchor for floating exchange rates with the SDR. The IMF verifies accounting and financial reporting, provides financial data, and publishes research on international banking and finance.

EXAMPLE **9.11**   *International IPRs*

International property rights IPRs involve protection of private property, one of the principles of English common law. Keith Maskus (1993) discusses international IPRs in the WTO negotiations. IPRs promote innovation because the owner enjoys monopoly power. IPRs may restrict the spread of technology. DCs have trade surpluses on IPR products. Patents and copyrights are involved with 20% of total US trade. The WTO hears complaints on IPR violations and some international actions have been taken on CD piracy, pharmaceutical patent infringement, and pirated books.

EXAMPLE **9.12**   *No Beef and Cheese Sandwich with Mustard*

Some cattle in the US are fed growth hormones. Scientific evidence indicates no associated health problems for the cattle or for people eating the beef. Nevertheless, the EU bans imports of US beef on the grounds that it is unhealthy. Certainly the competition is unhealthy for EU cattle growers. The WTO has ruled there is no reason to ban the beef. The US retaliated with tariffs on cheese, pork, and mustard. The WTO affords a platform to eliminate harmful trade barriers.

Section C Problems

C1. Explain the roles of the major organaizations of international political economy.
C2. Illustrate the pattern of trade and the gains from trade between the North and South with a production possibilities frontier for each region. Show the effects of Northern protection of its traditional industries. Discuss the income redistribution in both regions that would occur with free trade.

EXAMPLE **9.13**   *Mexico Libre*

During the 1990s Mexico made a dramatic switch in trade policy after decades of misguided import substitution and socialized industries. Mexico has become more open and competitive in free trade agreements with Chile, NAFTA, Columbia, Venezuela, Bolivia, Costa Rica, Nicaragua, and the EU. Productivity and income are rising substantially in Mexico.

D.   ECONOMIC INTEGRATION

A nation involves a government, borders, territory, language, culture, history, flags, currencies, border patrols, armed forces, and defense against other nations. International economics stresses barriers to trade, migration, and investment.

International economic integration leads countries toward common trade, legal, and economic policies. Deliberate steps encourage free trade, investment, and migration. Through international economic integration the political economy of a country changes and global economic efficiency improves.

The four steps of international economic integration are

- free trade area
- customs union
- common market
- monetary or economic union

EXAMPLE **9.14**   *The Mexican Connection*

The economies of the US and Mexico are intertwined in NAFTA. Trade between the two involves a good deal of intermediate products. In the top five categories of 2004, the three below are both exports and imports in $billion. This high level of trade within industry categories suggests manufacturing processes are highly integrated depending on labor costs and transport costs. The other two top US exports are Chemicals and Machinery at $9 billion apiece. The other two top Mexican exports are Oil & Gas at $14 billion and Apparel & Accessories at $7 billion.

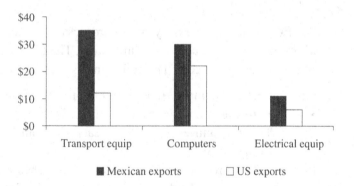

Free Trade Area

Protectionism is costly but difficult for governments to quit because protected industries offer politicians money and votes. Nevertheless countries enter free trade agreements. The US, Canada, and Mexico eliminated protection with NAFTA. Countries that agree to eliminate trade barriers enjoy gains especially in export industries and industries that use imported intermediate products.

A Free Trade Area FTA is the first step toward international economic integration, removing protection. An FTA removes the temptation of industry to rely on political payoffs, forcing industry to become efficient and innovative.

Countries form a free trade area FTA to legally eliminate protectionism.

In NAFTA there are no tariffs between the US, Canada, and Mexico. Governments give up their tax to protect traditional industries. National incomes increase with a more even international distribution of income. FTAs take trade policy out of the hands of shortsighted politicians.

There is concern that the world is breaking up into regional trade blocs that decrease global trade. If country A lowers its tariff on country B and not country C some exports from C could be diverted. Barry Eichengreen and Doug Irwin (1994) examine regional free trade agreements between 1928 and 1938 and find very little diverted trade.

NAFTA is a watershed in US trade policy since protectionism has been the hallmark of US trade policy. The GATT treaty and the WTO have slowly led the US toward free trade since World War II. Canada and the US were fumbling toward an FTA when Mexico approached them in the early 1990s. By making NAFTA a treaty the administrative branch of government has taken the power from Congress to levy tariffs for favored industries.

NAFTA sets up an environmental agency to monitor pollution in all three countries. Labor issues are slowing elimination of some tariffs. Specific industries remain exempt from NAFTA. Nevertheless NAFTA represents a step away from special interest legislation.

EXAMPLE **9.15**   *EU in Steps*

The EU has taken over 50 years to progress to its current stage. Progress occurs with free trade, investment, and migration. The EU has common migration policy, transport law, and taxes. The following is a short history of the EU.

1951   France, Germany, Italy, Belgium, the Netherlands, Luxembourg form the European Coal and Steel Community
1957   These countries sign the Treaty of Rome establishing the European Community (EC)
1968   EC removes internal duties and establishes a customs union
1972   Denmark, Ireland, the UK join the "snake" exchange rate
1985   Spain and Portugal join the EC
1986   Single European Act leads to a common market
1992   Start of common market with free labor and capital mobility
1999   Monetary union with the euro

Customs Union

The next step toward international economic integration is a customs union CU with common external tariffs and quotas. The step to a CU is much harder because each country has its own particular industries facing international competition from the rest of the world ROW. Industries might give up their protection from a neighboring country inside the FTA but still want protection from competing industries in the ROW.

A CU is an FTA with common tariffs and protection.

Importers in the FTA country with the lowest tariff can buy goods from the ROW and ship to the higher tariff country. If Germany has a 25% tariff on shoes and France has a 10% tariff, French importers buy Brazilian shoes in France and ship them to Germany as French goods. For an FTA to work smoothly, it must become a CU to avoid this tariff jumping.

An FTA is easier to form between countries with fewer common industries because there is less call for protection. A CU is easier to form for member countries with more common industries because they can agree on protection from the ROW. The step from an FTA to a CU is difficult.

EXAMPLE **9.16**   *Projected Gains from Integration*

Trade within the EU increases specialization across countries. Alasdair Smith and Anthony Venables (1988) project gains for German and Italian appliance industries but losses for those industries in the rest of the EU. Winning industries are office machines, fibers, autos, and footwear. Overall income gains are between 2% and 5%.

EXAMPLE **9.17**   *EFTA the CU*

The European Free Trade Association EFTA is a customs union of Austria, Finland, Iceland, Norway, Sweden, and Switzerland that is joining the EU. EFTA is the largest trading partner of the EU followed by the US. The EU is by far the largest trading partner of EFTA. EFTA is small and will gain the most due to improved terms of trade with the EU.

Common Market

The next step in international integration is a common market CM which is a CU without restrictions on international migration and capital. The EU is a CM with workers and firms free to move. The EU also has uniform policy for migration and international capital with the ROW.

There is discussion of creating a CM between the US and Canada. Both countries have restrictive immigration policies. It is a large step for the two to open their borders to each other's workers and firms. Common policies for international factor movements with the ROW would have to be adopted.

With free trade and factor mobility economies in a CM are almost completely integrated. Competitive markets create similar living standards throughtout a CM.

EXAMPLE **9.18**   *FTAA*

NAFTA establishes free trade between Canada, Mexico, and the US. The Andean Pact and Mercosur do the same for South America. There are also free trade agreements in Central America and the Caribbean. The next step is to tie them all together in the Free Trade Area of the Americas FTAA. Countries would benefit through free trade and investment. Open migration policy will meet resistance in Canada and the US. Open investment policy will meet resistance in Latin America.

EXAMPLE **9.19**   *ASEAN Common Market*

Workers and firms freely move throughout a common market. The Association of South East Asian Nations ASEAN includes Japan, China, South Korea, and the "tiger economies" of Southeast Asia (Brunei, Cambodia, Laos, Indonesia, Malaysia, Myanmar, the Philippines, Singapore, Thailand, and Vietnam). ASEAN is progressing to become a common market.

Monetary Union

The final step of economic integration is a monetary union MU with countries sharing the same currency. The step to an MU is the most difficult because the government monopoly on printing money allows more spending than tax revenue.

The EU has become an MU with the euro. Since World War II Germany has had low inflation. Italy, Spain, and Greece have histories of much higher inflation. With the euro, each government lost ability to control its money supply.

Economic integration has been proceeding slowly worldwide. Numerous free trade, customs union, common market, and monetary union agreements are in effect. The move toward economic integration in Central and Eastern Europe has had dramatic effects.

The most powerful influences leading the world toward international economic integration are increased investment and improved communication. Trade continues to grow in size and importance. MNFs weaken the effects of borders. Everyone has an interest in increasing productivity and income. Most people in the world live in poverty and many others live by standards well below the DCs. Getting more of the world into the mainstream of efficient economic activity is the main challenge facing economics.

EXAMPLE **9.20**   *Hey Buddy, Can You Spare Me an SDR?*

The International Monetary Fund IMF is the bank for government central banks. The IMF is bank for the banks of the banks. The SDR is an accounting money defined in terms of a basket of world currencies. With a stable international currency, central banks would lose their ability to print money to cover government deficits. Foreign exchange markets would be unnecessary. There would be no inflation.

Comparative Economic Systems and International Integration

The difference between capitalism and socialism is ownership of productive capital and natural resources. Private ownership of factors of production and decentralized decisions characterize capitalism. Government ownership and centralized command and control characterize socialism.

The Soviet Union, China, Cuba, Eastern Europe, and others had planned socialist economies with a system of material balance planning. Priorities for finished products and intermediate goods were planned and allocated. Nevertheless, a wide range of agricultural and consumer products were produced and allocated in markets. International trade and finance were controlled by the government. Trade by primitive barter was the rule.

The US is a predominantly capitalist economy with market allocation. Production that is efficient and profitable continues, while inefficient and unprofitable activity, ceases. The US has a socialized postal service, public housing, and welfare as well as partly socialized medical care and public support of some failed firms. Utility firms in the US have been government franchised monopolies since the 1930s. Nevertheless, markets determine most production as well as international trade and finance.

Countries in Eastern Europe were closed to international trade and investment since World War II but are now open to international markets. Foreign investment and trade between the Western capitalist economies and socialist Eastern Europe continues to increase. Russia is shaking off some of its socialist traditions. China has been a closed socialist economy but is integrating back into the world economy.

LDCs in South America, Africa, and Asia are choosing economic systems. Market economies rely on international trade and investment. Planned socialist economies restrict international commerce, unfortunate from a global perspective because of the potential gains from free trade and investment. LDCs would benefit from free enterprise and international commerce. DCs should eliminate all protection of imports.

Nations choose economic systems along the spectrum from market capitalism to command and control socialism.

EXAMPLE **9.21**   *China and the WTO*

As China integrates into the world economy, real incomes around the world are rising. China negotiated for 13 years before entering the WTO. Protectionist claims against China have been rising due to import competiton in labor intensive industries. China in inching toward a floating exchange rate for the yuan.

Section D Problems

D1. Eastern European countries were integrated closely with Russia in the Soviet Union. How did they benefit through disintegration of the Soviet Union?

D2. Explain whether two countries could have free international labor and capital movements with no FTA.

D3. Use factor abundance, factor intensity, and manufacturing wages to constrast the US trade with Canada and Latin America in Example 9.18.

EXAMPLE **9.22**   *Dump Dumping*

Antidumping laws are a protectionist relic. No firm will sell its output at a loss for very long. The real issue is whether US industry and labor groups will be forced to face international competition. Antidumping law may seem to protect existing industry but harms productivity, and other industry by limiting specialization. Chile claims US dumping laws are a protectionist instrument. US industry is at a comparative disadvantage because of higher priced inputs due to antidumping restrictions.

CONCLUSION

Free trade and investment remain the goal of international political economy. The trend toward international economic integration is improving living standards around the world. Strategic international economic policy has unintended consequences and is best avoided. The coming chapters turn to open economy macroeconomics.

Terms

Branch plant
Common market (CM)
Customs union (CU)
Externalities
Free rider problem
Free trade area (FTA)
Horizontal and vertical integration
International externality
Joint venture

Licensing agreement
Marginal social cost
Monetary union (MU)
Multinational firm (MNF)
Paradox of voting
Public goods
Rational ignorance
Transfer pricing

MAIN POINTS

- Multinational firms increase international economic integration, trade, and investment.
- International externalities call for economic policy coordination between countries.
- International political economy examines the causes and effects of political choice across countries. Income redistribution is the main result of policy choices.
- Nations integrate through steps to promote international trade and investment. Each country operates its economy somewhere on the spectrum between capitalism and socialism.

REVIEW PROBLEMS

1. Explain why the US has many MNF branches in construction, business services, and oil production.
2. Analyze what happens in a multiplant firm similar to Figure 9.1 if costs are the same in each plant.
3. Explain how price discrimination between foreign and domestic markets could lead a firm to establish an MNF branch.
4. Analyze what happens to the vertically integrated MNF in Figure 9.2 if costs rise in the foreign country with a new labor contract in the electronic component industry.
5. Smoke from a factory in country A falls across the border onto country B. Explain three ways to control this problem.
6. How can a government host encourage the positive externalities that come with MNF activity? How will domestic firms react?

7. The EU acts like a single nation and the separate countries in Europe like the states in the US. Predict whether this sort of international cooperation can spread.
8. Illustrate North and South trade with offer curves including protectionism in the North. What happens to the volume and terms of trade if this protectionism is lifted?
9. Speculate on why economic integration has not been successful in Africa or Japan.
10. What would be the economic effects of an FTA between the US and Japan? A CU? A CM? An MU? What are the politics of such agreements?
11. Answer the same questions as #10 for the US and the EU.
12. Predict what would happen if the MU between states in the US were eliminated and each state government could print its own currency.
13. What would be the consequences for the US if an FTA was formed for North, Central, and South America? A CU? A CM? An MU?

READINGS

Philip Martin (1993) *Trade and Migration: NAFTA and Agriculture*, Washington: Institute for International Economics. Migrant workers and NAFTA.

Gary Hufbauer and Jeffrey Schott (1994) *Western Hemisphere Economic Integration*, Washington: Institute for International Economics. Economic integration in North and South America.

Nora Lustig, Barry Bosworth, and Robert Lawrence, eds. (1992) *Assessing the Impact of North American Free Trade*, Washington: Institute for International Economics. Articles on assessing NAFTA.

Harold Crookell (1990) *Canadian-American Trade and Investment Under the Free Trade Agreement*, New York: Quorum Books. Changes for the two countries.

James Cassing and Steve Husted, eds. (1988) *Capital, Technology, and Labor in the Global Economy*, Washington: The AEI Press. Globalization of production and technology.

Jeffrey Arpan and David Ricks, eds. (1990) *Directory of Foreign Manufacturers in the US*, Atlanta: Georgia State University Business Press. Detailed data on foreign MNFs in the US.

John Carrol, ed. (1988) *International Environmental Diplomacy*, Cambridge: Cambridge University Press, 1988. Articles on the international politics.

Tom Tietenberg (1994) *Environmental and Natural Resource Economics*, New York: Harper-Collins. Very good on production externalities.

James Buchanan and Gordon Tullock (1962) *The Calculus of Consent*, Ann Arbor: University of Michigan Press. The classic in public choice economics.

Jeffry Frieden and David Lake, eds. (1987) *International Political Economy: Perspective on Global Wealth and Power*, New York: St. Martin's Press. Articles on international political economy.

Stephen Easton (1989) Free trade, nationalism, and the common man: The Free Trade Agreement between Canada and the US, *Contemporary Policy Issues*. Free trade from a Canadian viewpoint.

Paul Gregory and Robert Stuart (1985) *Comparative Economic Systems*, Boston: Houghton Mifflin. Perspective on different economic systems.

Melvyn Kraus, ed. (1973) *The Economics of Integration*, London: George Allen and Unwin Ltd. Articles on economic integration.

INTERNATIONAL MACROECONOMICS

CHAPTER 10

Balance of Payments

Preview

This chapter introduces the balance of payments BOP. Issues range from how to finance a trade deficit to what happens to the foreign currency of a trade surplus. A related issue is the effect of a government deficit on the BOP. The potential of government policy to influence the BOP is examined. This chapter examines:

- Import and export elasticities and the trade balance
- Components of the BOP
- The government budget and the BOP
- International roles of fiscal and monetary policies

INTRODUCTION

If the price of an import rises, import quantity falls. If imports fall enough, import spending falls even with the higher price. The imports of one country are the exports of another implying the balance of trade depends on how sensitive imports are to changing prices.

For economies dependent on trade, international price changes can be critical. For instance, changes in the price of oil cause adjustments for both exporters and importers.

Countries may not spend on imports what they earn from exports during a year. The current account in the balance of payments BOP includes trade in goods and services plus net interest payments. If the current account is not zero, there is international borrowing or lending in the capital account. This chapter describes the fundamental mechanisms of BOP adjustment in the current and capital accounts.

Government economic policy may influence the BOP. Fiscal policy refers to government spending and taxes. Monetary policy refers to government control of the money supply. This chapter examines now fiscal and monetary policies influence the BOP.

A.   ELASTICITIES AND THE TRADE BALANCE

Changing prices of traded goods affect export revenue and import spending. Changing prices of merchandise imports and exports affect the balance of trade *BOT* equal to export revenue minus import spending. The balance on goods and services *BGS* includes trade in services,

$$BGS = X - M.$$

Changing Export Prices and the BGS

A higher export price increases production and export revenue but domestic consumers pay the higher price. In Figure 10.1 at a world price of $10, exports equal 100 units of services. Production is 200 units and 100 units are consumed. Exporters can sell as much as they want at the international price. If price rises to $12 domestic consumers cut consumption to 75 and producers increase output to 225. Excess supply or exports expand to 150.

Selling more services at the higher price increases export revenue. The level of exports rises by 50, export revenue rises from $1000 to $1800, and total revenue of domestic firms rises from $2000 to $2700. Domestic consumers pay a higher price and consume less. Consumers spend $900 on 75 units, less than the previous $1000 on 100 units.

A higher export price is illustrated with the increase in foreign excess demand in Figure 10.2 consistent with Figures 10.1. The higher foreign

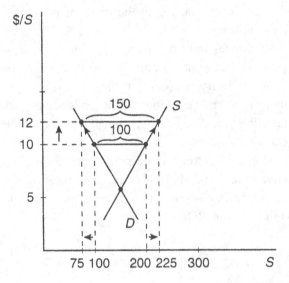

Figure 10.1
Increased Export Prices
When the price of exported services rises from $10 to $12 exports rise from 100 to 150. Producer surplus rises but consumer surplus falls.

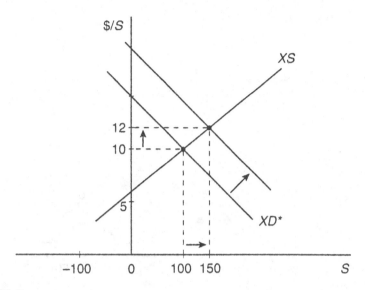

Figure 10.2
Increased Foreign Excess Demand
An increase in foreign excess demand XD^* raises the international price from $10 to $12 and raises the quantity exported from 100 to 150.

excess demand in Figure 10.2 is the cause of the higher price in Figure 10.1. In Figure 10.2 the price increase is endogenous, explained by the model. In Figure 10.1, the price change is exogenous, outside the model.

Increased export prices raise export revenue and the BGS.

EXAMPLE 10.1   *Price Taking Small Open Economies*

Are small economy exporters price takers? Arvind Panagariya, Shekhar Shah, and Deepak Mishra (2001) find that Bangladesh faces an import elasticity of 26 in textiles and apparel products. A 1% increase in the price of these products by Bangladesh reduces the quantity of exports by 26%, very elastic. These exporters in Bangladesh have no market power, making the price taking assumption reasonable.

Import Prices and the BGS

Imports are inversely related to price. An increase in the price of an import lowers quantity demanded and raises the quantity supplied.

Examples of increased import prices include the Organization of Petroleum Exporting Countries (OPEC) tripling the price of oil in the 1970s, bad weather in Colombia driving up the international coffee price, and dollar depreciation raising the price of imported cars from Germany.

Consider the exogenous increase in the price of imported manufactures from $5 to $7.50 in Figure 10.3. Domestic quantity demanded falls from 300 to 250.

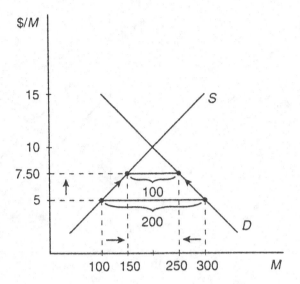

Figure 10.3
Higher Import Prices
An increase in the price of imports from \$5 to \$7.50 increases quantity supplied from 100 to 150. Domestic quantity demanded falls from 300 to 250. Imports fall from 200 to 100. Import spending falls due to the elastic imports.

Spending by domestic consumers increases from \$1500 to \$1875. The quantity supplied domestically rises from 100 to 150. Revenue of domestic firms rises from \$500 to \$1125.

Import spending falls from \$1000 to \$750, raising the *BGS*. Import spending may rise, however, depending on the import elasticity.

Import Elasticity

If there is little opportunity for adjustment to a higher import price, import demand is inelastic. A price increase then results in increased import spending.

If the price of imports and import spending are negatively related as in Figure 10.3 import demand is elastic. If consumers and firms adjust imports, import spending falls.

In the 1970s at the time of increased oil prices, consumers were driving large inefficient cars. Oil imports were inelastic and OPEC oil export revenue rose.

In the face of consistently high oil prices, cars became more fuel efficient. Houses were insulated and heating and cooling technology improved. Oil consumption fell. The quantity of oil supplied domestically increased. OPEC learned about import elasticity as their export revenue tapered and imports proved more elastic.

The import elasticity summarizes the relationship between import prices and spending,

$$\text{Import elasticity} = \varepsilon_{\text{imp}} = |(\%\Delta Q_{\text{imp}})/(\%\Delta P_{\text{imp}})|.$$

The symbol Δ means "change in" and $\%\Delta X$ is "the percentage change in X". Quantity Q_{imp} and price P_{imp} are inversely related.

To find percentage changes subtract the original level from the new one and divide by the average. In Figure 10.3, the $\%\Delta Q_{imp}$ is $(100 - 200)/150 = -.667 = -66.7\%$ and $\%\Delta P_{imp}$ is $(\$7.50 - \$5)/\$6.25 = 0.4 = 40\%$. The import elasticity in Figure 10.3 is $|-66.7\%/40\%| = 1.67$.

If the import elasticity is greater than one, demand for imports is elastic. Price and import spending move in opposite directions. If the import elasticity is less than one, the change in the level of imports is not large enough to offset the price change. Imports are inelastic and spending increases.

Whether a higher price for imports increases or decreases import spending is an empirical issue. Countries have different import elasticities.

There are higher import elasticities for goods that have more elastic supply, have more available substitutes, are a larger share of consumer budgets, and are luxuries.

EXAMPLE 10.2   *The Dollar and the BGS*

The US balance on goods and services *BGS* during the 1980s and 1990s is below. The trade weighted exchange rate 1/*e* shows the dollar appreciated. Export revenue first fell with higher priced US products as exports of machinery, transport equipment, apparel, and primary metals declined. Import spending on oil also increased sharply with higher oil prices. From 1986 to 1992 the *BGS* increased in spite of dollar appreciation. From 1992 to 1998 the *BGS* fell with the dollar appreciation.

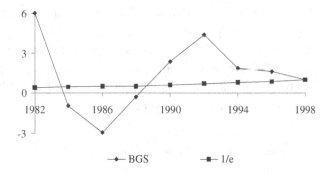

The Terms of Trade and the *BGS*

Consider a country exporting services in exchange for manufactures at international prices of $5 for *M* and $10 for *S*. The terms of trade *tt* or the relative price of exported services is 2.

The increase in the international price of *S* to $12 in Figure 10.1 improves *tt* to $12/$5 = 2.4.

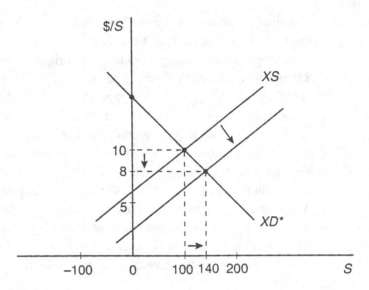

Figure 10.4
Improved Technology and Export Revenue
Increased excess supply of services drives down the price of exports and increases exports. The size and direction of the change in export revenue depends on foreign import elasticity.

Suppose the home country improves the technology of producing exports in Figure 10.4. The country sells more services as exports rise from 100 to 140. The change in export revenue depends on foreign import elasticity. The price of services falls from \$10 to \$8. Export revenue rises from \$1000 to \$1120. Foreign import demand is elastic.

If foreign import demand is inelastic, export revenue falls. Improved technology in export production then results in lower export revenue. If the level of exports rose to 115 with the same price decrease, export revenue would fall to \$920. This decrease seems paradoxical because improved technology is thought to be beneficial. This has been the history of agricultural production, improving technology and falling revenue.

EXAMPLE 10.3   *Markets Effects of the FX Rate*

Exchange rates have effects on many markets and the destination can be important. Nathan Childs and Michael Hammig (1987) trace regional exports of corn, wheat, soybeans, and rice from the US between 1968 and 1984. Soybean exports are sensitive to the exchange rate but corn exports are not. Rice and wheat exports to Europe and Asia are sensitive but exports to Latin America are not. The effects of the exchange rate are felt after two to three years in these export markets because of the time required for planning, planting, and harvesting.

Section A Problems

A1. In Figure 10.1 suppose the exogenous P_{exp} falls to $8, quantity demanded rises to 125, and quantity supplied falls to 175. Diagram this change in the export market and find the export revenue.

A2. In Figure 10.3, suppose quantity demanded falls to 270 and quantity supplied rises to 130 when the P_{imp} rises to $7.50. Find the import elasticity ε_{imp}. Explain what happens to the *BOT* with this increase in P_{imp}.

A3. Diagram an example of improved technology in export production and the international price decline based on Figure 10.4 with no change in export revenue.

B. THE CURRENT AND CAPITAL ACCOUNTS

The *BOP* has two main components, the current account *CA* and the capital account *KA*. Estimates of the *CA* regularly make the news and provide insight into international trade. They also lead to appeals for government policy.

A balance sheet shows current cash transactions, a positive credit when cash comes in and a negative debit when cash goes out. The sum of the entries indicates net cash flow.

Borrowing is a credit because cash comes in even though future debt payments must be made. Wealth holders can accumulate assets other than cash. If an asset is bought with cash, a debit is entered. If an asset is sold for cash, a credit is entered. The capital account *KA* reports borrowing and lending, the sale and purchase of assets.

EXAMPLE 10.4   *Japan, Inc*

> The role of Japan in trade and investment is discussed by Naohiro Amaya (1988). Savings rates in Japan are high relative to other countries. The *shinjinrui* (young wealthy) are spending more and saving less. The *keiretsu* business system entails dealing with firms in a close knit group or buddy system. The Japanese education system does not encourage innovation. Japanese business managers have trouble dealing with change and international competition.

BOP Accounts

A country keeps its balance sheet in the balance of payments. The *BOP* is the sum of the current account and the capital account,

$$BOP = CA + KA$$

Transactions involving current goods and services are in the *CA*. Investment transactions involving borrowing and lending are in the *KA*.

Components of the current account are the balance on goods and services (*BGS*) and net investment income (*NII*)

$$CA = BGS + NII$$

The *BGS* is the balance of trade (*BOT*) in merchandise plus trade in services (*TS*)

$$BGS = BOT + TS$$

TS includes international transactions for business or commercial services. Figure 10.5 summarises the *BOP* accounts

Since 1990 the *TS* has been positive and growing in the US. The *BOT* has been negative and falling. A summary of *BGS* trends in $billion for the US is in Table 10.1.

NII includes incoming payments on foreign stocks, bonds, and other assets. Incoming interest payments are credits. A positive *NII* indicates more payments on international assets than paid out. A negative *NII* indicates the country is a net borrower.

The capital account *KA* is the sum of direct investment *DI* and portfolio investment *PI*,

$$KA = DI + PI$$

International investment spending by firms in plant and equipment is *DI*. International portfolio investment by wealth holders with no control over the foreign operation is *PI*.

Table 10.1 Recent *BGS* in the US

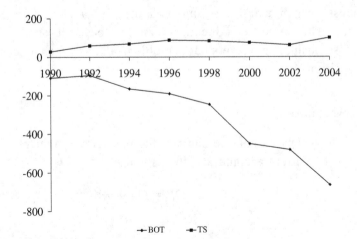

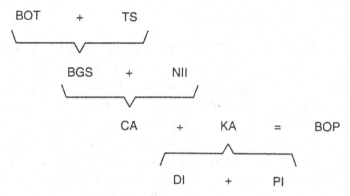

Figure 10.5
Element of the Balance of Payments
The balance of payments *BOP* is the sum of the current account *CA* and the capital account *KA*. The *CA* is the balance on goods and services *BGS* plus net investment income *NII*. The *BGS* equals the balance of trade *BOT* plus trade in services *TS*. The *KA* is the sum of direct investment *DI* and portfolio investment *PI*.

Distinguishing between *DI* and *PI* is difficult in practice with *DI* recorded for 10%, 25%, and 50% stock ownership held by the investor. Investment with less ownership is classified as PI. Roy Ruffin and Farhad Rassekh (1987) find *DI* and *PI* are with perfect substitutes with $1 of *PI* resulting in $1 less *DI*. The contribution to management of a branch operation is generally independent of stock ownership.

EXAMPLE **10.5**   *The History of US BOT*

Investment *I* has been stable except for a decline during the Great Depression. Government spending *G* replaced *I* during the 1930s, rose during the 1970s, and has declined slightly since. Both exports and imports grew during the last half of the 20th century. Recent *BOT* deficits are in line with history.

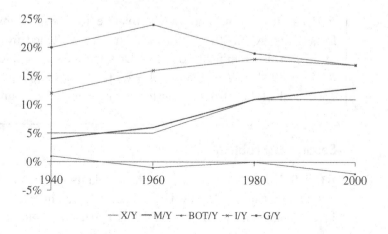

The Recent US *BOP*

A trend in the US is the *BOT* deficit. The last *BOT* surplus was in 1975. Domestic import competing industries use the *BOT* deficit to argue for protection. While the US has specialized less in manufacturing, it has specialized more in services. The *TS* surplus does not always make the news.

The *CA* in the US has historically been small compared to *GDP*. In the 1950s and 1960s the *CA* was a surplus of less than 0.5% of GDP. In the 1970s a deficit of 0.1% was the average. The typical US macroeconomics textbook included little international economics. During the 1980s the *CA* turned toward deficit. The *CA* deficit peaked at 4% of *GDP* in 1987 with imports 11% of *GDP* and exports 7%. Current account balances vary widely across countries, up to ± 20% of *GDP*.

The US has traditionally posted *DI* deficits as US firms establish foreign branch operations. A characteristic of *DI* is that management typically goes with the investment. European firms rely more on *PI*. Surpluses in *DI* during recent years in the US have been due to branch plants of foreign multinationals.

There is no clear trend since the 1970s in *PI* but the US generally represents a safe haven for investment funds. The volatility and volume of *PI* reflects increased competition in global financial markets. The New York Stock Exchange now must compete with financial centers worldwide as wealth holders diversify portfolios internationally.

A *CA* surplus in one country must be balanced by *CA* deficits of others. Taiwan, Japan, Germany, and China have had *CA* surpluses. A component of the recent *KA* surpluses in the US has been net official inflow, implying foreign central banks have been buying US government bonds.

The *BOP* data are estimated by survey with large margins of error. The statistical discrepancy some years is as large as the trade balance. Countries underestimate export revenue. Estimates of US exports to Canada are less than Canadian estimates of imports from the US. If that margin of error is applied to all trade, the *BOT* deficit disappears.

EXAMPLE 10.6   *FDI and International Capital*

FDI has been slow and steady relative to portfolio investment according to Robert Lipsey (2000). In the 1980s the US switched from the dominant source of *FDI* to the dominant host. In LDCs the main source of investment has been *FDI*. In 1994 *FDI* was about 1/3 of total international investment. There is a good deal of *FDI* from Japan to lower wage Asian countries.

Section B Problems

B1. US firms own and operate branch plants in Central America where apparel are exported to the US by US branch plants. These firms supply management, invest, and retain profits. Should this apparel be counted as imports?

B2. A Japanese carmaker that exports to the US decides to invest $100 million to build a plant in the US. Predict subsequent changes in the *BOP* and *NII*.

B3. In 1990 Mexico $X = 26.7$, $M = 29.8$, $TS = -5.7$, $NII = 3.5$, and $KA = 8.8$ in $billion. Find *BOT*, *CA*, and *BOP*. Find the change in *FX* reserves.

EXAMPLE 10.7 *Recent US BGS*

All four components of the US *BGS* have been growing with imports growing the fastest. These figures are in 2004 $billion. The *BGS* was nearly in balance through the 1970s but import spending on goods began to accelerate with higher oil prices in the 1980s. NAFTA and WTO trade agreements also had an effect during the 1990s as spending on cheap manufactured goods accelerated import spending. Exports of services are expanding but at a lower level. The net effect is a *BGS* near zero through the 1970s, a dip in the 1980s due to high oil prices, a recovery to near zero in 1992, then a decline based on rising oil prices and increased spending on imported manufactures.

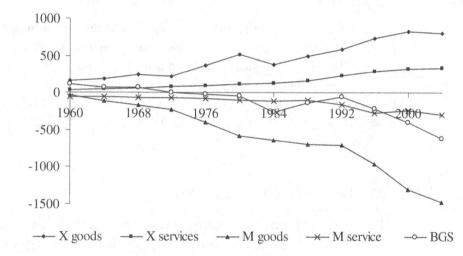

C. INTERNATIONAL DEFICITS AND SURPLUSES

The international credit market makes it possible for countries to borrow and lend. Borrowing to finance a current account deficit or lending of a current account surplus are examined in this section.

EXAMPLE 10.8 *Easy LDC Debt*

It has been too easy for LDC governments to borrow. In 2000 LDC debt was $2 trillion, 35 times their GDP. Debt service payments of the LDCs are about one-fifth of their exports. Lenders presume there will be no default on loans to governments. Such excessive credit will involve bankruptcy with taxpayers or equity holders paying.

International Debt and Equity

Household may spend more or less than their income during a year. Firms borrow to invest in capital goods or train labor. Firms assume debt by selling bonds or create equity by selling stock. A bond is a promise to pay a certain amount of cash at some future date. A stock entitles the holder to a share of future profit. Stocks represent ownership of the firm.

Countries include households, firms, and governments. Deficits and surpluses in the current account CA are expected and there is no reason a country should have a zero CA. If a country spends more on imported goods and services than it receives from exports, it must borrow or spend wealth.

Borrowing is typical for young and growing consumers, firms, and countries. When there is potential for future income, it is rational to borrow to invest. International lending and borrowing facilitate growth and stability.

EXAMPLE 10.9   *Expanding KA*

The US invests in the rest of the world as the rest of the world invests in the US. The capital account reports the change in net investment. Both outflow and inflow have grown especially during the 1990s. US investors prefer FDI in foreign countries and foreign investors prefer portfolio investment in the US. The US net KA has been positive since the 1980s, implying that *NII* will decline in the future. The incoming net investment, over 5% of GDP in 2004, raises productivity in the US.

The International Credit Market

If a household, firm, or country makes more income than it spends, it saves and becomes a lender. A period of individual saving typically happens at the peak of individual careers, after education and before retirement. Firms with positive profit either invest in new capital or become lenders. Countries with surpluses in their CA lend the surplus on the international credit market. The credit market for loanable funds involves lending and borrowing.

> *It is economically rational for some households, firms, and countries to be borrowers while others are lenders. Managed debt with a purpose has the potential to increase income.*

People have different habits and desires regarding wealth accumulation. Some firms want to expand while others maintain stable production and size. Countries vary in their desire for growth and wealth. In financial planning, what is wanted in the future is key.

EXAMPLE 10.10 *Baby Boom BOT*

> Baby boomers were born in the evidently busy years following World War II. The population group born between 1945 and 1955 is the largest in the US. Michael Bryan and Susan Bryne (1988) examine the influence of baby boomers on US trade and foreign investment. Boomers entering the workforce in the 1970s had low income but high earning potential. Their borrowing led to capital account surpluses and trade deficits. Boomers are now saving for retirement. As a result, the US will have a capital account deficit and *BOT* surplus.

A Borrowing Country

BOT deficits in the US have been in the range of $1000 to $2000 per household since the 1980s, evidence of sustained international borrowing. Much of this borrowing is spent on capital goods that raise productivity and the standard of living. Imports of capital goods are debits in the *BOT*. Growing countries borrow to accumulate capital goods. Foreign investors see a growing country as a good place for funds.

With a *CA* deficit a country borrows or sells assets that create debt as bonds or equity as stock. *CA* deficits are also financed by the sale of existing assets such as stocks, bonds, gold, or real estate.

EXAMPLE 10.11 *Government Deficits and Debt*

> Each government decides on services to provide and levies taxes to pay for them. Tax revenue T and government spending G reflect politics. G as a percentage of GDP has been on the rise. Italy, Greece, Spain, and Portugal have had high G deficits and debt burdens. The US has average G relative to GDP. Sweden has nearly balanced its government budget. Governments finance deficits by printing money or selling bonds, promises to pay bond-holders in the future.

Increased Foreign Assets

Foreign owned assets in the US have been increasing with recent *KA* surpluses as foreign investors buy US stocks, bonds, and other assets. Investors expect the US to grow. The *KA* surpluses indicate expected growth.

Foreigners own about 10% of the gross capital stock in the US. The US has historically bought more into the rest of the world than vice versa. Multinational firms continue to expand and invest around the world. International asset diversification has increased dramatically and the increased foreign lending and borrowing is a sign of a healthy global economy.

Section C Problems

C1. As the average age of a population rises from 30 to 50 predict what will happen to the *CA* and the *KA*.

C2. Explain whether Brazil or Austria would be more likely to have a *BGS* deficit.

C3. Diagram the international excess supply and excess demand for loans. What is the price of a loan? Show what happens if the borrowing country limits the quantity of foreign loans.

EXAMPLE 10.12   *The Ins and Outs of NII*

Receipts on US assets abroad have increased but payments on foreign assets have grown faster. Both in-payments and out-payments have increased. The figures are in 2004 $billion. Increasing interest payments in both directions reflect healthy economic activity.

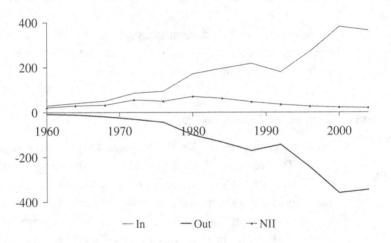

D.   FISCAL AND MONETARY POLICIES

International trade and finance are affected by economic policy. Two types of macroeconomic policy are:

- fiscal policy — government spending and taxation
- monetary policy — government control of the money supply

Fiscal and monetary policies affect the balance of payments. Economists differ in opinions about the effectiveness of fiscal and monetary policies. Some favor active policy intervention to deal with unemployment or inflation. Others favor passive policy, market adjustments, and balanced government budgets. This section introduces the influence of macroeconomic policy on international trade and finance.

The Government Budget Constraint

The government produces public goods. Examples of public goods are police, national defense, health inspectors, sewers, fire departments, highways, roads, parks, as well as clean air, rivers, and oceans. Governments play a positive role by providing public goods that might not be provided by the market economy. Markets fail to produce public goods because of free riders, people who do not pay and cannot be excluded from the good.

Taxes provide revenue for the government to produce public goods. When the government spends more than its tax revenue, it has a government deficit that creates national debt. The government can sell bonds to raise money.

A bond is a promise to pay the face value to the bondholder at a future date. Government bonds are bought by lenders willing to forego present consumption in favor of the interest premium and higher future consumption. Bonds are bought by consumers, firms, the central bank, foreign investors, foreign governments or foreign central banks. All exchange cash now for a promise of more cash later.

If a bond is bought by the central bank, it pays with new money. A government deficit then increases the money supply, amounting to monetary policy.

When a household or firm buys bonds, funds are transferred to the public sector. Government spending grows at the expense of consumption and investment spending. The demand for loans with the government's borrowing. The interest rate or the price of loans increases.

The government budget constraint reflects its cash flows. Let B represent total outstanding bonds, the national debt. The government must pay interest expense rB where r is the interest rate. Total government spending is $G + rB$. Subtract taxes to find the budget deficit, $G + rB - T$. The budget deficit must be financed by selling bonds ΔB or raising the money supply ΔM_S. The government budget constraint is

$$G + rB - T = \Delta B + \Delta M_S$$

Tax revenue T comes mainly from income taxes and profit taxes in developed countries. Compared to an income tax, a sales tax would result in more saving investment, and economic growth. Tariff revenue is important for LDCs.

EXAMPLE 10.13 *Foreign Stocks and Bonds*

The US holds of $6 trillion of private assets in foreign countries compared to $8 trillion of foreign owned assets in the US. Of the US assets abroad 37% were *DI*, 25% *PI*, and 11% bonds. The Western Hemisphere has the largest share of bond holdings at 42%. The EU accounts for 68% of the stocks and 38% of the bonds.

Fiscal Policy in the Open Macroeconomy

An increasing interest rate or cheaper bonds, other things equals, attract foreign investment. The demand for home currency in the foreign exchange market increases, appreciating the currency and pushing the *BOT* towards deficit.

> *Government deficit spending can lead to a trade deficit if higher interest rates attract foreign investment causing currency appreciation.*

This link between government deficits and trade deficits is called the twin deficits. The foreign exchange market is very busy and other influences may dominate. Decisions on government spending and taxes should be based on the costs and benefits of the particular programs or projects.

Figure 10.6 presents the channels of fiscal and monetary policies. Foreign purchase of government bonds can cause appreciation. Inflation resulting from expansionary monetary policy depreciates the currency. The effect of increased government spending on the *BOT* depends on the composition of imports consumed by the government relative to the private sector.

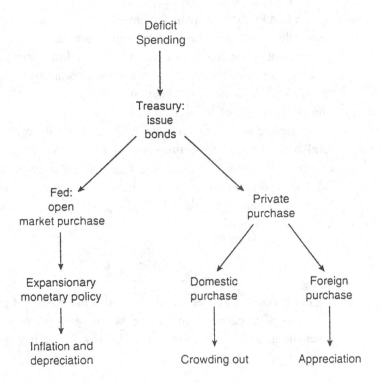

Figure 10.6
International Effects of Deficit Spending
Government debt created by deficit spending is financed by the sale of bonds. If the central bank makes a public bond purchase, the expansionary policy amounts to monetary policy. Private purchases crowd out consumption and investment spending. Foreign purchases appreciate the currency. Expansionary monetary policy can lead to inflation and depreciation if the growth rate of money exceeds the growth rate of output.

EXAMPLE 10.14   *Interest expense on National Debt in the US*

These figures show the breakdown on *G*, *B*, and *T* in the US. Interest on the national debt has risen to 15% of total government spending with tax revenue paying holders of US bonds who previously lent money to the government. About 1/10 of the national debt is held by foreigners.

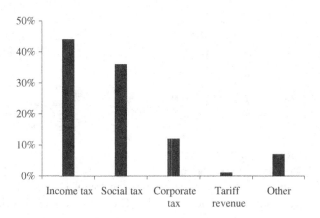

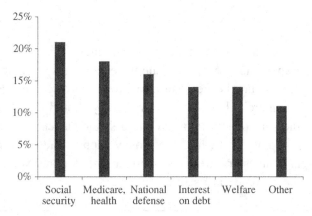

Monetary Policy and the *BOP*

Monetary policy can affect international trade and finance. Inflation occurs when the money supply grows faster than output. Inflation can have real effects through the credit and foreign exchange markets, but has little effect if correctly anticipated. Steady growth in the money supply leads to low or zero inflation.

Business cycles are alternating periods of recessions and booms and may be a natural part of a dynamic economy. Foreign business cycles can affect the domestic economy through exports.

As pictured in Figure 10.7, economies alternate between recession and expansion. The frequency of a business cycle is measured from peak to peak. The average business cycle in the US lasts four years.

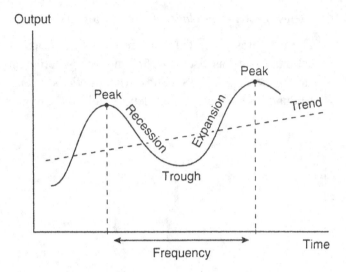

Figure 10.7
The Business Cycle
Output cycles around an underlying trend. Recessions lead from peaks to troughs, and expansions lead back to peaks. There are various theories of business cycles.

Central banks manage the money supply to influence the business cycle. Expanding the money supply encourages investment spendings and may end recession. The Fed can also lower the discount rate, the rate it lends money to commercial banks. Monetary policy should establish reliable money supply with the zero or low inflation and a stable currency on the foreign exchange market.

Steady growth of the money supply leads to a steady exchange rate. Traders and investors are able to make better plans when money growth, prices, and the currency are stable.

Section D Problems

D1. Describe how funds are borrowed from domestic and foreign sources when the government has a deficit. Explain how the foreign exchange rate is affected.
D2. When the government sells bonds to a foreign resident, what are the present and future effects on the *BOP*.
D3. Explain how government surpluses and the *BOT* are related.

CONCLUSION

International markets for goods, services, and assets are increasingly active. The world is becoming more integrated in trade and finance, and countries more dependent on each another. In some countries the daily exchange rate affects routine economic decisions. Exchange rates regularly make the news, have an impact on profit in many industries, affect prices of many goods and services, and influence foreign tourism. The next chapter studies the foreign exchange market.

Terms

Active versus passive policy

Balance of payments (*BOP*)

Balance of trade (*BOT*)

Balance on goods and services (*BGS*)

Business cycles

Capital account (*KA*)

Current account (*CA*)

International debt and equity

Net investment income (*NII*)

Direct investment (*DI*)

Export elasticity

Fiscal versus monetary policies

Government deficits and debt

Government bonds

Import elasticity

Inflation

Money supply

Portfolio investment (*PI*)

Trade in services (*TS*)

MAIN POINTS

- International excess supply and demand create adjustments in prices, imports, and exports. Import elasticities determine how price changes affect the BGS.
- The *BOP* reports international transactions in the *CA* and investment in the *KA*.
- *CA* deficits are no cause for alarm. Growing countries typically assume debt.
- Government deficit spending reduces private spending and raises national debt. Government borrowing affects interest and foreign exchange rates.

REVIEW PROBLEMS

1. Predict what will happen to foreign excess demand when lower prices are expected for home exports due to improved foreign technology. Explain happens to international prices, the level of exports, and export revenue.

2. Explain what will happen in the international market for manufactured goods when domestic income rises. Explain what happens to the international price, the level of imports, and import spending.

3. Explain what happens to import spending if the increase in import price to $7.50 in Figure 10.3 causes the quantity demanded to fall to 250 while domestic quantity supplied rises to 116.67.

4. If the price of *M* is $5 and the price of *S* is $12.50 find the relative price of *M* or the *tt* for the exporter of *M*. Do the same if the price of *S* is $7.50.

5. Find the elasticity and explain what happens to import spending when the quantity of imports rises from 100 to 125 with a fall in price from $10 to $8. Do the same if imports rise instead to 110, and to 130.

6. With 90 million households in the US, find the 1995 *BOP* account figures per household.

7. Explain current and expected future changes in the *BOP* when an investor in the US buys stock on the Tokyo stock exchange.

8. Suppose a US firm wants to open a manufacturing plant in Costa Rica. It can transfer $1 million of retained earnings to a bank in Costa Rica to build the plant. It could offer stock worth $400,000 in Costa Rica to raise funds. Describe the current and future *BOP* for the US and Costa Rica under each scenario.

9. An saying is that the way to get ahead in business is by using "other people's money". Explain the analogy with the *BOP* accounts.
10. Why do wealth holders diversify internationally?
11. Assume you were forced to live without borrowing or lending. How would your life be affected? How does this apply to international economics?
12. During the expansion and recession phases of the business cycle, explain whether there are *BOT* surpluses or deficits.
13. Justify whether you think congress should consider the marginal costs and benefits of each newly proposed fiscal program.
14. Explain the effect reducing import tariffs and imposing export taxes on the *BOT*.
15. Predict how wars in the Mideast affect the *BOP* accounts in the US.

READINGS

Robert Barro (1996) *Macroeconomics,* New York: McGraw-Hill. Analysis of monetary and fiscal policies.

Francisco Rivera-Batiz and Luis Rivera-Batiz (1985) *International Finance and Open Economy Macroeconomics*, New York: Macmillan. Macroeconomics for an open economy.

John Pool and Stephen Stamos (1989) *International Economic Policy: Beyond the Trade and Debt Crisis*, Lexington: Lexington Books, 1989. Facts on government and international debt.

James Rock, ed. (1991) *Debt and Twin Deficits Debate*, Mountain View: Mayfield Publishing. Links between governments deficit and trade deficit.

World Economic Outlook, Washington: IMF. Monetary developments, current and capital account balances, interest rates, exchange rates, and the international oil market.

CHAPTER 11

Foreign Exchange Rates

Preview

International trade, investment, and travel involve the foreign exchange FX market across countries with different currencies. This chapter covers:

- FX supply and demand
- Floating and fixed FX rates
- Stability and arbitrage of FX rates
- FX risk and inflation

INTRODUCTION

Currencies are bought and sold in the foreign exchange FX market, the largest market in the world. The exchange of goods, services, and assets between currency areas requires a currency exchange. There are billions of international transactions daily in the FX market exchanging mediums of exchange.

Demand for FX comes from domestic buyers of foreign products and assets. Supply of FX comes from foreign buyers of domestic products and assets. Supply and demand interact in the market to determine the market FX rate.

The setting for currency trading is a electronic global network linking private banks, FX brokers, traders, and government central banks. Figure 11.1 summarizes institutions of the FX market.

Although stock markets receives more publicity, the larger FX market offers more potential profit and loss. When the demand for a currency rises, so does its price in terms of other currencies. Rates of the three major traded currencies (dollar, euro, yen) are determined in an open market with minimal government involvement.These major currencies float in a free market.

Government central banks buy and sell currencies to affect exchange rates. Most countries have fixed exchange rates set like a price control. As with all price controls, fixed exchange rates lead to shortages of surpluses.

A depreciated or devalued currency implies more expensive imports. A government may devalue its fixed exchange rate to discourage imports and ease a trade deficit. An undervalued currency amounts to a tax on importing consumers and firms who pay a higher price for imports. A government might overvalue its fixed exchange rate to encourage foreign investment.

Fixed or managed exchange rates are inherently unsustainable due to the underlying market disequilibrium. Few governments, however, seem willing

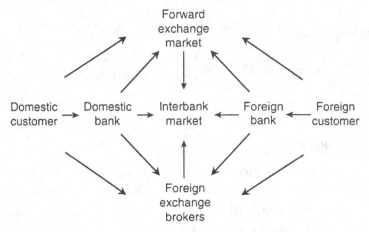

Figure 11.1
Foreign Exchange Trading
The electronic interbank market supports a vast amount of trading. Traders and investors buy and sell foreign exchange through local banks. Brokers bring buyers and sellers together, trading in search of profit. Future and forward exchange transactions moderate the risk of FX transactions.

to let the FX market work freely. This chapter examines the inefficiencies of governments trying to control the FX market.

A relatively high growth rate in the money supply leads to depreciation. Relative money supply differentials explain long term trends in exchange rates. Short term exchange rate changes are more difficult to predict.

Uncertainty about the exchange rate increases the risk of international transactions. A mechanism for avoiding exchange risk is the forward exchange market where a contract is signed to buy or sell foreign currency at some future date at a set rate.

A.   THE FOREIGN EXCHANGE MARKET

The FX market is based on the supply and demand of foreign exchange. Fundamental relationships involving exchange rates include

- The exchange rate link to prices of imports and exports
- The response of the *BOT* to depreciation or appreciation

The FX Market

An importer trades domestic currency for foreign currency on the foreign exchange FX market. Consider a US importer buying Japanese products. The importer can go through a bank to buy the yen to transfer to the bank of the Japanese exporter. Banks and import agencies specialize in currency transactions as well as import restrictions and customs paperwork.

Suppose the exchange rate of the yen is $0.008 in the FX market. As with any commodity, price is expressed in home currency. Apples cost $1/pound and

Japanese currency $0.008 per yen. One dollar trades for $1/.008 = 125$ yen. If the price of M is 625 yen in dollars is $\$0.008 \times 625 = \$5$. The decision of whether to import is based partly on the FX rate.

If the price of the dollar rises to yen/$\$ = 200$ the dollar price of M falls to $625/200 = \$3.13$. An appreciating currency lower the price of imports and increases the quantity demanded. If imports are elastic, import spending rises as does the quantity of foreign currency demanded.

This inverse relationship between $/yen and the quantity of yen demanded is illustrated by the demand for yen in Figure 11.2. The rise in yen/$ from 125 to 200 equals a fall in $/yen on the vertical axis from 0.008 to 0.005. The quantity of yen demanded rises from 20 to 30 trillion.

On the supply side, Japanese importers buying US exports sell yen in the FX market. If the price of business services is $10/S and the exchange rate 125 yen/$ the Japanese price of services is $125 \times 10 = 1250$ yen. If the yen/$ rate rises to 200 the yen price of services rises $200 \times 10 = 2000$ yen. At this higher yen price the quantity demanded of services is lower.

If foreign imports of services are elastic, spending and the quantity of foreign currency supplied fall. The quantity of yen supplied falls from 20 to 10 trillion in Figure 11.2 on the upward sloping supply curve.

The market exchange rate clears the market where the quantity of yen supplied equals the quantity demanded. In Figure 11.2 the equilibrium exchange rate is $/yen = 0.008 and the equilibrium quantity of FX traded is 20 trillion yen (per hour).

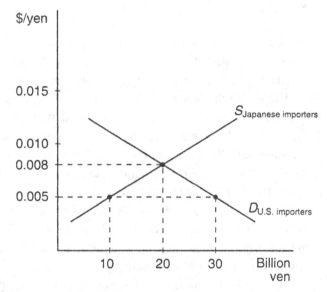

Figure 11.2
The Foreign Exchange Market
The demand (D) for FX comes from buyers of foreign goods in the home country. Supply (S) is based on buyers of home goods in the foreign country. Trade in goods, services, and assets goes through the FX market.

> *The FX market is based on the demand and supply of foreign currency. The price of foreign currency is in terms of home currency.*

EXAMPLE 11.1   *FX Rates*

Exchange rates change continuously and are quoted in newspapers and on the internet, and at banks, airports, and trading houses. In countries highly involved with international trade and investment, exchange rates are front page news and traders have windows on busy streets. In countries with quickly depreciating or appreciating currencies, the exchange rate influences everyday household and business decisions. Sample exchange rates are listed in US dollars below.

Dollar prices of foreign currencies	
	$/fc
Australian Dollars	0.93
Brazilian Real	0.57
British Pounds	1.54
Canadian Dollars	1.00
Chinese Yuan	0.15
Euro	1.34
Japanese Yen	0.01
Mexican Pesos	0.08

Depreciation

Depreciation occurs when a currency price falls in terms of foreign currency. In the $/yen market, dollar depreciation means $/yen rises. Depriciation lowers purchasing power for imports and makes exports cheaper abroad.

The key to the understanding FX market is the markets for the traded products and assets. Consider an increase in the demand for coffee from Colombia. In Figure 11.3 the demand for pesos shifts right. The volume in the FX market increases and the peso appreciates. The price of the peso rises from $/peso = 0.002 to 0.003. The dollar depreciates from 500 to 333 pesos.

As the dollar depreciates, the price of colombian coffee rises further. Suppose coffee cost 750 pesos/pound or $0.002 \times 750 = \$1.50$ at the original exchange rate. Depreciation increases price to $0.003 \times 750 = \$2.25$. The FX market strengthens the underlying price increase, encouraging substitution. Free foreign exchange markets increase market efficiency.

Depreciation from other sources also makes imports more expensive. Suppose central banks announce a plan to depreciate the dollar. If traders and investors expect the dollar to depreciate, the demand for foreign currencies increases and the dollar depreciates. Fewer market participants will want to hold dollars. When the dollar does depreciate, imports become more expensive.

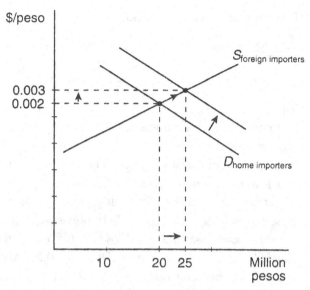

Figure 11.3
Increase in the Demand for Foreign Currency
This increase in demand raises the exchange rate from $0.002/peso to $0.003/peso. The quantity of pesos traded rises from 20 to 25 million.

Depreciation lowers import spending if imports are elastic. Simultaneously, exports become cheaper abroad and export revenue rises. Depreciation then leads to an increase in the *BGS*.

For depreciation to raise the *BGS* it is only necessary that home and foreign imports together are elastic. If import and export elasticities sum to more than one, the Marshall-Lerner condition holds.

> *Empirical evidence suggests the Marshall-Lerner condition holds given some months to adjust. Depreciation raises the BOT.*

EXAMPLE 11.2   *A Yen for the ¥*

The Japanese yen has a history of appreciating since WWII. This chart shows the upward path of $/¥ more than doubling. The growth rate in the supply of yen is kept low and the Japanese government budget balanced. As a long term strategy, yen assets remain attractive.

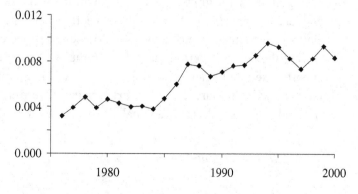

Depreciation and the BGS

The balance on goods and services BGS is export revenue less import expenditure,

$$BGS = p_X q_X - e p_M^* q_M.$$

The price of exports is p_X. Imports are priced in the foreign currency at p_M^* and converted to the domestic currency by the exchange rate e. Assume prices are constant and $BGS = 0$.

Depreciation means e rises. The higher e raises the quantity of exports q_X and lowers q_M due to effects on prices.

Suppose q_X does not adjust but q_M falls by 1% with 1% depreciation. The import elasticity is $\%\Delta q_M/\%\Delta p_M = -1$. Import spending and the BGS do not change.

Suppose q_X rises 0.5% and q_M falls 0.5% with the 1% depreciation. The export elasticity is 0.5 and the import elasticity −0.5. Export revenue then rises by 0.5% and import spending rises by 1% − 0.5% = 0.5%. The BGS does not change.

Suppose the export elasticity is 1 and the import elasticity is −1. With the 1% depreciation, export revenue rises by 1%. Import spending does not change. The BGS rises by 1%.

If the export elasticity plus the (negative of the) import elasticity is greater than 1 depreciation raises the trade balance.

If BGS < 0 stronger elasticities are required for depreciation to have a positive effect. If a country has international market power, depreciation increases export demand raising p_X and p_M^*. International market power strengthens the chance that a depreciation will raise the trade balance.

The large exchange rate swings since the 1980s provide experiments of changing currency values. The effect of a depreciating currency on the trade balance varies across countries and time but with evidence of a positive effect.

The J Curve

Depreciation may require time to have a positive effect on the trade balance with a temporary deficit. The J curve is the shape of the curve tracking the trade balance reaction to depreciation.

Figure 11.4 illustrates the J curve with depreciation at time d. Contracts for delivery at time d are based on the expected exchange rate. The surprise depreciation lowers the price of exports and raises the price of imports under contract. During the contract period the deficit in the BGS increases. With the quantity of exports fixed and price falling, export revenue falls. Import spending rises with the quantity of imports fixed and price rising. Over time, trade adjusts as exports rise and imports fall. The trade balance increases during this passthrough period.

A currency depreciation that raises the trade balance may cause a temporary deficit due to contracts pictured by the J curve.

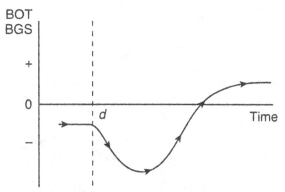

Figure 11.4
J Curve of a Depreciation
Depreciation causes import prices to rise and export prices to fall. A surprise depreciation
at time *d* temporarily worsens the trade balance with contracts set at agreed prices. Over
time, export and import quantities adjust.

EXAMPLE 11.3   *The FX Rate and Manufacturing*

The exchange rate affects the price of manufactures exported and the price of
intermediate products imported. Between April 1995 and August 1998 the dollar
appreciated 30%. US manufactured exports became more expensive and imported
intermediate products cheaper. Linda Goldberg and Keith Crockett (1998) examine exports as well as input purchases of US manufacturing industries. Industries most hurt by the appreciation were instruments, industrial machinery &
equipment, electronic & electrical equipment, tobacco products, and chemicals.
The appreciation benefited industries that export little but import intermediate
products: leather products, petroleum refining, printing & publishing, fabricated
metal products, and furniture & fixtures.

Currency Appreciation

Increased demand for exports causes foreign buyers to increase supply of their
currencies on the FX market. In Figure 11.5 increased supply of foreign currency
causes appreciation and increased FX trading. Appreciation raises foreign currency
prices of exports, strengthening the increased market price.

> *The accommodation and balancing effect of the FX market are reason to
> allow it to operate freely. Changes in the exchange rate work in the same
> direction as underlying prices.*

EXAMPLE 11.4   *FX and Local Industry*

Between 1975 and 1990 the dollar exchange rate had periods of large swings as a
result of erratic monetary policy. Henry Thompson and Kamal Upadhyaya (1998)
examine effects on two export industries, chemicals and primary metals in Alabama.

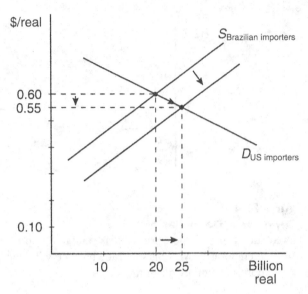

Figure 11.5
Increased Supply of Foreign Currency
This increase in the supply of Brazilian reals comes from increased demand for US exports in Brazil. The real falls from $0.60 to $0.55 as the quantity traded rises. Appreciation rises the price of US exports in Brazil reinforcing the market effect.

The chemicals industry in Alabama produces petrochemicals exporting about 1/4 of its output. Primary metals exports about 1/5 of its output. Chemical output in Alabama declined with appreciation between 1981 and 1985, then increased with depreciation from 1985 to 1990. Primary metals production rebounded with the dollar depreciation following 1985. A 10% appreciation lowered chemicals output by 2.8%, price by 1.4%, and revenue by 4.2%. For primary metals, decreases were 2.1% for output, 2.9% for price, and 5.0% for revenue.

Section A Problems

A1. Find dollar prices of imported cars costing 880,000 yen when the yen/$ exchange rate rises from 110 to 125.

A2. Illustrate the FX market for the euro with an equilibrium exchange rate of 0.85 €/$. Suppose the US announces an elimination of all restrictions on European imports after 6 months. Diagram how this announcement affects the exchange rate. Explain what happens to the price of EU products in the US.

A3. Suppose a US petrochemical company discovers an efficient way to produce liquid petroleum gas exported to Germany. Illustrate the effect on the euro FX market.

A4. Explain the effect of yuan appreciation on the trade surplus in China with J curve adjustment.

B.   MANAGED EXCHANGE RATES

Governments try to influence international trade and investment for various reasons. Managed exchange rates are one way for governments to influence prices of traded products and investment. This section examines

- Fixed exchange rates
- Foreign exchange licensing
- Black markets and FX market controls
- The pros and cons of managed exchange rates

Fixed Exchange Rates

Governments may want overpriced the exchange rate for cheap imports and foreign investment. An appreciated currency implies cheaper intermediate or capital good imports for domestic industry. An appreciating currency may attract foreign investors making it cheaper to pay debt in foreign currency.

In Figure 11.6 the market exchange rate between dollars and pesos would be $0.0005/peso. Suppose the peso government wants to keep the exchange rate at $0.0006. This fixed exchange rate creates an excess supply of 4 billion pesos.

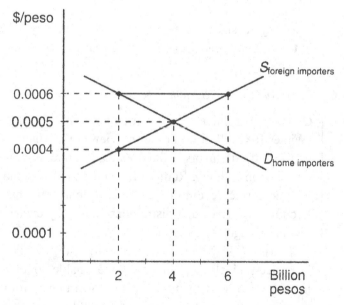

Figure 11.6
A Fixed Exchange Rate
At the official fixed exchange rate of $/peso = 0.0006 the peso is overvalued. There is an excess supply of 6 − 2 = 4 billion pesos. The peso central bank depletes its FX reserves.

At the fixed exchange rate, the excess supply of pesos equals excess dollar demand of $2.4 million. The peso central bank would have to sell $2.4 million of its FX reserves. Supporting a currency by depleting FX reserves generates a loss. The peso ultimately depreciates when the peso central bank depletes its FX reserves.

The peso central bank may want to undervalue its peso to stimulate exports. At $e = 0.0004$ in Figure 11.6 export prices in dollars would be lower than at the market rate 0.0005. The peso central bank would increase is FX reserves with the BGs surplus. Imports are more expensive in the peso country making this undervalued exchange rate ultimately unpopular.

Fixed exchange rates do not last indefinitely, helping some in the economy but hurting others.

EXAMPLE 11.5   *Fixed and Managed FX Rates*

Governments do not typically allow FX markets to operate freely but ultimately market forces cannot be denied. About 150 currencies are fixed, almost a third to some basket of currencies and another third to a particular currency. Central banks want their exchange rate policy difficult to predict. Central banks prefer to say their exchange rates are "managed" but "fixed" or "rigged" are more descriptive.

FX Licenses

One way to sustain the FX price of a currency without depleting FX reserves is to limit imports with foreign exchange licenses.

EXAMPLE 11.6   *Views on the FX System*

Conflicting opinions attract attention. The *Journal of Economic Perspectives* (Winter 1988) illustrates differing views on exchange rate reform. Ronald McKinnon (Stanford) favors a fixed exchange rate system managed by central banks focusing on stability. Rudiger Dornbusch (MIT) counters that floating rates work with no correct level to fix currencies. John Williamson (Institute of International Economics) agrees that disruptions caused by exchange rate swings are large but favors managed target zones.

In Figure 11.7 there is a license for only 15 billion pesos where peso supply is perfectly inelastic. Importers are unable to buy more foreign currency or imports. If peso demand falls, the government would have to decrease licenses to keep the value of the peso at $0.0006.

Governments also curtail tourism of their citizens and prohibit the purchase of foreign assets. People cannot leave the country with more than a fixed amount of cash. Investors are not allowed to buy foreign assets.

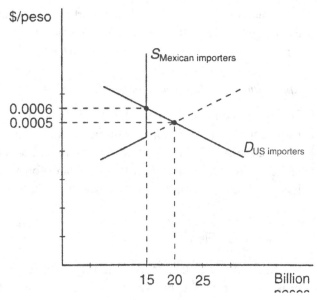

Figure 11.7
Foreign Exchange License
The peso government can support its currency by licensing the sale of pesos to 15 billion. The peso is propped above its market rate of $0.0005.

EXAMPLE 11.7   *Devaluation and the BOT*

A devaluation is a decrease in a fixed exchange rate. Governments must reset fixed exchange rates when inflation rate vary. Daniel Himarios (1989) reports on the effects of 60 devaluations of fixed exchange rates prior to 1973. Devaluations raised the *BOT* in 80% of the cases. There were immediate increases in the *BOT* as well as lagged effects a few years after a devaluation. Similar results occurred for 15 countries with fixed exchange rates between 1975 and 1984. There were J curves for Salvador, France, Greece, and Zambia. Murli Buluswar, Henry Thompson, and Kamal Upadhyaya (1996) find devaluations had no effects on the trade balance for India.

Black Markets

A black market for foreign exchange arises if the fixed rate is too far from the market rate. The black market rate is the market rate less the risk of penalty for illegal transactions. With an overvalued peso, US tourists, importers, and investors would be tempted by a black market rate.

An artificially supported peso is expected to devalue. Such expectations ensure the peso will stay low since nobody wants to hold pesos when they are devalued.

Merchants dealing with tourists are happy to accept "hard" currency at a rate more favorable to tourists. Black market trading is illegal as armed guards often remind tourists at border crossings.

Some governments allow black market transactions in what is called a parallel exchange market. Official markets operate alongside the black market, settling for a share of transactions at the official rate.

EXAMPLE 11.8   *Appreciation and Import Competition*

Dollar appreciation during 1980–1985 reduced prices, domestic production, and labor demand for 38 import competing manufacturing industries as shown by Ana Revenga (1992). There was a 6% reduction in the labor force and a 1.5% reduction in wages. Reduced labor demand forced the labor market down along its supply curve with a supply elasticity of 0.25.

Fixed versus Float

Speculators feed on market instability and enjoy exchange rate changes. FX brokers "churn" the market for higher turnover and fees. while floating FX rates seem like a lot of trouble, consider a fixed artificially high exchange rate. Central bank support eventually collapses and the currency is devalued. All speculation is on the down side of the fixed exchange rate.

There remains disagreement over floating versus fixed exchange rates. Exchange rates have fluctuated greatly since the early 1970s. The US dollar dropped 13% from 1974 to 1979, rose 63% by 1985, then fell 62% by 1990. Starting at $/yen = 0.05 an imported car costing 2,000,000 yen would cost $20,000 in 1974, $22,600 in 1979, $14,200 in 1985, and $23,000 in 1990.

High oil prices during the 1970s and 1980s led to large current account deficits for oil importing countries. Governments inflating their way out of debt had depreciating exchange rates. Governments increased spending to ease the recession due to high oil prices.

Perhaps a more regulated FX market would be more efficient. The Bretton Woods fixed exchange rate system operated from the end of World War II until the oil price hikes of the 1970s. The US was the dominant economy and the dollar the standard for all currencies. The Bretton Woods system is remembered as reliable and stable. The gold standard of the late 1800s or some other standard would seem more stable.

Any fixed exchange rate system would have collapsed under the economic upheavals since the 1970s. The Bretton Woods system succeeded only because the US was the dominant economy. Europe and Japan had been devastated by World War II. US monetary focused on a steady price level and a reliable currency standard.

The last three decades of the 20th century were characterized by oil price instability, LDC debt, the emergence of Japan, European integration, success of newly industrializing countries, high levels of international investment, the collapse of Soviet and Chinese communism, and large inflation differentials. The level and intensity of international transactions continues to grow. There is little chance to restart a fixed exchange rate system.

Fundamental forces determining the supply and demand of FX are little affected by central bank management these days. Active exchange rate intervention exacerbates exchange rate volatility.

Each country chooses its inflation rate through a political economic process. When inflation rates vary across countries, exchange rates adjust. A single international currency is feasible but the money supply would be beyond the control of any government. For better or worse, the world economy will operate with floating exchange rates.

EXAMPLE 11.9   *FX Policy*

Peter Kenen (Princeton) argues that governments should intervene to stop runs on FX markets. Ronald McKinnon (Stanford) argues for active management of FX rates. John Williamson (Institute for International Economics) favors active intervention and recommends joint action by central banks. Jacob Frankel (IMF) thinks better fiscal and monetary policy should be the focus. Martin Feldstein (Harvard) believes market forces should be allowed to determine FX rates.

Section B Problems

B1. Suppose China wants to undervalue the yuan. Diagram the FX market for yuan and illustrate the artifically low exchange rate. How could the central bank sustain this rate? Why would it want to?

B2. How could the Chinese government use FX market controls to keep the yuan below its market value?

B3. Justify your opinion on fixed versus floating exchange rates.

C.   FOREIGN EXCHANGE TRADING

The FX market involves buying and selling foreign currency. Topics in foreign exchange trading include:

- Expectations and exchange rates
- Stability of exchange rates
- Triangular arbitrage across currencies

Expectations and FX Rates

Traders expecting a currency to appreciate will increase demand in the FX market. The increased demand appreciates the currency. Market expectations make themselves come true.

Much of the hourly and daily changes in FX rates is due to traders looking for short term gains. Long term investors want to hold assets in currencies expected to maintain or appreciate. There is motivation for investors with cash in high inflation countries to buy assests in low inflation countries.

Expectations influence the spot exchange market. Expectations explain the dollar depreciation that started in 1985 when the central banks of Germany, France, Britain, Japan, and the US announced they would act together to sell dollars. Traders and investors expected the dollar to depreciate. The volume of central bank sales was trivial but trader expectations moved the market. In 1989 the dollar appreciated in spite of dollar sales by central banks. Central banks control their money supplies, determining inflation and exchange rates.

EXAMPLE 11.10   *Charts versus Fundamentals*

Chartists look for FX rate behavior in patterns of trends, break points, shoulders, cliffs, spikes, and bubbles. Fundamentalists examine underlying theory and variables that affect exchange rates. Fundamentalists may have the right idea but theory and practice differ. An increase in the relative growth of a money supply leads to depreciation, but when? Jeffrey Frenkel and Kenneth Froot (1990) report that chartists are more prevalent among FX traders. Most foreign exchange trading takes place between financial firms, banks, and brokers but small FX traders are increasing their market share.

FX Rate Speculation

Debate continues over exchange rate speculation. Economist Milton Friedman argued since the 1950s that speculation would lower exchange rate fluctuation. Figure 11.8 shows the market for yen at two different times. On the left, the exchange rate at time 0 is e_0. At a later time, the exchange rate is e_1 on the right. Supply S_1 is less S_0.

Speculators who correctly anticipate the coming change will buy yen at time 0 and sell them at time 1. Buying yen at e_0 and selling them later at e_1 yields a speculative profit. The profitable speculators dampen exchange rate variation over time. The increased D_0 raises e_0 and increased S_1 lowers e_1.

Unprofitable speculators would increase variation of e but they would soon be out of business. Only profitable speculators persist. Speculation must reduce exchange rate fluctuation, transferring currencies from times when they are plentiful to times when they are scarce.

Detractors argue speculators jump on the bandwagon of a trend in the exchange rate and create a speculative bubble. If the yen is appreciating, speculators buy yen on the expectation the trend will continue. The buying pushes the yen up faster and further. When the climb stops, speculators rush to sell yen, causing it to crash. Speculators make a profit creating a bubble and selling at the peak.

While the debate continues, speculation on the exchange rate will remain part of the international economy. Fixed exchange rates or central bank intervention

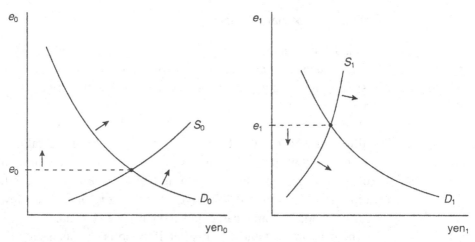

Figure 11.8
Stabilizing Profitable Speculation
The supply and demand for yen at time 0 is pictured on the left and later at time 1 on
the right. S_1 is less than S_0. Speculators at time 0 who anticipate the higher e at time 1
will buy yen now increasing D_0 and e_0, and sell yen later increasing S_1 and lowering e_1.
Profitable speculation reduces FX variation.

create speculation on one side of the market. Free exchange markets remain
the best system.

EXAMPLE 11.11 *Currency Game*

Investors put effort into trading currencies for profit. The top ranked fund
managers lost 1% trading currencies during 2004 after earning 1% the previous
year. Other years the gains and losses have been larger. Trading currencies is
riskier than trading other assets but with a higher than average return. Exchange
rates are difficult to predict.

EXAMPLE 11.12 *Official Foreign Exchange*

The foreign exchange reserves of the Fed are only a small fraction of the daily
volume of FX trading. The Federal Reserve Bank of New York summarizes
foreign exchange transactions an abridged 1998 report:

> The Fed intervened in the FX markets on June 17 selling $833 million dollars
> for yen. The yen had fallen 4.1% against the dollar during the quarter. The
> intervention was carried out in coordination with Japan. In the following
> days, the yen strengthened.

The yen could only have strengthened due to anticipated a change in Japanese
monetary policy. The $833 million purchase of yen had no effect. The
daily volume of trading was over 100 times that amount. The Fed had
$14 billion of foreign exchange reserves, a drop in the daily bucket of FX
transactions.

Stability of Exchange Markets

Demand for foreign exchange has a negative slope and supply a positive slope if import demands are elastic. Evidence suggests import demand is elastic at least over long time periods. The FX market may, however, be unstable over short time spans.

The equilibrium in Figure 11.2 is stable. An exchange rate above the equilibrium $/yen = 0.008 implies excess supply and a falling exchange rate. If $/yen = 0.009 traders see their yen inventories increase and dollar inventories decline, and respond by discounting yen. If the exchange rate is below the equilibrium at $/yen = 0.007 buyers clamor for yen but too few are offered to meet demand. Yen are scarce and their price is bid up.

There is an unstable FX market if imports are inelastic causing supply to have a negative slope. Suppose supply slopes downward as in Figure 11.9. A lower $/yen rate leads to an increase in the quantity of yen along the supply curve. The supply of yen might slope downward during the contract period of the J-curve. At $/yen = 0.009 there is an excess demand and $/yen is bid up. At $/yen = 0.007 there is excess supply of yen and $/yen falls. The exchange rate would crash or skyrocket over a short time period.

On an hourly or daily basis, there can be substantial exchange rate movement. Traders are looking for equilibrium. With short term movement in the exchange

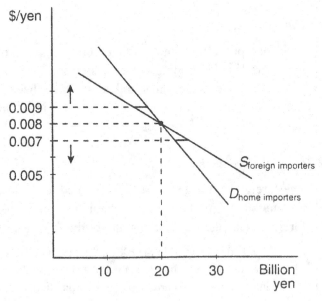

Figure 11.9
An Unstable FX Market
At any price above the equilibrium rate, excess demand raises the exchange rate. At any price below the market equilibrium, excess supply lowers the exchange rate. Instead of stabilizing, the exchange rate would rise or fall without bound.

rate, some traders profit while others lose. High risk and returns keep the FX market busy.

Large swings in the dollar occurred during the 1980s. The dollar appreciated 87% from 1980 to 1985, then depreciated 42% by 1988. The large dollar appreciation during the early 1980s raised import spending and lowered export revenue. These changes indicate import elasticity. The recession at the time can be attributed to low export production and imports of cheap foreign products. As the dollar depreciated after 1985, import prices rose and export revenue climbed. The US experienced trade surpluses early in 1991.

Exchange rates have been volatile but FX markets are reliable in the long term.

EXAMPLE **11.13** *Predicting FX Rates*

Economists are often asked to do the impossible and will do so for a fee. Predicting exchange rates is impossible. The popular press is full of conflicting "wisdom" about what has happened in exchange markets. For instance, *The Economist* magazine reported in May 1989 that rising US output caused the dollar to appreciate because foreigners wanted dollars to buy US products but then slower US output growth caused the dollar to appreciate because of the perception that there would be no inflation! Every FX trader has their own reasons for trading. No single theory will explain all exchange rate movements but relative money supplies explain long term exchange rate movements.

EXAMPLE **11.14** *FX Trading Banks*

The magazine *FX Week* publishes news on the foreign exchange trade. An October 1999 issue lists the foreign exchange revenue of US banks for the third quarter. Citigroup reports the largest FX revenue at $358 million, followed by Chase Manhattan with $199 million, and Bank of America with $138 million. FX traders make commissions on volume and do not care about the direction of change. Consider the comments of a dealer at one New York bank: "There was some good movement, but it came mainly in the latter part of the quarter. That activity kept FX desks reasonably busy and generated some good profit making opportunities. Volatility was not as high as in 1998 when the Asian and Russian crises were breaking out."

Triangular Arbitrage

The millions of banks, brokers, and traders in the FX market instantaneously know market rates online and through interbank electronic links. Brokers "make" the market, continuously matching buyers and sellers. The market making is electronic. The FX market is highly competitive, not partly monopolized like the US stock market with the Stock Exchange. Thousands of brokers and traders operate on minuscule volumes in the FX market.

Any difference in FX rates results in an opportunity for triangular arbitrage. Suppose exchange rates are mark/$ = 2, yen/mark = 62, and yen/$ = 125. A trader could take yen, buy marks, and then buy dollars at $62 \times 2 = 124$ yen/$. This cross rate is lower than the 125 market rate. Traders will buy dollars at the cross rate and sell at the market rate for a profit of 1 yen per dollar. Arbitrage decreases demand for the dollar, pushing together the cross rate and market rate.

Trillions of dollars of currency are involved in continuous triangular arbitrage. Among any three currencies, there are two independent exchange rates. Cross rates between any two currencies determine the value of the other currency through triangular arbitrage. Among any number n of currencies there are $n - 1$ independent exchange rates. Triangular arbitrage occurs continuously to keep the rates in line.

Many banks have an FX desk that trades currencies. In large US cities especially near the Canadian and Mexican borders, foreign currency circulates alongside the dollar. FX traders specialize in quick service at FX windows. Airports have FX windows where travelers can buy and sell foreign currencies. There is an increasing volume of FX trading on the internet.

The FX market is a vast competitive market made up of many traders, buyers, and sellers.

EXAMPLE 11.15   *Growth in the FX Market*

The volume of trade in the FX market has grown over 10% annually since the early 1990s according to the Bank for International Settlements BIS. The volume of exports is a small fraction of the volume of FX trading. Spot FX transactions are about a third of total FX transactions. Trading is focused geographically in three major centers. London handles the greatest volume. New York is the major center in the Americas. Tokyo is the major center in Asia. The FX market never closses.

Section C Problems

C1. If the South Korean won/$ rate is 1050, the peso/$ rate is 175, and the won/peso rate is 5.95, find profit starting with $1000.

C2. Suppose the demand for yen slopes upward due to inelastic demand for Japanese bonds. Diagram an unstable exchange market with upward sloping demand. Describe its behavior.

D.   FOREIGN EXCHANGE RISK

Exchange rates ultimately reflect inflation and currency purchasing power but unpredictable changes in exchange rates make exchange rate risk an element of trade and finance.

EXAMPLE 11.16 *The Euro Market*

> The euro fell relative to the US dollar in 1999 when it was introduced. US products in Europe became more expensive than they had been at the start of the year as European products became cheaper in the US. The supply of euros is controlled by the European government in Belgium. Without the ability to create money, national governments in Europe have to more nearly balance their budgets. The euro exchange rate will depend on growth rates of money supplies. Both the US and Europe have the stated monetary policy goal of low inflation. If that occurs the value of the $/euro exchange rate will stabilize. Between 1999 and 2010, however, the euro ranged from $0.85 to $1.50.

Inflation and the Exchange Rates

Inflation occurs when the general price level rises. If the price level P is $/good, its inverse goods/$ represents the purchasing power of the dollar.

Currencies have been generally inflating since the 1950s, some more than others. Some periods of deflation with the price level falling have occurred through history. Consumers and firms can adjust to inflation and depreciation.

If one currency is expected to inflate more than another, international interest rates will reflect the inflation differential. The real interest rate is the return on an investment after the erosion of inflation. The real interest rate does not vary much over time or between countries aside from risk. The nominal interest rate is the real interest rate plus an inflation premium. Nominal interest rates vary due to inflation differentials.

The Fisher equation named after economist Irvin Fisher is expressed

$$i = r + \pi$$

where i is the nominal interest rate, r is the real interest rate, and π is expected inflation.

If the nominal interest rate is 6% then $100 becomes $106 at the end of a year. Suppose inflation for the year is 5%. The purchasing power of the $106 is discounted to find the real interest rate, 6% − 5% = 1%.

Suppose expected inflation is 25% for the peso and 5% for the dollar. Expectations are based on the history of inflation in each country as well as expected monetary policies. A 28% nominal interest rate in pesos equals a real interest rate of 3% and a nominal interest rate of 8% in dollars. Investing at those nominal interest rates yields the same purchasing power. The expected increase in purchasing power from investing in either country is 3%.

Nominal interest rates are observed. Comparing of real interest rates involves expected inflation. The difference between nominal interest rates in two countries with competitive exchange and financial markets is the market expectation of the difference between the two inflation rates. If nominal interest rates are 18% for the peso and 8% for the dollar, the peso would have a 18% − 8% = 10% discount against the dollar.

Holding foreign currency involves exchange risk. Investors diversify currency holdings to dissipate risk. Currencies can be ranked according to potential for unexpected depreciation.

Nominal interest rates in currencies with higher expected inflation must be discounted. Differences in nominal interest rates reveal how the market discounts currencies.

EXAMPLE 11.17 *The Trade Weighted Dollar Exchange Rate*

The importance of each country in US trade is used to weight the dollar exchange rate. Trade with country i is $T_i = X_i + M_i$ and the sum of trade with all countries is T. The weight of country i is its share of total trade $W_i = T_i/T$. The trade weighted exchange rate is $E = W_1E_1 + \cdots + W_nE_n$ where E is that currency rate. From 1973 when floating exchange rates started until 1981, the dollar remained around $E = 30$ (1999 = 100). The dollar then appreciated strongly to 1986. A slight depreciation followed but an appreciation began in 1991. By 1998 the dollar reached 100. Long term appreciation indicates that the money supply of dollars has fallen relative to the money supplies of US trading partners.

EXAMPLE 11.18 *Peso Crashes*

The Mexican government tries to keep the peso above its market rate. The supply of pesos increases to support government spending. An excess supply of pesos is created at the fixed exchange rate as in Figure 11.6. To meet the excess demand for dollars Mexican international reserves fell 70% in 1994. The supply of pesos continued to grow with the peso overvalued. Finally the government devalued the peso by 15% leading to speculation that the peso was ready for a crash. Over the next 3 months the peso fell 50% relative to the dollar. The price of imports skyrocketed in Mexico as real income fell. Such episodes occur periodically in Mexico. Fixed exchange rates will not support a currency out of line with underlying price levels and money supplies.

Forward and Future Exchange

There is risk in international transactions because of unexpected exchange rate changes. Contracts for goods and services are written for future delivery. Investors hold long term assets denominated in foreign currency.

To avoid FX risk, traders and investors can hedge in the forward exchange market with a contract to buy or sell foreign currency at a date in the future for a price set today. The supply and demand for forward exchange come from traders and investors wanting to settle prices of transactions or earnings in their own currency.

The forward exchange market reflects what market participants think the exchange rate will become. Rapidly inflating currencies are discounted with forward rates below spot rates. Currencies with low inflation have premiums.

Future contracts for standard quantities and time have developed. Transaction costs of future contracts are very low. The forward and future rates are unbiased predictors of the exchange rate.

Speculators trade foreign exchange when they believe the exchange rate will turn out to be different from the forward rate. Suppose the current spot rate for South Korean won is 760 won/$ and the 3 month future rate 780. Suppose a speculator thinks the won will drop to 800 won/$. The speculator will sign a contract to sell won at the forward rate of 780 and buy won later in the spot market. This speculation is leveraged since no current payment is required to make the contract.

Forward and future FX markets offer hedgers a way to avoid risk, and speculators a way to assume risk.

EXAMPLE 11.19 *Trading FX Futures*

Futures contracts are for standard quantities of foreign currency at specified dates. For instance, contracts list for 12.5 million yen on Wednesdays. Investors and speculators match wits buying and selling future contracts. Foreign exchange is traded in futures markets alongside gold, oil, cotton, and beef as in the following quotes are for 30 day future contracts. A trader could buy or sell yen at yen/$ = 94.94. The spot price of yen that day was yen/$ = 106 indicating investors expected the yen to depreciate. Speculators buy future contracts hoping to outguess the market. The change column shows the percentage change from the previous day.

	Price	Change
¥ FUTURE	94.94	0.14%
£ FUTURE	162.06	0.05%
C$ FUTURE	68.19	−0.06%
GOLD 100 OZ FUTURE	289.30	−0.58%
CRUDE OIL FUTURE	23.00	0.61%
COTTON FUTURE	51.11	0.02%

Section D Problems

D1. Suppose current price levels are $P = \$/\text{good} = 100$ and $P^* = €/\text{good} = 150$. If the same goods are consumed in each country and there is free trade, what is the current exchange rate $\$/€$? Five years later, $P = 120$ and $P^* = 160$. What should the exchange rate be? Explain which currency depreciated.

D2. Suppose the nominal interest rate is 12% and inflation is 9%. Find the real interest rate. Starting with $100 find the nominal and real return to saving. If expected inflation rises to 15% but the real interest rate does not change, find the nominal rate. Find the nominal and real returns to $100.

EXAMPLE 11.20   *Volatile Central Banks*

Central banks intervene in FX markets trying to stabilize a currency. Richard Baillie and William Osterberg (1997) find evidence that intervention is destabilizing. Daily foreign exchange interventions by the US, German, and Japanese central banks increase exchange rate variability. Traders view central banks as unpredictable and unreliable.

CONCLUSION

The FX market is a vast deep market with increasing numbers of firms and consumers participating. As a country integrates more into the world economy, its foreign exchange market becomes more important. The influence of the exchange rate on daily economic life cannot be overlooked. The next chapter turns attention to issues of international finance and the international role of money.

Terms

Black market FX	Future and forward contracts
Cross rate	Import license FX control
FX discount & premium	J curve
Expected inflation	Managed FX rate
Fischer equation	Market exchange rate
Fixed exchange rate	Marshall-Lerner condition
Forward exchange rate	Parallel exchange markets
FX reserves	Real and nominal interest rates
FX risk	Spot exchange rate
FX speculation	Triangular arbitrage

MAIN POINTS

- FX markets are large, busy, electronic, efficient, vital, and the most important market for many countries.
- The demand for foreign exchange comes from domestic buyers of foreign products and assets. Supply comes from foreign buyers of domestic products and assets.
- A depreciating currency raises the domestic price of foreign goods and lowers the foreign price of domestic goods. Depreciation generally leads to an increase in the trade balance.
- A government may artificially fix or manage its exchange rate to meet some policy goal. Theory and experience, however, recommend market exchange rates.
- High inflation rates are associated with high nominal interest rates and depreciating currencies. Currencies expected to depreciate are discounted by forward and future exchange rates.

REVIEW PROBLEMS

1. Suppose the domestic demand for Japanese cars is $Q = 10,000 - P$ where P is the dollar price. Find the quantity of Japanese cars costing 1 million yen that would be demanded when the exchange rate is $1/e$ = yen/\$ = 110 and then 125. Plot the quantity of yen demanded to buy the autos at these two exchange rates.

2. Find yen prices of US rice costing \$4.50 per bushel when the yen/\$ exchange rate is 110 and then 125. Demand for rice is $Q = 9,000,000 - 10,000\ P^*$ where P^* is the yen price. Find the quantity of yen supplied at both exchange rates. Plot the corresponding supply of yen.

3. Start with \$1000 and find a way to make a profit if won/peso = 6.05, won/\$ = 1050, and \$/peso = 0.00571.

4. Suppose the EU launches a number of communications satellites improving their telecommunications industry. Given that the US exports telecommunications services, diagram the effect on the FX market.

5. Find the short run percentage change in import spending and export revenue due to 5% depreciation when the short run import elasticity is 0.3 and the short run export elasticity is 0.4. Describe what happens to the trade balance.

6. If the long run import elasticity is 1.5 and the long run export elasticity is 1.2 find the long run percentage change in export revenue and import spending due to the 5% depreciation. Does the trade balance rise or fall in the long run?

7. Illustrate the effect on the foreign exchange market of a limit on cash that can be taken on foreign travel.

8. Explain how a central bank supporting its currency by buying a surplus of its own currency taxes its citizens.

9. Which groups of economic agents demand pesos in the forward market? What happens to the quantity of pesos demanded when the forward price of pesos rises? Who supplies pesos forward in the market?

10. "Despite repeated central bank intervention, the US dollar rallied to highs of 1.7095 marks, 151.35 yen, and $1.6155/pound." Illustrate with an FX market diagram.

11. Suppose the spot exchange rate for Kuwait dinar is $/dinar = 3.60 and the six-month forward rate is 3.65. Explain whether the dinar has a forward premium or discount.

12. In the example of Korean won, calculate profit if the speculator signs a contract to sell 10 million won and the spot rate turns out to be exactly what was expected. Find profit in dollars if the spot rate instead falls to 750 won/$.

READINGS

Mike Melvin, *International Money and Finance* (1989) New York: Harper & Row. Lively text with excellent coverage of the FX market.

Paul Krugman (1989) *Exchange Rate Instability*, Cambridge: The MIT Press. Examines the surprising volatility of exchange rates during the 1980s.

Leland Yeager (1976) *International Monetary Relations*, New York: Harper & Row. A classic.

Federal Reserve Bank Bulletins. Monthly bulletins with analysis of the FX market, available online.

A number of foreign exchange sites on the internet include various commercial trading and information on the FX market.

CHAPTER 12

International Money and Financial Markets

Preview

Finance refers to lending and borrowing in credit markets. International financial markets involve lending and borrowing across borders. This chapter covers:

- The international credit market
- Relationship between foreign exchange and international credit markets
- Money, international prices, and exchange rates
- Relative money supplies and international financial markets

INTRODUCTION

Money is a medium of exchange that facilitates trade. People trade with money in the form of checks, credit cards, and cash. The scarcity of money reflects resource scarcity and economic choice.

To balance income and spending, lenders and borrowers trade in credit markets. The interest rate is the return on a loan and the cost of borrowing.

Countries can be net lenders or borrowers in the international credit market. Each country would have its own autarky credit market but all countries benefit through the international credit market. International interest rates are the result of lending and borrowing across countries.

Money is a unit of account for products and assets. International price comparisons are made through the exchange rate. Money is also a store of value. An inflating currency is a poor store of value as it depreciates in the FX market. Currency trading takes place as investors look for currencies that are a better store of value.

International financial flows are reported in the capital account of the balance of payments. Interest payments on international loans are reported as net investment income in the current account. Borrowing countries experience cash inflow and capital account surpluses but future deficits in net investment income. Lenders have cash outflows, capital account deficits, and future surpluses in net investment income.

While interpreted as bad news, a trade deficit and international borrowing are signals a country is expected to grow. LDCs must incur debt to acquire capital goods and repay debt as output expands.

Stocks, bonds, certificates of deposit, futures contracts, options, swaps, and overnight paper are financial instruments involved in international finance. Arbitrage trading occurs internationally among financial intermediaries including banks, investment houses, and brokers.

The main role a government should play in international financial markets is to manage its deficit spending and control its money supply growth. Money supply growing relative to the rest of the world depreciates the currency with the foreign exchange rate reflecting monetary and fiscal policies.

A.   THE INTERNATIONAL CREDIT MARKET

This section covers international credit markets and financial accounting.

EXAMPLE 12.1   *International Credit Markets over the Centuries*

International credit markets were highly integrated in the 1890s but disrupted by two World Wars and the Great Depression. International investment relative to output reached a low during the 1950s and 1960s. Since the late 1970s international investment has increased but in real terms remains below the level of the 1900s. Markets for foreign exchange and investment encourage international credit markets.

Two Senses of "Capital"

Capital has two meanings in economics. In microeconomics, capital is an input in production. Productive capital is the machinery and structures combined with labor and natural resources to produce output. In finance, capital refers to credit.

The two meanings are connected. When a firm borrows from a bank, sells bonds, or sells stocks, it typically invests in productive capital to increase future production. Debt and equity purchase new productive capital input.

Consumers can expand consumption beyond income by borrowing. Governments can increase spending beyond tax revenue by selling bonds. If a firm lacks cash for a worthwhile investment project, it can borrow in the credit market.

A firm deciding whether to invest in a project looks at its rates of return. Suppose a new machine is expected to create net profit of $40,000 per year for an indefinitely long lifetime. The net benefit of the machine is the $40,000 per year it adds to profit. If the machine costs $1 million, its rate of return is $40,000/$1,000,000 = 4%.

To determine whether investing in the machine is worthwhile, the opportunity cost of the $1 million has to be considered. Suppose the rate interest rate is 3%. With no inflation, this 3% is the real interest rate. If the firm has $1 million cash, it could become a lender and earn $30,000 but the machine offers more.

If the market interest rate were 5%, the firm could earn $50,000 by lending and should not invest in the machine.

If the firm has no cash on hand, it could borrow to invest in the machine. Suppose it costs $35,000 per year to pay back the principal and interest on a loan of $1 million. Yearly benefits from the machine of $40,000 outweigh the costs of $35,000. If borrowing costs were $45,000 per year, the purchase of the machine would not be profitable.

Financial capital is translated into productive capital by firms borrowing to invest in new capital plant and equipment.

Investment spending varies inversely with the interest rate. A higher interest rate leads to fewer investment projects.

EXAMPLE 12.2   *Emerging Stock Markets*

Financial capital is transformed into productive capital when firms sell stocks and bonds to spend on investment projects. The major international stock markets in New York, Tokyo, and London are in the news daily but smaller stock markets are critical. There is a high degree of variation in returns across emerging stock markets as well as across firms and industries in each country. Emerging stock markets have high average rates of return but high risk.

The Credit Market

At higher interest rates, the quantity of loans demanded decreases and saving increases. Demand and supply for credit as loanable funds LF are pictured in Figure 12.1. The real interest rate r is the price of borrowing and the return to lending. The real interest rate equals the nominal interest rate minus expected inflation in the Fisher equation,

$$r = i - \pi$$

If $r = 5\%$ saving $100 today results in $105 of purchasing power next year. From the borrower's viewpoint, borrowing $100 will cost $5 of goods and services. From the lender's viewpoint, $5 worth of goods and services will be gained next year by not consuming $100 now.

At $r = 4\%$ the quantity of loans demanded $12 billion is greater than the quantity supplied $8 billion. Financial intermediaries perceive this excess demand and ration by increasing the interest rate. At $r = 6\%$, there is excess supply of $4 billion. Idle reserves would spur banks to lower the interest rate. At the market equilibrium 5% the quantity of credit supplied equals the quantity demanded.

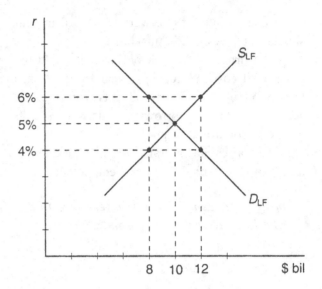

Figure 12.1
The Domestic Credit Market
The real interest rate *r* represents the real expected return. The demand for loanable funds LF is the return on various investment projects in order of returns. At higher interest rates, the quantity of credit demanded is lower. The supply of credit comes from those with liquidity willing to sacrifice current spending. Higher interest rates increase quantity of LF supplied. Equilibrium occurs at 5% with $10 billion credit.

EXAMPLE 12.3   *International Default*

Bad loans, debt problems, default, and bankruptcy are hardly new to the international economy. Relative to output, international lending was higher a century ago. Barry Eichengreen (1991) surveys the history of bad debt. Latin American countries defaulted on their loans in the 1820s followed by US states during the 1830s and 1840s. Latin American countries defaulted again in the 1880s along with Egypt, Greece, and Turkey. During the Great Depression of the 1930s every debtor country defaulted. Defaulting countries perform better than those continuing the struggle to pay back bad loans. Lenders always make new loans because of high potential returns. Bankruptcy practice allows bad domestic loans to be written off but there are no international bankruptcy laws.

The International Credit Market

International financial intermediation occurs when banks match lenders and borrowers in different countries.

At the international interest rate of 4% the small open economy in Figure 12.1 can borrow all it wants. There will be an inflow of $4 billion. This inflow is a capital account surplus, KA > 0. If the world interest rate were 6%, the surplus of $4 billion is exported with a KA deficit as the country lends internationally.

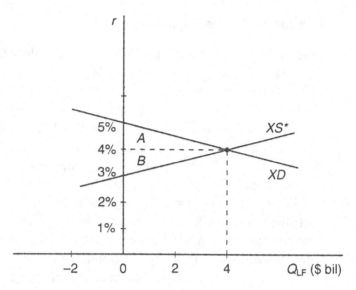

Figure 12.2
The International Credit Market
The excess demand XD for credit from the home country slopes down. The home autarky return is 5%. The excess supply XS* from the foreign country slopes upward. The foreign autarky return is 3%. The international equilibrium $r = 4\%$ results in $4 billion of loans from the foreign country.

A small open economy takes the international interest rate. The economy borrows if the international interest rate is lower than the domestic autarky interest rate but lends if the international interest rate is higher.

The international loanable funds market between two large economies in Figure 12.2 is similar to the excess supply and demand of products. Home excess demand XD for credit is derived from Figure 12.1.

The foreign country has different lenders and borrowers. Note that the foreign autarky interest rate $r^* = 3\%$ is less than the home autarky interest rate $r = 5\%$. At $r = 4\%$ home excess demand for credit equals foreign excess supply, $XD = XS^*$. The home country borrows $4 billion from the foreign country.

Borrowers are better off in autarky at home and lenders in the foreign country. On the other hand, lenders at home suffer lower returns as they compete with foreign lenders. Borrowers abroad pay more than they would in autarky because they have to compete with home country borrowers.

Net international gains are represented by triangles A and B in Figure 12.2. Net gain a for the home country is the area between XD and the international interest rate, area A equal to $1/2(.01 \times \$4 \text{ bil}) = \$20$ million.

The foreign net gain is the area between foreign XS* and the international interest rate 4%, area B equal to $1/2(.01 \times \$4 \text{ bil}) = \$20$ million. International gains are the sum of the two, a total of $40 million.

International Investment Accounting

Financial flows enter the capital account KA of the *BOP* as foreign investment. Borrowing countries report surpluses as a positive number, and lending countries deficits as negative numbers.

Net investment income NII enters the *BOP*. Suppose home investors have a stock of $2200 billion invested abroad, while foreigners have $1675 billion invested at home. If the international interest rate is 4% then 0.04 × $2200 billion = $88 billion is received as investment income while 0.04 × $1675 billion = $67 billion is paid. The NII is then $88 billion − $67 billion = $21 billion. This surplus in NII was reported by the US in 1998.

Estimates of the KA and NII are done by survey. Some years it is not clear whether the US is a net debtor or creditor due to the statistical discrepancy. International financial activity is expanding too quickly for government surveys.

Multinational firms MNFs account for an increasing share of international finance. The development of international banks is analogous. Transactions within firms are difficult to track.

Imagine the branch of a US bank operating in Mexico buys $1 million of new stock in a new industrial plant in a free trade zone in Texas that plans to employ Mexicans. Suppose 49% of the stock of the Mexican bank is owned by a bank in Spain, while 60% of the deposits in the Mexican bank belong to investors in Texas. Machinery in the assembly line is assembled by a firm based in Michigan importing components from China. Such international activity presents a quagmire for national income accounting. International investment accounting offers only a rough estimate.

International Financial Policy

Governments try to control and influence international financial flows. Governments can place direct controls on international investment. LDCs forbid the outflow of investment. Many governments are reluctant to allow inflows fearing the influence of foreign interests.

A concern is the share of GDP paid abroad as interest. Markets determine if there has been too much borrowing. If a country borrows to finance consumption, it soon loses ability to repay debt and lending stops. Financial markets, not governments politicians, should govern financial flows.

A government may protect its own financial industry but the country suffers due to the resulting inefficiency. Foreign investment and competition in banking and investment are outlawed in some countries. A trip to a bank can then be painful with transactions done by hand, people waiting hours to cash a check, and slow uncaring government workers.

There will always be political pressure for controls on international investment. International competition, however, forces banks to become more competitive. Financial intermediation becomes more efficient in the face of competition.

EXAMPLE 12.4   *Global Financial Instability*

International trade and finance slow during a financial crisis. Frederic Mishkin (1999) notes that lending of financial intermediaries stops, interest rates rise, and uncertainties increase during crises. Gerard Caprio and Patrick Honohan (1999) find political interference in bank regulation is a common theme in every crisis. Jeffrey Sachs (1995) advocates an international bankruptcy court. Paul Krugman (1998) advocates controls on capital outflows but Sebastian Edwards (1999) shows they are ineffective. Barry Eichengreen (1999) advocates controls on capital inflows. Henry Kaufman (1998) advocates the IMF become an international financial regulator. Jeffrey Garten (1998) proposes a single world currency and central bank. Kenneth Rogoff (1999) advocates equity financing. Stanley Fischer (1999) advocates transparent international credit standards. Two points are clear. International competition makes banking systems more efficient. Balanced government budgets would eliminate a good deal of instability.

Section A Problems

A1. Draw the foreign credit market for credit leading to the foreign excess supply in Figure 12.2.

A2. Find the investment income due on the international loans in Figure 12.2. Explain which country makes the payment.

A3. Find NII given a 5% interest rate at home and a 6% interest rate abroad with a home owned investment stock abroad of $1470 billion and a foreign owned stock at home of $1346 billion. Explain whether there is a surplus or deficit for NII.

A4. If there is a 5% increase in the home owned stock abroad in the previous problem while the foreign owned capital stock at home increases 39%, find the KA and the NII.

EXAMPLE 12.5   *LDC Defaults*

During the 1970s OPEC oil embargoes created high oil profit and surplus of credit. These funds filtered through international banks as loans to LDCs. Many were loans to LDC governments with the incorrect perception of no chance of default. Nominal interest rates were high due to high inflation. In the late 1970s and early 1980s many LDCs suffered in a worldwide recession precipitated by high oil prices. Loan funds were wasted. Paying back the loans was impossible for the LDCs. Many defaulted. Rudiger Dornbusch and Franco Modigliani proposed the debt be paid in currency that would have to be spent locally. Some of the debt was forgiven as taxpayers in the DCs covered the losses. A more efficient option is to let inefficient banks go bankrupt. Their stockholders suffer the loss. Other more prudent banks quickly take their place.

B.   FX RATES AND INTERNATIONAL FINANCE

International financial transactions involve currency exchange in the foreign exchange market. Exchange rates affect and are affected by international financial transactions. First, exchange rates change prices of foreign financial assets. Second, expected or future exchange rates determine returns to foreign assets. When investors buy or sell foreign stocks and bonds, exchange rates are affected. This section examines these links between exchange rates and international financial markets.

International Portfolios

The large numbers of international financial transactions are carried out electronically between large international banks and financial intermediaries. Traders adjust portfolios internationally to spread risk and to avoid overexposure to a particular currency.

International financial transactions occur due to trade, exchange rate hedging, foreign direct investment spending, and international portfolio diversification. Banks and other financial intermediaries arbitrage across credit and exchange markets, looking for profitable transactions across foreign currencies and international interest rates.

Exchange rates affect stock prices, bond markets, and other financial assets. International financial transactions, in turn, affect exchange rates.

Suppose the nominal interest rate is 20% in a country with peso currency. The price of a perpetuity bond paying 100,000 pesos per year indefinitely would be $100,000/.20 = 500,000$ pesos since 500,000 pesos earns 100,000 pesos interest every year. Suppose the current spot exchange rate is $e = \$/pesos = 0.002$ and both the dollar and peso have the same inflation rate. The dollar price of this perpetuity bond would be $0.002 \times 500,000 = \$1000$. An unexpected peso devaluation to $e = 0.0015$ would decrease the dollar price of the bond to $0.0015 \times 500,000 = \$750$. Whether the peso bond has suddenly become a bargain depends on the expected future peso depreciation.

EXAMPLE 12.6   *The FX Rate and Foreign Investment*

An appreciating dollar means assets in the US become more expensive for foreign investors. Kenneth Froot and Jeremy Stein (1988) find that a 10% dollar appreciation lowers FDI by a few percent. Over half of direct investment DI in to the US goes to mergers and acquisitions with no impact on the management of the US firms. Interest rate differentials and expected depreciation affect portfolio investment while the level of the FX rate has no effect.

Depreciation Discounting

An issue on an international investor's mind is expected deprecation. What will a 100,000 peso premium of a perpetuity bond be worth next year? If investors expect the peso inflation rate to remain at its historical average of 20% and the dollar at 4%, the peso is expected to lose 16% every year relative to the dollar. If the exchange rate is $e = 0.002$, the 100,000 peso bond premium is worth $200. One year from now the 100,000 peso premium is expected to be worth 84% as much, $168. Two years from now, the 100,000 pesos is expected to be worth $125. The dollar value of the bond must be discounted 16% every year. The present value of the peso bond is 100,000/(0.20 + 0.16) = 277,778 pesos. At the exchange rate $/pesos = 0.002 the peso bond would sell for $556. If the peso and the dollar had the same expected inflation, the peso bond would sell for $1000. The difference of $444 is the depreciation discount. Default risk may also be an issue with the peso bond. Suppose peso bonds have a history of defaulting 12% of the time and dollar bonds an average of 4% of the time. An additional 8% risk discount would be placed on the peso bond. The present value of the peso bond would be 100,000/0.44 = 227,273 pesos or $454.

International bond prices are discounted by expected depreciation and default risk.

EXAMPLE 12.7   *Country Risk*

Country risk ratings summarize the history and perception of whether loans will be repaid. Borrowers in countries with high risk ratings have to pay a high borrowing rate. LDCs generally have the highest risk ranking and pay the highest interest rates. Investors can earn more but face higher default risk. A few of the top and bottom countries in a recent ranking are below. Tunisia has the median ranking of 50 and Jordan the mode of 38.

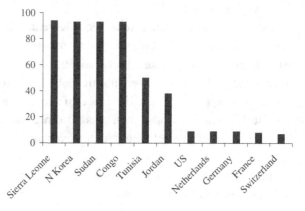

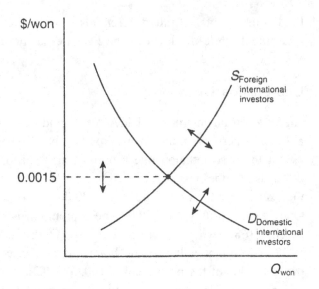

Figure 12.3
International Finance and the FX Market
Demand for won slopes downward partly because a lower $/won implies cheaper Korean assets in the US. The quantity of won demanded to buy Korean assets increases. Supply of won slopes upward partly because a higher $/won exchange rate implies cheaper US assets in Korea. Changes in investment opportunities shift FX supply and demand.

International Investment Influence on the FX Market

The effects of international financial markets on the FX market is illustrated in the market for Korean won in Figure 12.3. Demand for won is based in part on domestic investors who are potential buyers of Korean financial assets. The demand for won slopes downward. As $/won rises, the price of Korean assets in the US rises, the quantity demanded in the US falls, and the quantity of won demanded falls.

The supply of won comes from Korean investors as buyers of US assets. As $/won rises, the price of US assets in Korea falls, the quantity of US assets demanded in Korea rises, and the quantity of won supplied rises. The supply of won slopes upward.

Suppose the expected return on Korean investments rises because of an announced policy of increased privatization in Korea. Investors in the US will want to buy more Korean stocks and bonds because Korean firms are expected to prosper under the new economic policy. The demand for won rises, causing the won to appreciate and the price of Korean assets to rise further.

The FX market works in the same direction as the underlying asset market. Government policy interfering with the exchange market hinders this complementary effect.

International investors try to anticipate government intervention. Erratic behavior in international financial markets has been cited as evidence of the need for more government regulation. The erratic behavior, however, typically results from market participants trying to anticipate government intervention.

A saying in FX circles is to watch what the central bank is doing, and do the opposite. With central banks intervening, market participants turn their attention away from market fundamentals. FX traders, hedgers, and speculators should operate in a market free of central bank interventions and control.

No scheme of managed exchange rates or regulated financial markets could have handled the financial upheavals since the 1970s. Innovations occur with increased competition that forces banks and financial intermediaries to become more efficient. Banks favor regulation and enjoy the lack of competition in a government regulated franchise monopolies, but competition in banking and financial markets should be the rule.

EXAMPLE 12.8   *News and the FX Market*

FX traders keep up with the news on trade deficits, investment flows, inflation rates, economic trends, and policy. Graig Hakkio and Douglas Pearce (1985) examine empirical links between the FX rate and economic news. They find only one type of news has immediate and consistent impacts, news about money supply growth. Exchange rates adjust to money supply news after about 20 minutes. If the US money supply increases unexpectedly, traders expect the dollar to depreciate and begin selling dollars right away. Prior to money supply announcements, there is decreased exchange rate movement as traders wait for the news.

Covered Interest Arbitrage

Asset markets are linked internationally with FX markets through international banks and financial intermediaries. Suppose an investor with $100 in the US can earn the domestic interest rate of $i = 3\%$. At the end of the year the investor has $103. The Malaysian interest rate is $i = 6\%$ and the current spot rate is $e = \$/R = 0.26$ where R is the ringgit. The $100 can be exchanged into $100/0.26 = R385$ that will yield $385 \times 1.06 = R408$ at the end of the year.

The investor can take the position and leave it open but may want to turn the ringgits back into dollars at the end of the year. With an open position the investor waits until the end of the year to sell the 408 ringgits on the spot exchange market. There is risk of ringgit depreciation during the year.

This foreign exchange risk can be eliminated by the forward exchange market. A forward contract to sell 408 ringgits at the end of the year can be made in the forward exchange market. The forward exchange rate is for transactions at a date in the future for a rate set now.

The forward rate f will invariably be close to $f = \$/R = \$103$. The reason is that 408 ringgits will convert back to $103 at that forward rate. If returns were not equal, traders could make risk free arbitrage profit. Covered interest arbitrage transactions continuously link international asset and exchange markets.

The FX market is very quick and much larger than the more publicized stock markets. Stock trading involves only an exchange of claims to future profit. FX trading supports the entire system of international trade and investment.

Unexpected exchange rate movements can result in large profit or loss international investors. Some large banks have gone bankrupt due to their FX operations.

Covered interest arbitrage is the relationship

$$(1 + i) = (1/e)(1 + i^{*})f$$

An investor with $1 can earn $(1 + i)$ buying a home bond. The alternative is to convert the $1 to foreign currency (divide by e), buy a foreign bond with return $1 + i^{*}$, and cover the earnings back into dollars (multiply by f).

If one side of covered arbitrage is larger than the other, there are four markets that simultaneously restore equilibrium. Profit makers push the four markets as shown in Figure 12.4 the example of ringgit-dollar arbitrage.

Suppose the Fed increases the supply of credit by selling bonds. The interest rate i falls in the upper left domestic credit market. Investors notice the higher return on covered foreign bonds. The first step to buy a foreign bond is to buy the foreign currency. The demand for ringgits rises, pushing e higher in the lower left quadrant. The supply of credit in Malaysia rises, pushing the interest rate i^{*} down in the upper right quadrant. Investors cover their earnings back into dollars. Ringgits are sold forward, increasing the forward supply and lowering f. All of these changes (higher e, lower i^{*}, and lower f) lower the right side of the arbitrage equation.

Covered interest arbitrage works through spot exchange markets, international credit markets, and forward exchange markets.

EXAMPLE 12.9   *Differences in Inflation and Interest Rate*

Recent Inflation and interest rate differences compared to the US show that a larger inflation rate difference implies a larger nominal interest rate difference. Currencies inflating rapidy depreciate and sell at a discount in the forward FX market. Interest arbitrage ensures the link between exchange and interest rates.

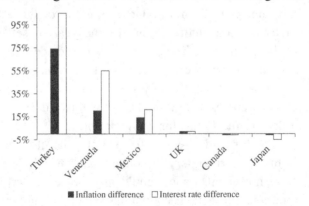

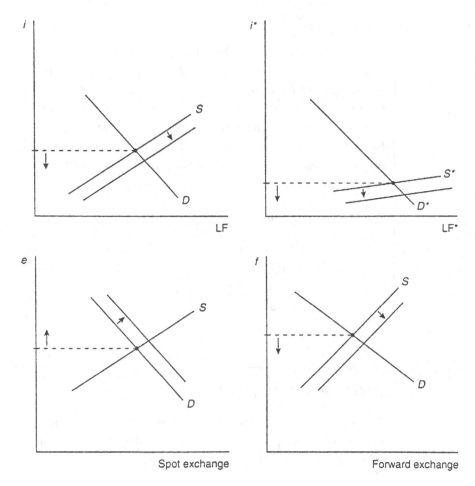

Figure 12.4
Interest Rate and Exchange Rate Markets
Covered interest arbitrage equates the return to riskless international investments in
the equilibrium $1 + i = (f/e) (1 + i^*)$. If i falls with a credit expansion, the demand
for spot exchange rises, the supply of foreign loanable funds rises, and the supply of
forward exchange falls. Market adjustments maintain the arbitrage condition.

Section B Problems

B1. With the example of the perpetuity bond paying 100,000 pesos per year,
suppose the dollar is expected to have inflation of 2%. Find the dollar value of
the peso bond. Do the same if expected inflation is 6%.
B2. Diagram and explain what happens in the FX market in Figure 12.3 when
the domestic interest rate falls, the foreign interest rate rises, faster growth is
expected in the US economy, and political unrest breaks out in Korea.
B3. In the example of CIA find the profitable position if the forward exchange
rate is $/ringgit = 0.26. Do the same if the forward rate is 0.24.

EXAMPLE 12.10 *IRP not Quite*

Interest rate parity holds because investors watch interest rates. These recent effective real interest rates subtract the rate of depreciation from the rate of interest. A bond paying over 100% in Turkey may sound like a deal but inflation eats the return. Before the fact, investors know interest rates but not depreciation. Investments are made on the basis of expectations about future exchange rates. The highest and lowest three countries are compared to the US. High variation in the effective interest rate implies international investment has high risk but high return.

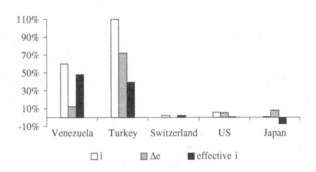

C.   INTERNATIONAL MONEY

This section examines the link between money supplies and price levels. Inflation occurs when the price level rises faster than output and the purchasing power of money falls.

What is Money?

The functions of money are

- medium of exchange
- store of value
- unit of account

Money as a medium of exchange makes commerce possible. Barter is direct trade of one product for another. Primitive societies use barter as households trade hides for corn, meat for labor, and so on. Money allows people to specialize and trade. Some barter continues to take place to avoid taxation or financial constraints. International commerce requires an international medium of exchange, the foreign exchange market.

Money as a store of value allows delayed spending. Some money must be stored. An inflating currency is a poor store of value. With hyperinflation money is spent quickly before it loses value.

Money is a unit of account. If a car is worth $20,000, a shirt $25, and a night on the town $50, the car is worth 800 shirts or 400 nights out. Relative prices are fundamental but people become accustomed to valuing products in their currency.

Only certain commodities can perform all of the functions of money. Gold might be a decent store of value and unit of account but is too heavy for a medium of exchange. Ice cream could be a medium of exchange but would not store value. Paper clips could be money if their supply could be limited.

The money supply is controlled by government central banks. Government monetary policy directly controls the monetary base. The banking system is made up of commercial banks that accept deposits and make loans. This financial intermediation expands the monetary base to the money supply. The link between the money supply and the price level determines how well money performs.

Money and the Price Level

The demand for money depends on the goods and services it can purchase. The price level P is the average price of all products, P = \$/good. Its inverse $1/P$ = goods/\$ is the purchasing power of money.

As P rises the purchasing power of money falls. Less products can be bought with each dollar. Money that loses purchasing power with inflation is a poor store of value. When P rises people hold more stocks, bonds, gold, jewelry, real estate, or foreign currency.

The money market in Figure 12.5 has the price of money $1/P$ on the vertical axis. The demand for money slopes downward due to increased purchasing power. The supply of money is the vertical line at \$1 trillion.

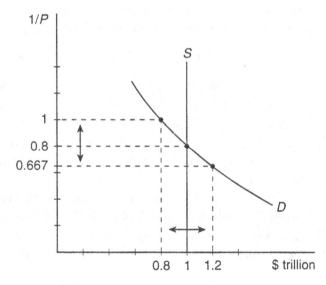

Figure 12.5
The Money Market
The demand for money slopes downward because a higher price level P implies a lower price of money $1/P$ and a higher quantity of money demanded for the same transactions. The equilibrium price level is $1/1.25 = 0.8$. If the money supply increases to 1.2 the price of money drops to $1/1.50 = 0.667$. If the money supply falls to \$0.8 billion, the price of money rises to 1.

A money supply of $1 trillion and price level of 1.25 are roughly the US 1990 levels of M1 and consumer price index (1982 = 1). M1 is cash and demand deposits that can be withdrawn by check. The price index of 1.25 indicates prices were 25% higher in 1990 than in 1982. Where supply and demand meet, the price of money is $1/P = 1/1.25 = 0.80$ and the price level $P = 1.25$. Increasing the money supply to $1.2 trillion would lower the price of money to $1/1.5 = 0.67$ and raise P to 1.50. Lowering the money supply to $0.8 trillion would raise the price of money to 1 and lower the price level to 1.

Let M_s be the money supply and V its velocity, the average number of times each dollar changes hands per year. The product MV is the value of all transactions in the economy. The price level is P and Q the quantity of output. The product PQ is the value of output or GDP.

The quantity equation is $M_s V = PQ$.

If M_s increases by 20% to $1.2 trillion in Figure 12.5 and both V and Q are constant then P increases by 20% to 1.5. Velocity V is in fact generally constant. Real output is not affected by money growth as long as monetary policy is stable. If M_s falls by 20% and Q is unchanged P would then fall by 20%.

Currencies with rapidly increasing supply have higher inflation.

Some of the demand for a currency is foreign. Suppose investors expect the dollar to appreciate relative to the other currencies. The demand for dollars increases. Increased demand drives up the price of the dollar. The price level P falls. In the FX market, the demand for dollars rises and the dollar appreciates.

A currency with relatively low inflation will appreciate in the FX market.

The US dollar plays an important role on the international scene with about a quarter of international transactions carried out in dollars. Governments and banks over the world keep reserves of dollars. Many countries peg their currencies to the dollar. If the dollar inflates with oversupply, global inflation is a result. The same can be said about the other two major international currencies, the euro and the yen.

The dollar has a record of moderate but steady inflation. Goods that now cost $100 would have cost $79 in 2000 and $18 in 1970. Inflation erodes the purchasing power of the dollar but, most other currencies have higher inflation. The yen and euro have had lower inflation than the dollar during recent decades.

EXAMPLE 12.11   *Money Growth and Inflation*

Inflation is fueled by money supply growth. For the average price of all products to rise, the money supply must expand. These figures illustrate the link between money supply growth and inflation across countries in 1998.

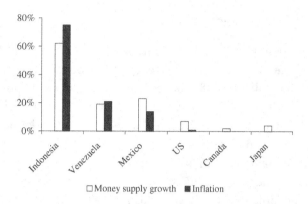

Fiat Currencies versus Monetary Standards

Governments control their money supplies, affecting the FX market. The international monetary system is an extension of national monetary systems.

Fiat currency is paper money that has to be accepted by law as a medium of exchange. Government central banks print money. Fiat currency is not backed by gold, silver, or any other commodity. The US government stopped redeeming dollars for gold in 1933 and stopped defining the dollar in terms of gold in 1971. Instead, the dollar carries "This note is legal tender for all debts, public and private" as its own endorsement.

Under the gold standard of the 1800s governments exchanged gold for paper money, or vice versa. Currency notes were equivalent to a defined amount of gold. The US experimented with a bimetal standard for a period during the late 1890s with the dollar defined in both gold and silver. The Bretton Woods fixed exchange rate system lasted from the end of World War II until the early 1970s attempting to fix exchange rates at familiar levels.

The international floating exchange rate system at present is the result of flat currencies. Currencies seek their market exchange rates. Most minor currencies are fixed and tightly managed by government central banks. Central banks routinely intervene in FX markets attempting to influence rates.

EXAMPLE 12.12   *The Great Contraction*

The Great Depression resulted from poor government monetary policy. There was a decline in the US money supply and extremely high tariffs. Bennet McCallum (1989) builds a model of the US economy and tests what would have happened with steady growth in the money supply. Linking money supply growth to output, the US economy would have grown steadily. A fixed money supply growth rule would take away discretion of the Fed to control the money supply. The result would be less inflation and smoother output growth.

Money Standards

The gold standard lasted from the late 1800s until World War I with the English pound as the major currency. The pound was worth 0.234 ounces of gold and the dollar 0.048 ounces, freezing the dollar/pound exchange rate at $0.234/0.048 = 4.87 = \$/£$. Other currencies had their own gold equivalents. All currencies were accepted all over the world because they were redeemable into gold. The lack of foreign exchange risk in international commerce created favorable conditions for international commerce and economic growth.

Under the gold standard, growth in the money supply is limited by the government supply of gold. Immigration and output growth in the US outpaced growth of the money supply, causing deflation. The demand for money grew faster than supply causing the price of money $1/P$ to rise. There was pressure to expand the money supply but gold was scarce.

The solution was a bimetal standard, defining the dollar in terms of silver as well as gold. If the official price of silver was too high, traders could buy cheap silver in the market to trade with the government for gold. Bad money chased out good money. Gold was hoarded.

The principle that only bad money circulates is Gresham's law, named after a British banker in the 1500s. Coins then actually contained the metals worth their stamped value. The crafty banker shaved coins and hoarded the shavings. Anyone who found an unshaved coin (good money) would store it or shave it. Only shaved coins (bad money) circulated.

EXAMPLE 12.13 *Causes of the Great Depression*

The Great Depression lasted for about ten years following the stock market crash of 1929. International trade virtually halted with Hawley-Smoot tariffs and restrictive tariffs worldwide. The loss of imported intermediate and capital goods stopped economic growth. Reduced trade lowered income and slowed recovery. Harold Cole and Lee Ohanian (1999) point out that the National Industrial Recovery Act (NIRA) of 1933 encouraged cartels that restricted output and raised prices, contributing to the depression. NIRA was designed to stimulate the economy but had a negative effect.

Collapse of the International Gold Standard

World War I largely stopped international commerce and disrupted the international monetary system. Following the war, countries tried to return to the gold standard but governments increased money supplies to pay back the war expenses. Inflation raised prices in Europe.

Exchange rates from the gold standard era proved unworkable. The British pound was worth more at the government gold exchange window than in goods and services. The British gold supply dwindled as traders cashed in pounds for gold. The overvalued pound made British exports uncompetitive. The UK dropped the gold standard in 1931. The dollar remained redeemable in terms of gold and became the standard international currency. Investors wanted the stability provided by gold and traded dollars for gold. US government gold supplies dwindled and the government stopped redeeming dollars for gold in 1933.

Governments then devalued currencies repeatedly to make exports cheaper abroad. Inflation was high worldwide. German hyperinflation created the economic instability that allowed the Nazi party to take control. In misguided efforts to save jobs, high tariffs were imposed worldwide. The US passed the infamous Smoot-Hawley Tariff Act. International investment dwindled due to the high exchange risk. The Great Depression of the 1930s led to World War II.

EXAMPLE 12.14   *Safe Haven*

The US is a safe haven for international investors. The US has political stability with no imminent military threat and prospects for continued growth. Higher defense spending makes the US appear to be an even safer haven. Robert Ayanian (1988) and Vittrio Grilli and Andrea Beltratti (1989) show that defense spending raises the demand for US assets and dollars. Increased defense spending causes dollar appreciation.

The Bretton Woods System

The international monetary system collapsed during World War II. After the war all nations wanted a stable monetary system with no inflation. An international conference was held in Bretton Woods, New Hampshire to create such as system.

A gold exchange standard evolved. Currencies were defined in terms of gold but were not redeemable. The dollar was defined as 1/35 ounces of gold and became the international standard. The US held more than half the world's gold stock at the time. Other currencies were defined in terms of the dollar. The English pound was defined as $2.80, the Japanese yen $0.0028, and the German mark $0.24. The International Monetary Fund was created to as a bank for the central banks to help governments kept these exchange rates.

Bretton Woods fixed exchange rates operated under an adjustable peg system. A country with a trade deficit could borrow from the IMF to meet the cash shortage. If a country had a chronic trade deficit, the IMF would eventually allow it to depreciate.

During the 1950s international trade and investment grew at slow but steady rates. Money supplies grew at low rates and there was no inflation. Europe and Japan rebuilt. The US had *BOT* deficits, suggesting the dollar should depreciate. If the dollar lost value in terms of gold, anyone holding gold would enjoy a profit. In anticipation, the price of gold was bid well above the official price of $35 per ounce. The Bretton Woods system managed to hold together even through US inflation during the Vietnam War.

The dollar had not been redeemable for gold since 1933 but the US government continued to redeem foreign government dollars for gold. The US gold stock steadily declined as other governments, notably the French, accumulated gold stocks. As the US gold stock declined, the credibility of the Bretton Woods system suffered. In 1971 when President Nixon cut the dollar from its definition in terms of gold, the Bretton Woods fixed exchange rate system collapsed.

EXAMPLE 12.15   *Declining Purchasing Power*

The inverse of consumer price index CPI since 1952 shows the decline in the purchasing power of the dollar. There was slight deflation during the 1920s and 1930s but inflation during World War II and up to 1950. During the 1950s and 1960s there was low inflation. Starting in the late 1960s through the early 1980s inflation rates were high. During the 1980s and 1990s inflation declined. The Fed has the responsibility for controlling the money supply. Government budget deficits are the cause of the high growth rates in the money supply and the resulting inflation.

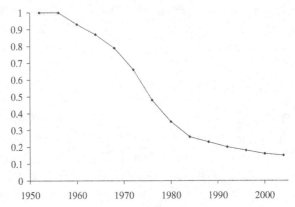

International Money and Floating Exchange Rates

International differences in inflation, and growing international commerce caused the Bretton Woods system to collapse. Fixed exchange rates failed, not for the first time. The price of gold was bid up by investors who saw it as a safe haven. By 1973 the world had adopted floating exchange rates. During the 1920s there was a period of floating exchange rates. Canada floated its dollar during the 1970s.

With floating exchange rates, each government determines its own money supply and inflation. It might be little surprise that both increased during the 1970s. International banks increased their FX operations. Foreign exchange brokers and traders set up shop. Speculators attempted to outguess the market and make FX profits. Hedging and speculating in foreign exchange increased. The FX market quickly grew into a lively worldwide business.

The floating exchange rate system is not entirely free. Governments intervene to influence their currencies, some imposing direct controls. The system is a managed float. The IMF is a bank for government central banks, making loans to governments short on cash. The IMF supplies its own money, the special drawing right SDR for transactions between central banks. The SDR is part of each nation's FX reserves and monetary base.

The floating exchange rate system has worked through oil embargoes, debt crises, surpluses, emerging economic powers, banking failures, government defaults, and rapidly increasing global commerce. Any fixed rate system would have collapsed.

> *Economic theory and history teach that governments should let markets operate. Floating exchange rates have proven capable of handling international commerce.*

EXAMPLE 12.16   *The FX Rate and Inflation*

Kenneth Kasa (1995) reports that 60% of the trend during the 1970s and 1980s in the $/mark rate was due to the inflation differential between the two currencies. The dollar depreciated 5% annually versus the mark as US inflation exceeded German inflation by 2%. For $/yen only 20% of the exchange rate trend was due to the inflation differential. The dollar depreciated an average of 5% per year versus the yen but inflation in the US exceeded Japan by only 1%. Japanese labor productivity growth was 2% higher than in the US.

Section C Problems

C1. Explain how well each of the following that have been used would perform each of the functions of money: beaver tails, tobacco, dried buffalo chips, beads, and large boulders.

C2. Can the supply of money come from private banks? Describe how a private money supply system, would operate. Diagram the supply curve. How would the international monetary system operate?

C3. Any commodity standard of money ties the value of money to a certain quantity of some commodity. Explain which of these commodities would function better as money standards: gold, oil, wheat, and a stock market price index.

D.   INTERNATIONAL MONEY AND FINANCE

Money supplies and monetary policy affect international finance. The foreign exchange market transmits international monetary signals reflecting underlying monetary policies.

Government Bonds and the Money Supply

Governments create national debt with deficits from spending more than tax revenue. Governments can raise cash for deficit spending by selling government bonds. A bond is a promise to pay the bondholder face value on maturity.

Government borrowing increases the demand for loanable funds and interest rates. The increased supply of bonds lowers bond prices. Higher interest rates (lower bond prices) attract foreign investors, at least disregarding the risks of default and inflation. Demand for the domestic currency rises, causing it to appreciate leading to a current account deficit.

The link between the government and trade deficits is called the twin deficit.

Governments can also finance deficit spending with increased money supply. Monetary expansion is carried out predominantly by open market operations. The government prints new bonds, selling them to acquire cash to pay its bills. The central bank buys the new bonds with newly printed money. If the supply of money grows faster than output, there is inflation.

Government deficits can be financed by bond sales or by expanding the money supply.

EXAMPLE 12.17 *Dollarization*

Imagine money from heaven with a stable value. Prices would be stable. Investment and economic growth would be encouraged. The government could not print inflate its way out of fiscal deficits. Governments would have to rely on taxes and bond sales for spending. Panama adopted exactly such money, the US dollar. William Gruben and Sherry Kiser (1999) discuss how dollarization would allow Latin American countries to avoid their periodic currency collapses due to irresponsible fiscal and monetary policies.

International Money Supplies and Price Levels

During the 1700s David Hume wrote about the relationship between money, prices, and trade in the price-specie flow mechanism. When the money supply in increases, its price level increases. Higher prices cause the country to export less as its products become more expensive. Imports increase because they become relatively cheaper. The trade deficit creates an outflow of cash. As a result, prices fall pushing the process toward balanced trade. Through the influence of prices, specie (currency) flows internationally to balance trade.

The link between the money supply and inflation is illustrated in the classical quantity equation,

$$MV = PQ$$

Suppose the money supply M is \$1 trillion and GDP or Q is \$4 trillion. On average, each dollar changes hands four times during the year. The \$1 trillion of money supports \$4 trillion of transactions. Money velocity V equals 4.

If the government increases M while output Q and velocity V remain constant, P must rise. If M rises to \$1.1 trillion P will be 1.1. The 10% increase in M causes an increase of 10% in P.

There is overwhelming evidence of a positive relationship between the money supply and inflation over time within each country, and across countries.

Purchasing Power Parity and the Real Exchange Rate

Trade links money supplies, prices and exchange rates. Most products can be traded. Even haircuts in Iowa include clippers from Germany, vacuum cleaners from Japan, workers from Mexico, and so on.

Purchasing power parity PPP would hold if all goods and services were freely traded,

$$P = eP^*$$

P is the home price level, P^* the foreign price level, and e the exchange rate. Arbitrage implies equal product prices since any price difference generates trade that eliminates it. PPP is based on the law of one price that arbitrage equalizes prices of goods across locations.

There is empirical evidence supporting PPP. Transport costs, protection, and nontraded goods weaken PPP but it tends to hold. In a weaker form, relative PPP says that percentage changes in P is matched by percentage changes in e and P^*.

Suppose $P = 1.25$ euro and $P^* = 125$ yen. The real exchange rate comes from the PPP relation

$$e_R = P/P^*$$

The real exchange rate is €/¥ = e_R = 1.25/125 = 0.01. The real exchange rate anticipates long term changes in exchange rates. If the market exchange rate is €/¥ = 0.012 the yen and Japanese products are overvalued. Japan would run a current account deficit, depreciating the yen. Predicting the timing of such depreciation is difficult.

Deviations from PPP diminish over time. Kenneth Froot and Kenneth Rogoff (1995) show half of the deviation from PPP erodes after 4 years.

EXAMPLE 12.18 *Big Mac PPP*

Big Mac prices provide insight into purchasing power across currencies. *The Economist* tracks prices of Big Macs that anticipate exchange rate adjustment. Big Macs are produced locally with standardized products including a wide range of labor and capital as well as local intermediate products. Figures below show the Big Mac price in each country relative to the US price of $2 long with the FX rate e. The dollar was undervalued against the won, yen, and pound, but overvalued against the Canadian and Singapore dollars. Currencies tend to move as predicted by the last column although the timing is difficult to predict.

Country	Big Mac P^*	P/P^*	e	% Difference
South Korea	2400 won	1188	666	−44%
Japan	370 yen	183	133	−27%
Britain	1.26 pounds	0.62	0.59	−5%
Canada	2.15 C$	1.06	1.19	13%
Singapore	2.80 S$	1.39	1.96	41%

EXAMPLE 12.19 *1930s PPP*

In 1931 the UK gave up the gold standard. Speculation turned against the pound and it depreciated 30% versus the dollar. The relative price of US goods rose 10% as described by S.N. Broadway (1987). Two years later PPP was 40% out of line. The US then dropped the gold standard, the dollar depreciated, and P/P^* fell. PPP returned by 1934.

EXAMPLE 12.20 *C$ and Prices*

The Canadian dollar declined 25% relative to the US dollar during the 1990s. According to PPP prices of products in Canada were too low at the end of the decade. Charles Engel (1999) discusses why prices in Canada stayed out of line. Firms price to market temporarily absorbing exchange rate changes. If demand in Canada is lower or more elastic, firms will price discriminate and charge lower prices. Investors might have expected the Canadian dollar to depreciate keeping Canadian asset prices low.

Relative Money Supply and the Real Exchange Rate

The relationship between the relative money supply M/M^* and the real exchange rate P/P^* is shown in Figure 12.6. If $M^* = 76$ billion Swiss francs and $M = \$1000$ billion, $M/M^* = 13.2$ and $P/P^* = 1.12/1.07 = 1.05$. These are the 1989 money supplies and consumer price indices (1985 = 1) for Switzerland and the US. If M increases by 10% to $\$1.1$ trillion with outputs and M^* constant, M/M^* rises to $1100/76 = 14.5$, P rises by 10% to 1.232, and the real exchange e_R rises to 1.15.

Countries with higher money supply growth have higher inflation and depreciation.

The positive relationship in Figure 12.6 is well established over long time periods. Countries with high inflation rates and depreciating exchange rates in recent history include Mexico, Brazil, Israel, and Greece on the drachma. Countries with the lowest rates of inflation and appreciating exchange rates include Germany, Switzerland, and Japan.

Inflation helps debtors paying off fixed term loans but hurls creditors. If lenders and borrowers anticipate inflation, its has no real effect. Economic variables can

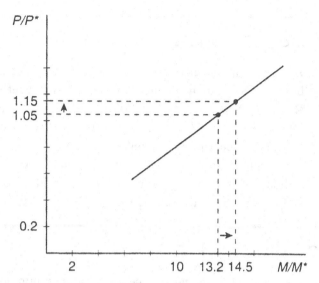

Figure 12.6
Relative Money Supplies and the Real FX Rate
PPP implies the relative price level P/P^* is the real exchange rate e_R. Increasing M relative to M^* causes a higher e_R and depreciation of the home currency.

be reduced to real terms and people think in real terms. Businesses in countries with high inflation quote prices in stable currencies, even for local domestic customers.

If inflation is predictable, it has little impact on international trade and investment.

Inflating currencies ultimately depreciate. Inflation values currencies against products while exchange rates value currencies against each other.

Exchange rates ultimately follow real exchange rates. Inflating currencies depreciate.

Control of the Money Supply

Countries choose their money supply growth rates and price levels. Money supply growth is the result of economic processes including central bank control of the money base, commercial lending, and aggregate spending. The primary job of the central bank is to control the money supply.

Control of the money supply is a central issue of economic policy. A competitive banking system with efficient financial intermediation is essential for a successful economy. The link between government deficits and money supply growth suggests that governments wanting to control inflation should first control their budgets. When a government spends more that it collects in taxes, the temptation is to create new money to pay for the spending.

Section D Problems

D1. Explain the difference between the Chinese government or a US citizen buying US bonds to finance a government budget deficit.

D2. If $P = \$1.25$ and $P^* = 200$ pesos, find the real exchange rate in terms of $/peso. If the market rate is e = 150, explain which currency is overvalued. Explain which currency should appreciate.

D3. Suppose in Figure 12.7 the foreign money supply M^* increases to 79.8 billion Swiss francs with M remaining at $1 trillion. Find the relative money supply and the real exchange rate.

CONCLUSION

International trade and finance are becoming more integrated, involving firms and consumers from more countries. Domestic industries are involved in producing for export. Imports enter domestic production and consumption.

International finance is crucial for economic production. Countries are becoming increasingly interdependent. The gains from international finance are sizeable.

The basic lesson of international economics is to reap the benefits of open international trade and finance. Free international financial markets are a step toward healthy international economic activity.

Terms

Adjustable peg	Hyperinflation
Bimetal standard	Open market operations
Covered interest arbitrage	Price-specie flow mechanism
Fiat currency	Purchasing power parity (PPP)
Forward exchange rate	Real exchange rate
Gold exchange standard	Real interest rate
Gold standard	Special drawing rights (SDR)
Gresham's law	

MAIN POINTS

- Credit markets match lenders and borrowers, determining interest rates and the quantity of loans. International credit markets determine international interest rates borders.
- Exchange rates and international interest rates are linked through triangular arbitrage and covered interest arbitrage.

- Money supply relative to output determines the price level. Changes in the money supply and output determine the inflation rate. Relative money supplies ultimately influence exchange rates.
- Price levels are linked across trading partners through purchasing power parity.

REVIEW PROBLEMS

1. Explain which group in an economy, would favor restricting foreign investment, borrowers or lenders.
2. Show what happens in Figure 12.2 if households in the home country start saving more because of tax reductions. Explain the international adjustment.
3. Suppose the home country decides to restrict the inflow of foreign capital in Figure 12.2 to $2 billion. Show what happens to interest rates.
4. Explain the difference when foreign investors in Figure 12.2 buy private versus government bonds.
5. The Mexican government historically limited foreign ownership of firms in Mexico to 49%. This restriction was lifted inside NAFTA. Predict the long term effects on the peso/$ exchange rate.
6. In the example of international inflation and arbitrage, suppose US credit contracts. Explain adjustments in the other markets.
7. Suppose the supply of loans in the foreign country decreases in the international financial market of Figure 12.4. Explain the effects on the credit market and FX market.
8. Suppose Kia builds a new $10 billion automobile plant in the US raising 50% of the funds through the issue and sale of new stock in US. Explain how the new plant affects the US capital account and exchange rate. Explain how the US balance of trade is ultimately affected.
9. Starting with the money market in Figure 12.5, show and explain what happens if foreign investors expect the dollar to depreciate.
10. Discuss the following quote:

    News that the US trade deficit fell in November pushed dollar down against the euro. The dollar later recovered in a technical correction of the euro which was overbought in the euphoria over events in Eastern Europe.

11. Suppose the dollar is put on a bimetal standard. The government defines the dollar as 0.0025 ounces of gold and 0.185 ounces of silver and stands ready to trade paper dollars for either gold or silver. In the market, the price of gold is $393.75 and the price of silver is $5.25/oz. Explain what arbitragers will do. What will happen to government stocks of gold and silver? Explain which is the bad money.
12. Describe the link between the government surplus and the trade surplus.
13. Explain three reasons PPP might not hold.
14. Explain whether a country with a relatively young population more or less likely to have unexpected inflation. What about a country with a relatively wealthy population?

READINGS

Gary Smith, *Money, Banking, and Financial Intermediation* (1991) Lexington. Introduction to monetary economics.

Symposia: New institutions for developing country debt (1990) *Journal of Economic Perspectives*. Proposals for dealing with LDC debt.

Ron Jones and Peter Kenen, eds. (1985) *Handbook of International Economics*, vol II, Amsterdam: North-Holland. Surveys of international monetary economics.

Central Bank Watch, the American Banker Newsletter Division. Periodical to keep international bankers abreast of central banks.

International Trade Finance Report, Morgan Williams Group, online articles and information on international finance.

Ronald McKinnon (1993) The rules of the game: International money in historical perspective, *The Journal of Economic Literature*. A look at the game played by central banks.

CHAPTER 13

Open Economy Macroeconomics

Preview

This chapter introduces open economy macroeconomics covering:
- Microeconomic foundations
- The closed microeconomic model
- The open economy macro model
- Macro policy, inflation, and the exchange rate

INTRODUCTION

Macroeconomics paints the big picture of an economy and its interaction with the rest of the world. The major macroeconomic variables are national income, unemployment, inflation, the interest rate, balance of payments, and the exchange rate. Macroeconomics focuses on how government spending, taxes, and money supply influence these variables. In an open economy the government also has international investment and exchange rate policies. Government policies influence what is produced, how it is produced, and how income is distributed.

The fundamental model of the open economy is based on an aggregate production function and optimal decision making by households and firms. Saving and foreign investment feed the capital stock. Output goes into consumption, investment, government spending, and net trade. The balance of trade and international capital are critical for a successful open economy.

A. MICRO FOUNDATIONS

The foundation of macroeconomics is neoclassical production, overlapping generations (OLG) savings, and optimal investment.

Neoclassical production links the capital stock and labor force to production. Saving in the OLG model is an optimal lifetime process. Optimal investment by firms is based on their opportunities and expectations. These microeconomic models provide a foundation for the open economy macroeconomic model.

EXAMPLE 13.1   *US National Income Accounts*

The comparisons below scale components of spending in the US economy. Consumption spending C is about 60% for services and 40% for goods. About two thirds of investment spending I is by firms, the rest by households on housing. Government spending G not including transfer payments aimed at income redistribution is almost as large as I. Export revenue X and import spending M involve mostly goods although the share of services in X has grown to about one third.

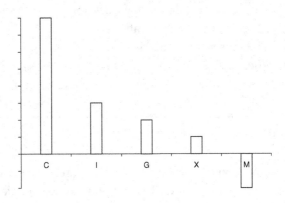

Aggregate Production

The economy produces aggregate output Y with inputs capital K and labor L in the neoclassical production function

$$Y = A\,f(K,\,L)$$

where A represents technology. Increased inputs of K or L raise Y but with diminishing marginal productivity. Holding K constant, an additional worker raises Y but each contributes diminishing amounts. There is a positive cross productivity effect with more of one input raising productivity of the other.

Improved technology A raises output holding inputs constant although capital imbeds technology. Macroeconomics focuses on adjustments in the economy over a few quarters or a year, making it safe to assume constant technology.

The Cobb-Douglas production function scaled to the US economy is

$$Y = A\,K^3 L^7$$

where r is the return to capital and w the wage. Inputs are paid marginal products in competitive input markets, $r = MP_K$ and $w = MP_L$.

Figure 13.1 shows the per capita production function

$$y = A\,k^3$$

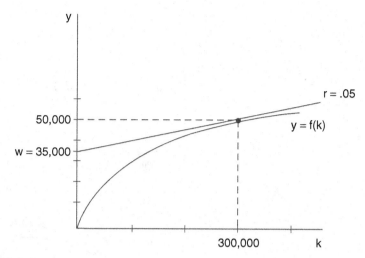

Figure 13.1
The Macro Production Function
This production function is scaled to $k = \$300,000$, $y = \$50,000$, and $w = \$35,000$.
Income per capita y is an increasing function of the capital labor ratio k. The per capita
production function is concave due to diminishing marginal returns.

where y is income per capita Y/L and k is the capital/labor ratio K/L. In the
example, $Y = \$10$ trillion, $L = 200$ million, and $y = \$50,000$. The labor share
of national income is $wL/Y = 70\% = 0.7$ and $w = \$35,000$.

If the return to capital is $r = 5\% = .05$ the capital share of income is rK/Y
$= 30\% = .30$. Assuming a $\$1$ unit of capital input $K = \$60$ trillion and $k =$
$\$300,000$. The scaled production function in Figure 13.1 is $y = 1137\, k^{.3}$.

Labor and capital generate national income as the sum of payments to the
factors of production, $Y = wL + rK$. Dividing by L, per capita income is the
wage plus capital income per capita

$$y = w + rk.$$

The slope of the tangent to the production function in Figure 13.1 is the capital
return $r = .05$ and the intercept of its tangent with the y axis is the wage w.
Higher k implies y and w rise while r falls. An increasing capital labor ratio k
raises per capita income y.

*Income per capita y is an increasing concave function of the capital/labor
ratio k.*

EXAMPLE 13.2   *Production Function Plots*

Output per capita y is typically an increasing concave function of the capital
labor ratio k as the plots below illustrate. The first is the US economy from
1950 to 1990 in thousands, the second a plot of countries in 1990.

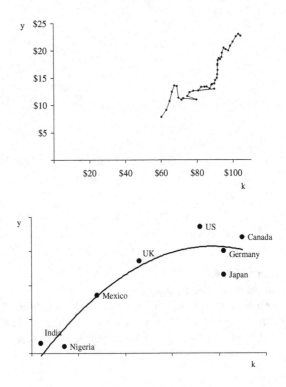

EXAMPLE **13.3**   *History of Economic Growth*

This long term growth in per capita income *y* in thousands of dollars is from Maddison (1991). The UK was the early leader. The US and Canada CN lead but Japan JP and Germany GE closed the gap after World War II. The LDCs in the second graph have lower *y*. Korea KO has been accelerating while India IN and China CN have progressed very little. Colombia CL has grown slowly but steadily. Argentina AR was high in 1870 but grew slowly and fell back with socialism.

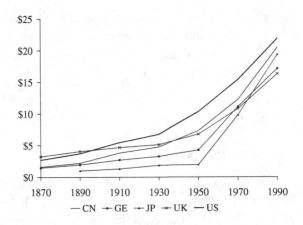

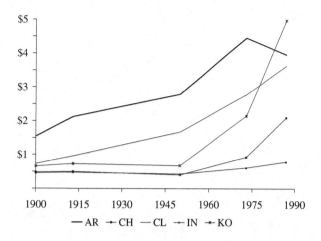

Savings and the OLG Model

The decision to save depends on the interest rate and preferences about consuming now or later. Young workers save some income to retire. Social security schemes that tax workers to pay retirees directly erode saving.

In the overlapping generations OLG model, households live off savings plus interest earnings when they retire. Workers retire, retirees die, the next generation begins work. There are always two generations, young workers and retired capital owners. The capital stock is purchased by young workers from the old retirees.

Figure 13.2 illustrates the optimal saving decision. Labor income is the wage w along the horizontal axis. Workers can transfer labor income to retirement, earning interest rate r. The maximum potential retirement income is $(1 + r)w$. In the example $w = \$35,000$ and $r = 5\%$ making potential retirement income $\$36,750$.

The line connecting w with $(1 + r)w$ is the intergenerational budget constraint. The household can select any point along the line according to its time preferences. In the example $\sigma = 0.2$ and saving is $0.2 \times \$35,000 = \$7,000$. Consumption in youth is $\$28,000$. Saving earns 5% interest making retirement consumption $\$7,350$.

Social security supplements retirement income by taxing young workers, an inefficient scheme that lowers the intergenerational budget line making both workers and retirees worse off. Social security taxes reduce income in youth, lower total saving, and put households on a lower budget line. The transfer earns no interest, leaving youth and retirees worse off.

A higher interest rate r would encourage saving by raising the opportunity cost of consuming during youth. The increased saving S means a higher saving rate σ.

Intertemporal preferences differ. Households that are frugal and plan ahead have preferences biased more toward the future, save a larger share of income,

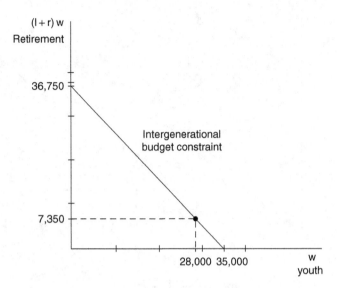

Figure 13.2
Optimal saving in the OLG Model
Labor income w is saved and transferred to retirement at the interest rate r. With $r = .05$ wages of \$35,000 transfer to $1.05 \times \$35,000 = \$36,750$ potential retirement income. The optimizer consumes \$28,000 while working and $1.05 \times \$7,000 = \$7,350$ while retired.

and enjoy higher income in retirement. Countries with higher discount rates consume more out of income and save less.

EXAMPLE **13.4**   *Saving and Investment in the US*

Saving and investment relative to GDP S/Y and I/Y during the last half of the 20th century generally moved together and trended upward slightly after 1960. Negative real interest rates in the 1970s were due to high inflation. These trends suggest influences other than the interest rate influence investment and saving.

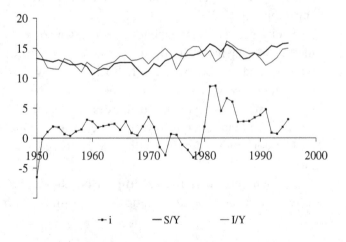

Section A Problems

A1. Find per capita income y and the wage w in Figure 13.1 if $k = \$200,000$ and $r = 6.6\%$. Explain the difference from the wage in the text example. Diagram the change in position on the production function.

A2. Find the capital labor ratio k for income per capita y to be $\$60,000$ in Figure 13.1. If $r = 3.3\%$ find the wage w. Diagram these two points on the production function.

A3. Suppose workers in the OLG model of Figure 13.2 save 30% of their income. Find their consumption with work and retirement. Diagram their optimal saving.

A4. Compare the indifference curve in the previous problem with one that leads to the optimal consumption in Figure 13.2. Explain the increased saving.

B.   CLOSED ECONOMY MACROECONOMICS

Two sides of the economy are production versus money. The interaction of the product market and money market determines national output, employment and the interest rate.

Aggregate Production

A closed economy has no international trade or investment. Output goes to domestic consumption, investment, and government spending. For a closed economy, output Y equals spending,

$$Y = C + I + G.$$

Consumption spending C is for current goods and services. Investment spending I by firms adds to the capital stock for future production. Government spending G provides public and other goods and services.

Lending and borrowing are critical to the macro economy. Some economic agents have less cash than they want to spend this year, while others have more. Lending and borrowing in the credit market allows households to save for retirement, firms to borrow for expanded production, and the government to spend beyond its ability to tax.

A bond is a promise to pay back a loan with interest. Assume bonds are risk free in the credit market. The simplest example is a perpetuity bond paying a perpetual income stream. The price of a perpetuity securing a $1 payment forever at an interest rate of $r_B = 5\% = .05$ is $p_B = 1/r_B = 1/.05 = \$20$. At the 5% interest rate $20 earns $1 interest payment per year forever. A lower interest rate implies a higher bond price with more money required to yield the same $1 income stream. If r_B falls to 4% then p_B rises to $25.

A firm considering an investment project will compare its projected rate of return to the interest rate. The opportunity cost of spending on an investment project is buying a bond. Firms short of cash can borrow at the interest rate and spend on projects with higher expected rates of return. At lower interest rates, more investment projects become attractive and investment spending increases.

Suppose every decrease of the interest rate r by .01 raises investment spending I by \$0.4 trillion. The investment function in Figure 13.3 with $r = .05$ and $I = 2 trillion is $I = 4 - 40r$.

Firms wanting cash for profitable investment projects can also sell stocks as equity promising the holder of the stock a share of future profit. Stock dividends depend on uncertain profits making stock returns riskier than fixed bond rates. To compensate for the risk, stock returns must be higher on average that bond rates. Since the 1800s stock returns in the US have averaged 6% while bond rates have been 2%. A firm wanting to borrow can sell bonds or borrow from financial intermediaries that match borrowers with lenders.

Economic agents save out of income for future spending. The rate of saving is σ and total saving σY. National income minus consumption is $Y - C = I + G$. Output not consumed equals saving S in the closed economy,

$$S = \sigma Y = I + G.$$

In the example $\sigma = 0.2$ and $S = 0.2 \times \$10$ trillion $= \$2$ trillion.

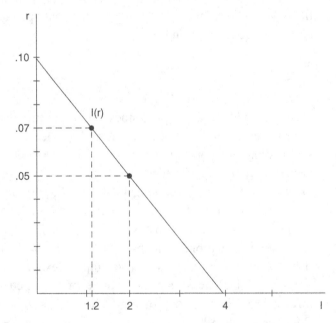

Figure 13.3
Investment Function
The investment function $I = 4 - 40r$ yields investment spending of \$2 trillion when $r = .05$. If r rises to .07, I falls to $4 - 2.4 = \$1.2$ trillion.

The IS curve in Figure 13.4 shows combinations of r and Y where $S = I + G$. Higher Y implies an increase in S. The interest rate r has to fall to increase I to return to product market equilibrium where investment equals saving ($I = S$ or IS).

The IS curve has a negative slope. In the example $S = .2Y$ and $I = 4 - 40r$ leading to the IS curve in Figure 13.4,

$$r = .1 + 0.25G - .005Y.$$

On the right side of the IS curve there is excess saving, $S > I$. On the left side there is a saving shortage with $I > S$. Output Y adjusts so the economy remains on its IS curve.

Moving down the IS curve, the lower r implies the economy moves to a higher capital/labor ratio k along its production function in Figure 13.1. The wage w and per capita income y are higher with the higher k. There must have been available capital, the capital slack allowing the economy to move down its IS curve.

Moving down the IS curve, national income increases and the interest rate falls.

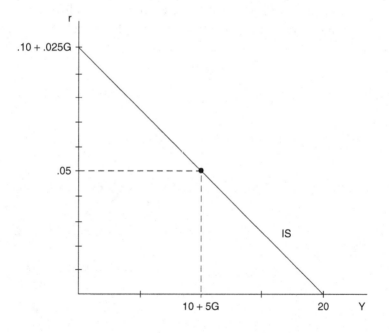

Figure 13.4
The IS Curve
To the right of the IS curve, saving is greater than investment. If $r = .05$ then $I = \$2$ trillion on the investment function in Fig. 13.3. The IS curve is the combinations of r and Y that satisfy $S = I + G$.

EXAMPLE 13.5   *Macroeconomic relationships*

Macroeconomics searches for simple relationships among GDP, unempolyment inflation, deficit spending, and the trade balance. High output growth might be expected to lower unemployment, but higher unemployment benefits increase the incentive to remain unemployed. Inflation might stimulate growth but lower money supply growth in the 1990s had no effect on output. Expansionary fiscal policy is thought to stimulate output but the link is weak and may be negative. Unemployment and inflation often move in the same direction. Trade deficits do not necessarily lower output growth. Government budget deficits may not relate to trade deficits. There are few simple rules of thumb in macroeconomics.

Capital and Labor Markets

The demand for capital input in Figure 13.5 is its marginal product, $MP_K = D_K$. Firms hire capital when its marginal product is greater than its price. The marginal product of capital from the production function is $MP_K = 341K^{-.7}L^{.7} = 341k^{-.7}$. If $r = .05$ capital input is $K = 60$ trillion given $L = 200$ million and $k = 300,000$. If r fell to .04 then K would rise to 84 trillion along the capital demand curve D_K.

Firms rent capital from its owners who are ready to supply machinery and equipment. To move down the IS curve, idle capital must be utilized.

Figure 13.6 shows the labor market. The demand for labor D_L is its marginal product $MP_L = 796k^{.3}$ in the example. Firms hire labor according to its marginal productivity MP_L. In the example with $K = \$60$ trillion, firms employ 200 million

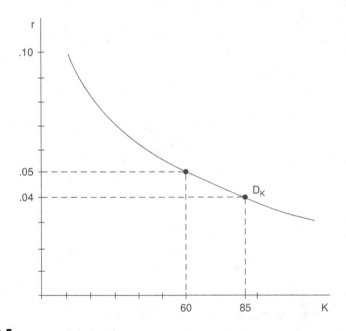

Figure 13.5
The Demand for Capital
The marginal product of capital $MP_K = 341k^{-.7}$ comes from the production function $Y = AK^{.3}L^{.7}$ or $y = 1137K^{.3}$. If r rises then K has to fall for an increase MP_K.

workers at $w = \$35,000$. If w were to raise to $\$40,000$, the quantity of labor demanded would fall to 128 million.

Increasing Y on the IS curve, K input increases raising MP_L and w. Firms will hire more labor due to increased productivity. The total amount of labor available is L_{tot}. The unemployment rate $u = (L_{tot} - L)/L_{tot}$ declines when L increases. Consistent with the declining r along the IS curve, k increases.

Higher output along the IS curve increases capital input and the capital/labor ratio.

EXAMPLE 13.6   *The Capital Stimulus of Trade*

When a capital abundant DC opens to trade, the return to capital increases with increased production and exports of capital intensive products. The higher return to capital encourages saving, shifting the economy with accelerated capital accumulation. Richard Baldwin (1992) finds these capital gains range up to 8% across a number of European countries.

The Money Market

Money is a liquid asset required for transactions but holding money involves a lost opportunity to buy bonds and enjoy future return. Liquidity demand is a function of income and the interest rate,

$$L = L(\overset{+}{Y}, \overset{-}{r}).$$

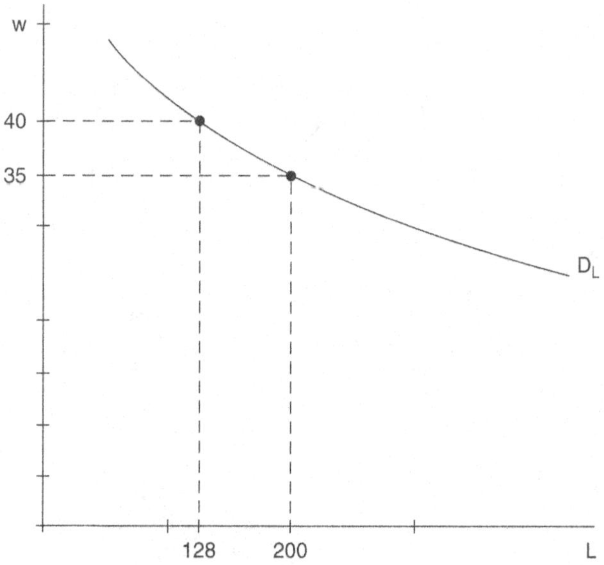

Figure 13.6
The Demand for Labor
Labor demand is its marginal product derived from the production function. Firms hire labor to adjust its marginal product MP_L to the wage w. In the example $MP_L = 796k^{.3} = \$35,000$ and $L = 200$ million.

Spending requires liquidity for transactions leading to the positive effect of Y. A higher interest rate makes bonds more attractive lowering the demand for liquidity.

The government central bank controls the real money supply M_s through the commercial banking system. The central bank directly controls its credit C_{CB} in the reserves of commercial banks. The total money supply M_s is a multiple, $M_s = \mu C_{CB}$ where μ is the money multiplier.

Money market equilibrium occurs along the LM (liquidity = money) curve,

$$M_s = L(\overset{+}{Y}, \overset{-}{r}).$$

The LM curve slopes upward since an increase in Y would have to offset by a higher r to keep money demand L equal to supply M_s. The interest rate r adjusts to keep the economy on its LM curve.

The money supply M_S is a policy variable controlled by the central bank. Expansionary monetary policy increases M_s shifting the LM curve to the right.

If $M_s = \$1.3$ trillion, the ratio of cash to income equals $\$1.3/\$10 = 0.13$. An additional $\$100$ income increases the demand for liquidity by $\$13$. If the elasticity of liquidity demand with respect to the interest rate is -1 the marginal effect of r on L is $\$1.3/.05 = -26$. The money demand function is then $L = 1.3 + .13Y - 26r$. With $M_S = 1.3$, the *LM curve* in Figure 13.7 is

$$r = .005Y.$$

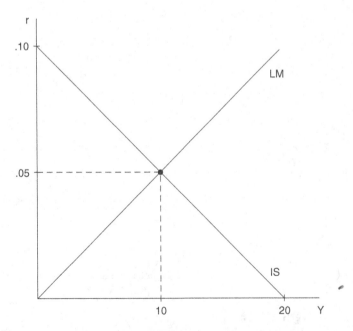

Figure 13.7
The ISLM Closed Economy
The LM curve $r = .005Y$ intersects the IS curve $r = .1 - .005Y$ at the closed economy ISLM macro equilibrium $r = .05$ and $Y = 10$ assuming $G = 0$.

The closed economy ISLM model in Figure 13.7 has equilibrium where the IS and LM curves intersect at $r = .05$ and $Y = 10$ trillion assuming $G = 0$.

The ISLM model determines the interest rate and output that clear the product and money markets.

EXAMPLE 13.7   *Money Supply Growth, Inflation, and the Real Interest Rate*

An increase in the money supply lowers the real interest rate but can lead to inflation. This chart tracks the annual growth rate of the US money supply along with the inflation rate and the real interest rate during the last half of the 20th century. Rising money supply growth rates lead to inflation. The Fed does not specify an inflation target. The real interest rate was negative during the 1970s due to the very high inflation rates.

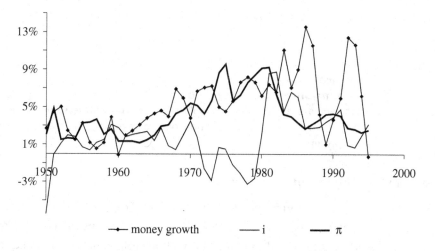

Monetary Policy

Monetary policy refers to control of the money supply M_s. Expansionary monetary policy is an increase in M_s shifting the LM curve to the right in Figure 13.8.

An increase in the money supply moves the economy down the IS curve, raising output Y and lowering the interest rate r. The 10% increase in M_S from $1.3 to $1.43 trillion lowers r from 5% to 4.75% and raises Y from 10 to 10.5.

The falling r implies a higher bond price with investment spending increasing to $2.1 trillion along the investment schedule $I(r)$ in Figure 13.3. The capital/labor ratio k in Figure 13.1 increases from $300 to $327, output per capita y rises from $50,000 to $51,300, and the wage w rises from $35,000 to $35,900.

The political motivation for expansionary monetary policy is unemployment. This labor market stimulus is possible if there is idle capital. Such a transitory stimulus occurs over a short time span of one quarter to a year.

Continued expansion of the money supply leads to inflation with no impact on the labor market. The ISLM model in Figure 13.8 assumes no inflation.

Economic growth is a gradual process that results from saving, and investment. Expansionary monetary policy does not permanently affect economic growth.

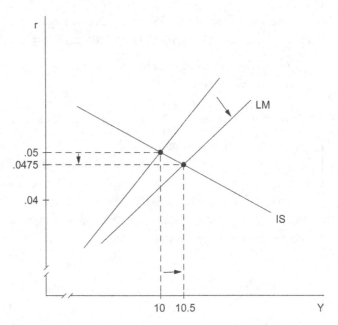

Figure 13.8
Expansionary Monetary Policy
An increase in the money supply shifts the LM curve to the right, lowering the interest
rate and raising output. Inflation occurs if the output does not keep pace with money
supply growth.

EXAMPLE 13.8   *The End of the Drachma*

Greece provides an example of the effects of money supply growth on GDP.
Beginning in the 1970s Greece pursued expansionary government spending and
industrial subsidies combined with unsustainable welfare and retirement programs.
Government deficits were financed by increasing supply of money. Inflation rates
of 25% through the 1980s disrupted economic incentives. There were also high
tariffs and tight restrictions on international investment. The government lost its
ability to increase the money supply when Greece joined the euro zone resulting
in government default.

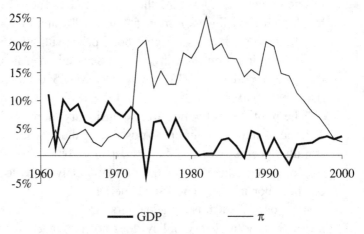

Fiscal Policy

Fiscal policy refers to government spending G and taxes T. Start with $G = T = 0$ and let G increase to examine the effects of expansionary fiscal policy. Lowering T has the same effect aside from income redistribution. Saving equals investment plus government spending, $\sigma Y = I + G$. An increase in G shifts the IS curve to the right.

Figure 13.9 shows the effects of an increase in government spending equal to 1% of GDP or $100 billion in the example. The IS curve shifts to $r = .1025 - .005Y$. Output Y rises from $10 to $10.25 trillion and the interest rate from 5% to 5.125% along the LM curve. The higher capital return reduces capital input and k falls along the production function in Figure 13.1. There is increased labor employment along the labor demand curve with a lower wage, the unemployment rate u falls. There must be unemployment slack for the increase in G to raise Y.

Capital owners are better off but income per capita y falls to $49,600, w falls to $31,600, and k falls to $293,000 in Figure 13.1. The economy switches toward more labor intensive production due to the lower relative price of labor. Investment spending drops from $2 to $1.95 trillion along the investment schedule in Figure 13.2 implying slower growth. The reduced investment spending is the crowding out of government spending.

Firms determine the level of employment according to labor demand. There must be available workers not employed and willing to work for a lower wage to

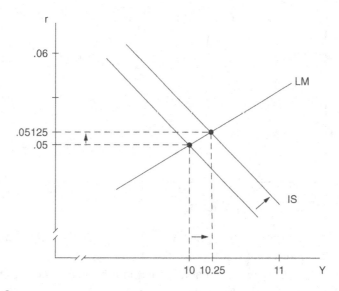

Figure 13.9
Expansionary Fiscal Policy
An increase in government spending G with taxes T constant, or a decrease in T with G constant, shifts the IS curve to the right. Output expands with increased labor employment but the wage falls. With full employment of labor, the LM curve is vertical and there is no increase in output due to expansionary fiscal policy.

increase output. Expansionary fiscal policy is certainly not capable of increasing output indefinitely. Fiscal expansion may succeed in stimulating short term employment but is an inflexible tool for active macroeconomic management. Declining investment and growth suggest it is wise to address unemployment directly through the labor market.

Another critical related issue is the effect of government debt. If $G > T$ the government must either borrow or increase the money supply. Expanding the money supply amounts to monetary policy that can be pursued on its own merit with no increase in government spending.

Government borrowing implies future taxes. Ricardian equivalence notes that taxpayers understand the future tax liability and increase their saving to pay the future tax. This increased saving lowers the IS curve back to its original position in Figure 13.9 making the fiscal expansion ineffective.

EXAMPLE 13.9   *Inflation, Unemployment, and Trade in Portugal*

Portugal is a small open economy that joined the EU in 1992. Unemployment did not respond to expansionary fiscal policy, government deficits, and inflation in the 1970s. When trade increased in the 1980s, unemployment fell. A decline in unemployment began in 1985 and continued with free trade in the EU. Trade increased from 1985 to 2000. Fiscal and monetary policies were ineffective

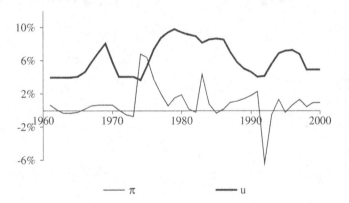

Section B Problems

B1. Show and explain what happens to the capital and labor markets when the interest rate rises along the IS curve.

B2. Use input demands to explain how an increase in the interest rate r affects capital and labor employment.

B3. Show and explain the effects of a decrease in the money supply in the ISLM model.

B4. Show and explain the effects of an increase in taxes in the ISLM model.

C. THE OPEN MACRO ECONOMY

An economy open to international trade and investment responds differently to macro policy. The exchange rate, trade balance, and international investment play roles in the open macro economy. Policy makers in the open economy choose the exchange rate system and rules for foreign investment.

Income and the Balance of Payments

The balance on goods and services BGS is part of the national income statement of an open economy,

$$Y = C + I + G + BGS$$

where $BGS = X - M$, export revenue X minus import spending M.

Total domestic spending $C + I + G$ is absorption A. To derive national income Y from absorption A, add export revenue X since it is produced but not consumed, and subtract import spending M since it is consumed but not produced. National income for the open economy is

$$Y = A + BGS.$$

Including the BGS and government spending G in the example $X = \$1$, $M = \$1.4$, and $BGS = -\$0.4$ in trillions. Absorption $A = \$10.4$ is made up of $C = \$7$, $I = \$1.4$, and $G = \$2$. National income is $Y = A + BGS = \$10$.

The trade balance BGS depends partly on the exchange rate. In terms of the euro $e = \$/€$. Depreciation $e\uparrow$ is a decrease in the price of domestic currency.

The relative foreign price level P^*/P is the real exchange rate e_R. For present purposes, assume P and P^* are constant and focus on the nominal exchange rate e.

Depreciation raises the BGS given the Marshall-Lerner condition of elastic trade. Assuming export plus import quantities are elastic, depreciation raises the BGS.

Higher foreign income Y^* raises X since the foreign country spends more on imports. Higher home income Y raises import spending M. The BGS function

$$BGS = B(\overset{+}{e}, \overset{+}{Y^*}, \bar{Y})$$

is part of the open economy IS curve, $\sigma Y = I + G + BGS$. For fixed levels of saving $S = \sigma Y$ and government spending G, a trade deficit reduces investment.

EXAMPLE 13.10   *Trade Prices and the BOT in Korea*

Price indices of imports and exports in Korea generally rose during the 1970s and 1980s with a bump during the oil embargo of the late 1970s. The *BOT* was negative with a dip due to the higher price of oil. Import prices leveled out during the early 1990s falling slightly behind export prices, an improvement in the terms of trade. Nevertheless the *BOT* became more negative. Starting about 1995 import prices began to outpace export prices with slightly falling terms of trade but the trade balance began a climb into surplus. Imports and exports are elastic.

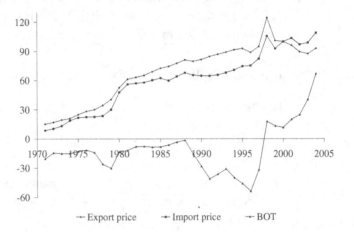

The balance of payments *BOP* is the sum of the current account *CA* and the capital account *KA*, *BOP* = *CA* + *KA*. A deficit in the CA implies a cash outflow for current goods and services. With a *CA* deficit, there is offsetting international borrowing in a *KA* surplus.

In the example *CA* = −*KA* = −$0.4 trillion. As a whole, the country borrows with the promise to repay in the future. The *CA* deficit lowers domestic investment *I* similar to the effect of an increase in government spending *G* but there an increase in foreign investment *FI*. Countries with *CA* surpluses lend to countries with *KA* surpluses.

A small country faces the interest rate r^* in the global bond market. If $r^* > r$ the home country is an international lender. If $r > r^*$ the home country borrows.

International lending and borrowing for a large country impacts international interest rates. If $r^* > r$ the home country increases the supply of loans lowering r^*. In the home country, the supply of loans decreases raising r and lowering the price of home bonds. Arbitrage leads toward international interest rate equalization.

Both r and r^* enter the capital account

$$KA(\overset{+}{r}, \ \overset{-}{\bar{r}^*}).$$

An increase in r creates an inflow of cash to buy home bonds. An increase in r^* creates cash outflow to buy foreign bonds.

The balance of payments is the sum of the current and capital accounts in the BP curve

$$BOP = BP(\overset{+}{\bar{e}}, \ \overset{+}{\bar{Y}^*}, \ \bar{Y}, \ \bar{r}^*, \ \overset{+}{r}) = 0.$$

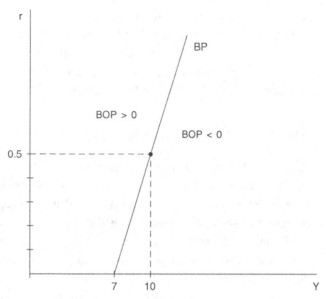

Figure 13.10
The BOP Curve
The *BOP* curve shows combinations of *Y* and *r* where *BOP* = 0. To the right *BOP* < 0.
To the left *BOP* > 0.

The BP curve in Figure 13.10 is part of the open economy ISLMBP model. It slopes upward since an increase in *Y* that lowers *BOP* has to be offset by an increase in *r*.

The BP curve can be derived from the marginal propensity to import and the interest rate effect on the capital account. If the marginal propensity to import is constant at $M/Y = 0.14$ an increase of $100 in income increases import spending by $14. If the elasticity of the *KA* with respect to *r* equals one, the marginal effect of *r* on *KA* equals 8 when *KA* = $0.4 trillion and *r* = .05. The scaled BP function in Figure 13.10 is $BOP = 0 = 1 - .14Y + 8r$ or $r = -.125 + .0175Y$.

This BP curve is combinations of *r* and *Y* where *BOP* = 0. To the right of the BP curve there is a *BOP* deficit and to the left a *BOP* surplus. The BP curve shifts right with depreciation or devaluation $e\uparrow$, higher foreign income Y^*, or a higher foreign interest rate r^*. A flatter BP curve indicates a higher degree of international capital mobility since less of an increase in *r* is required to offset an increase in *Y*. With perfect international capital mobility the BP curve is flat at the international interest rate r^*.

EXAMPLE 13.11   *The History of the US BOP*

During the 1800s the US was a growing debtor country with a capital account *KA* surplus and current account *CA* deficit. Foreign investment went into railroads, infrastructure, and agriculture. By the late 1800s output had climbed and there was a *CA* surplus. Following the Great Depression and two World Wars, there was a *KA* deficit as the US invested in Europe and Japan. Investment income then led to a *CA* surplus up to 1980. Increased import spending on oil and consumer goods then outpaced exports of resource based production, high tech manufactures, and business services. For the last few decades, the US has a *CA* deficit and *KA* surplus.

The Open Economy ISLMBP Model

The IS, LM, and BP curves determine the interest rate r, national income Y, and either the exchange rate e or the money supply M_s. A floating exchange rate is determined by the equilibrium. With a fixed exchange rate, the money supply adjusts to the macro equilibrium.

Figure 13.11 shows the open economy equilibrium at point A where the IS, LM, and BP curves intersect. Adjustments lead r, Y and either e or M_S toward the equilibrium.

There are market adjustments toward the macro equilibrium. For instance, if $Y = 10$ but $r = .04$ at point B in Figure 13.11 there is excess demand for output below IS, excess demand for money to the right of LM, and a *BOP* deficit to the right of the BP curve. A rising interest rate would lower demand for money and raise the capital account. The excess demand for money at point B is an

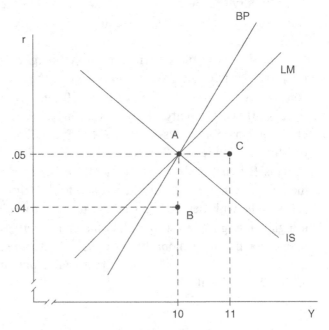

Figure 13.11
The ISLMBP Macro Model
The IS, LM, and BP curves combine into the ISLMBP model. At point A, the product, money, and international markets are in equilibrium.

excess supply of bonds, pushing the price of bonds down (the interest rate up). The rising interest rate attracts foreign investment raising *BOP*. Market forces push the economy toward point A although the path may not be a straight one since the rising interest rate lowers investment spending.

From point C where $Y = 11$ and $r = .05$ there is excess supply of output, excess demand for money, and a *BOP* deficit. The interest rate rises to eliminate both the excess demand for money and the *BOP* deficit, and output falls to eliminate the excess supply of output. The *BOP* deficit also causes depreciation or the money supply to fall with a fixed exchange rate.

EXAMPLE 13.12 *The Dollar and the BOT, 1950–2000*

A history of the dollar exchange rate 1/e is shown below with the *BOT* in 1992. During the 1950s the US had a *BOT* surplus. With the fixed exchange rate, foreign exchange reserves and gold holding grew. Starting in the late 1950s there was a growing *BOT* deficit with foreign assets depleting. When the dollar was cut loose from its official gold price in 1973, the dollar depreciated and the *BOT* deficit shrank. After a brief turnaround in 1975 the dollar depreciated and by 1980 there was a *BOT* surplus. Starting in 1981 the dollar appreciated sharply and the *BOT* fell into deficit. In 1986 these trends reversed with the dollar depreciating and the *BOT* climbing back toward zero. In the early 1990s the *BOT* deficit began to grow with increased spending on oil and labor intensive imports.

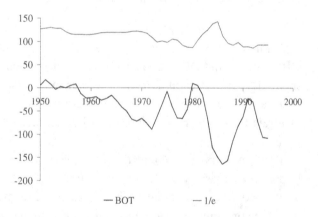

Monetary Policy with a Flexible Exchange Rate

Expansionary monetary policy shifts the LM curve to the right, moving the economy from point A to B in Figure 13.12. There is a *BOP* deficit to the right of the BP curve. A 10% increase in M_S lowers r from .05 to .0475 and raises Y from 10 to 10.5. At point B there is a *BOP* deficit with the economy to the right of the BP curve, $BOP = 1 - .14Y + 8r = -.09$ is with a *BOP* deficit of $90 billion.

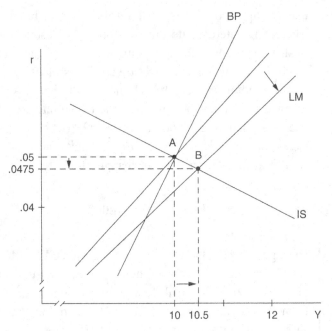

Figure 13.12
Expansionary Monetary Policy
An increase in the money supply shifts the LM curve right moving the economy from point A to B where there is a *BOP* deficit. With a flexible exchange rate the currency depreciates, shifting the BP curve out to point B. With a fixed exchange rate the money supply diminishes, returning the economy to its original position at point A.

With a flexible exchange rate, depreciation shifts the BP curve to point B. The effects of the monetary expansion are a lower interest rate, increased investment spending, a lower capital account, higher output, depreciation, a higher trade balance, and a decrease in the capital account. Home investment increases relative to foreign investment. Capital and labor markets adjust exactly as in the closed economy.

Policy makers may be under pressure, however, not to let the currency depreciate. Import prices rise with depreciation. Foreign investment falls since earnings are discounted when converted back to foreign currency.

Exchange market intervention to prop up the currency may follow expansionary monetary policy. The possibility of government intervention leads to erratic exchange rate movements. Traders focus more on government policy than underlying market fundamentals.

EXAMPLE 13.13   *Money Growth and the Exchange Rate*

Over long time periods money supply growth has a fundamental effect on the exchange rate. The chart tracks money supply growth and the dollar exchange rate. Exchange rates were fixed upto early 1973. The rising money supply growth led to depreciation up to 1981. During the oil crises of the 1970s and 1980s the dollar was a safe haven. Beginning in 1986 the dollar depreciated up to 1990. Monetary policy should limit money supply growth to eliminate inflation. If trading partners follow suit, exchange rates would stabilize following purchasing power parity. Erratic monetary policy leads to exchange rate variability.

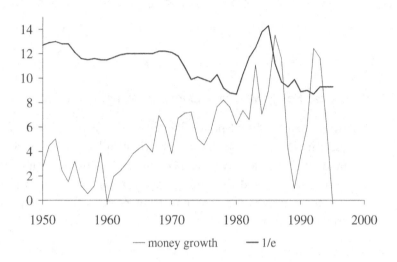

Monetary Policy with a Fixed Exchange Rate

With a fixed exchange rate, the monetary expansion and *BOP* deficit at point B in Figure 13.12 lead to a decrease in the money supply. The economy spends more on imports than it makes on exports with money leaving the economy. The LM curve shifts left and the economy returns to point A. Monetary expansion is ineffective with a fixed exchange rate.

A government with a fixed exchange rate may not "play by the rules" increasing the money supply to offset the cash outflow due to the *BOP* deficit. The money supply M_S is a multiple μ of the sum of central bank credit C_{BC} and foreign exchange reserves FX_R,

$$M_S = \mu(C_{BC} + FX_R).$$

The *BOP* deficit at point B drains FX_R lowering M_S. An offsetting increase in C_{BC} is sterilization of the *BOP* deficit.

EXAMPLE 13.14   *Price Levels and Real Exchange Rates*

Price levels vary quite a bit across countries, even developed countries. High income and demand raise prices for goods and services. Price levels in LDCs are much lower. Relative price levels vary in this sample by a factor of 4.

Fiscal Policy with a Flexible Exchange Rate

Expansionary fiscal policy increases output but generates a balance of payments deficit. The IS curve shifts to the right in Figure 13.13. Start assuming $G = T = 0$ and let G increase by 1% of GDP or $100 billion. Output Y increases from $10 to $10.5 trillion and the interest rate r rises from 5% to 5.125%. The shift in the IS curve moves the economy from point A to B but with a *BOP* deficit to the right of the BP curve.

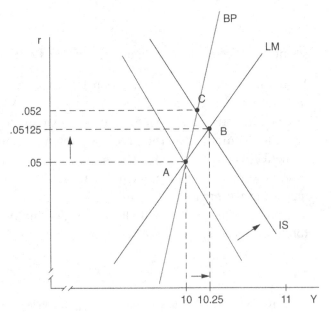

Figure 13.13
Expansionary Fiscal Policy
An increase in government spending or a decrease in taxes shifts the IS curve moving the economy from A to B where BOP < 0. The currency depreciates shifting the BP curve out to point B making the fiscal policy effective. With a fixed exchange rate, the money supply falls shifting the LM curve in and moving the economy to point C. Fiscal policy has a larger effect on the interest rate but a smaller effect on output relative to a closed economy.

The government deficit generated by the increased spending leads to a balance of payments deficit. This link is called the twin deficits. Governments that run fiscal deficits cause *BOP* deficits.

With a flexible exchange rate the *BOP* deficit causes depreciation and a shift of the BP curve to point B. On the BP curve $BOP = 1 - .14Y + 8r = -\$60$ billion at point B. Depreciation raises the *BGS* from −$400 billion to −$340 billion to return the *BOP* to zero.

EXAMPLE 13.15   *Dollar Depreciation in 2003*

The US trade deficit narrowed in November 2003 as civilian aircraft and capital good exports led a 3% jump in export revenue. Exports had been rising steadily with dollar depreciation. Concern over the government deficit was credited with causing depreciation. EU policymakers meanwhile were concerned that euro appreciation would stifle an export led recovery.

Fiscal Policy with a Fixed Exchange Rate

At point B in Figure 13.13 there is a *BOP* deficit caused by expansionary fiscal policy. With a fixed exchange rate, the money supply M_S decreases as the economy spends more than it makes internationally. The fall in the money supply shifts the LM curve left to point C. With a fixed exchange rate, the fiscal expansion leads to an offsetting monetary contraction.

In the example there is a *BOP* deficit of −$60 billion as M_S falls from $1.3 to $1.24 trillion. From point B to C in Figure 13.13 r rises from 5.1% to 5.2% and Y falls from $10.2 to $10.1 trillion along the new IS curve. The *BGS* falls $14 billion due to increased imports.

Fiscal expansion creates less of an increase in output but more of an increase in the interest rate relative to a closed economy. This higher interest rate implies more of a decrease in investment spending. The higher domestic interest rate attracts more foreign investment.

Total investment, domestic plus foreign, falls. At point C with $r = 5.2\%$ in Figure 13.13, domestic investment falls to $1.92 trillion along the investment schedule in Figure 13.2. This decrease of $80 billion in domestic investment is less than completely offset by the $14 billion increase in foreign investment. Total investment falls by $64 billion. Foreign investment only partly replaces domestic investment.

Expansionary fiscal policy may temporarily lower unemployment. It is no accident that governments increase spending as election time approaches in the political business cycle. Expansionary fiscal policy may increase output but lowers investment and economic growth. Government debt and future tax liabilities make expansionary fiscal policy even less attractive.

EXAMPLE 13.16   *China's Command an Control Yuan*

China has begun a process of opening to the world economy with growing international trade and investment. One indication of its potential role in the world economy was the rising international price of oil due to increased demand in China. Foreign investment is funding the transition from state command and control to free markets. China maintains a fixed exchange rate with an undervalued yuan making Chinese products cheaper abroad and export revenue artificially high.

Competitive Devaluation

Competitive devaluation of a fixed exchange rate generates a trade surplus, raises national income, and lowers the interest rate. Devaluation for the home country is revaluation for the foreign country with exactly the opposite effects. Policy retaliation can be expected from foreign countries.

Devaluation shifts the BP in Figure 13.14 to the right. The economy remains in domestic equilibrium at point A with a *BOP* surplus. The money supply increases, shifting the LM curve and moving the economy to a new equilibrium at point B.

With an exchange rate elasticity of the *BGS* equal to one, a 10% competitive depreciation generates a 10% increase in the *BGS* from −$400 to −$360 billion. The money supply increases from $1.3 to $1.34 trillion in the money market equilibrium $M_S = 1.3 + .13Y − 26r$. At point B national income Y increases from $10 to $10.15 trillion and the interest rate falls from 5% to 4.9% along the IS curve.

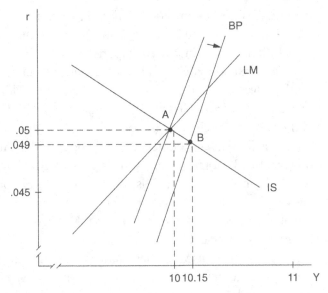

Figure 13.14
A Competitive Devaluation

A competitive devaluation shifts the BP curve creating a trade surplus at point A. Foreign exchange reserves and the money supply increase, shifting the LM curve to point B. The competitive devaluation stimulates output and lowers the interest rate.

The foreign country has a revaluation with a trade deficit, decreased money supply, lower national income, and higher interest rate. Countries become entangled in competitive devaluations and retaliations. One country devalues and the other retaliates with a devaluation of its own. Ultimately there is no effect except to create confusion that discourages trade and investment. There are negative long term consequences when traders and investors pay more attention to government policy makers than market fundamentals.

Inflation typically occurs with devaluation. The increased output and lower real interest rate in Figure 13.14 assume no inflation. Price levels rise following competitive devaluation and inflation lessens the positive effects in Figure 13.14.

EXAMPLE 13.17   *The Exchange Rate in Korea*

This chart shows the history of the won exchange rate e, balance of trade *BOT*, and *GDP*. In the late 1970s the won appreciated and the *BOT* fell. When the won depreciated in 1979 the *BOT* increased until 1986. The won then appreciated sharply and the *BOT* soon fell. In 1996 the won sharply depreciated with the Asian crisis and the *BOT* began a steady climb. The effects of depreciation on *GDP* are negligible.

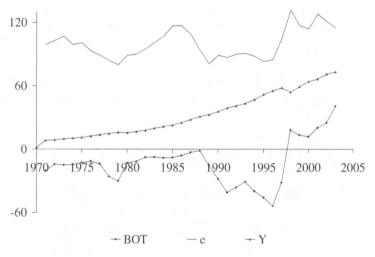

EXAMPLE 13.18   *Asian Exchange Risk and Exports*

Depreciation should affect trade and raise export revenue, but the risk associated with increased exchange rate volatility can discourage trade. WenShwo Fang, YiHao Li, and Henry Thompson (2005) find evidence of negative risk effects in 3 of 8 Asian countries in monthly data 1979–2002. The currencies depreciated from 1% to 5% on a yearly basis. Risk as standard deviation ranges from 2% to 7%. The chart shows that the small yearly effects of depreciation on export revenue in Singapore, Taiwan, and Japan were outweighed by large risk effects. The units are percent effect on export revenue. The Philippines, Thailand,

and Indonesia gained about 2% export revenue per year due to depreciation. Risk had no impact in Malaysia, the Philippines, Thailand, and Indonesia in spite of their higher risk levels. Singapore and Taiwan had the lowest risk but the highest risk effects, almost 8% per year in Singapore. Traders not used to exchange volatility are most vulnerable. Negative risk effects dominate positive effects of depreciation.

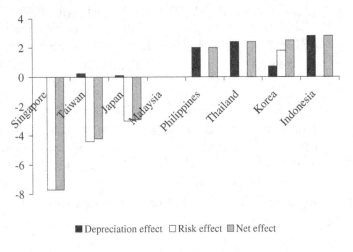

Section C Problems

C1. Suppose investment $I = 2$, government spending $G = 1$, absorption $A = 11$, export revenue $X = 6$, and national income $Y = 15$. Find consumption spending C, import spending M, and the BGS. Find the real exchange rate with the home price level $P = 1.1$ and foreign $P^* = 1.5$.

C2. Derive the open economy IS equation $\sigma Y = A - C + BGS$ from the national income equation.

C3. Show and explain the effect on the BP curve of
    (a) an increase in foreign income Y^*
    (b) an increase in the foreign interest rate r^*
    (c) a revaluation of the domestic currency.

C4. Show and explain the effects of a decrease in the money supply in the open ISLMBP economy with
    (a) a flexible exchange rate
    (b) a fixed exchange rate.

EXAMPLE **13.19**   *Dollar and US Tourism*

The weak US dollar during the 2000s made travel to the US a bargain but the US share of international travelers declined from 8% in 1994 to 6% in 2004. There is increasing competition from new destinations such as Dubai, Budapest, and China. US foreign policy and tight security discourage travelers. Declining export demand shifts the BP curve in Figure 13.14 to the left.

D.   THE FX RATE AND INFLATION

Inflation is the direct result of expansionary policy. Inflation, an increase in the price level P, lowers the real money supply M_S/P and shifts the LM curve left. Inflation raises the price of exports relative to imports. This section examines the effects of inflation in the open economy model of aggregate supply and demand.

Money and the Exchange Rate

The real money supply M_S/P equals demand for cash balances $L(Y, r)$. Purchasing power parity $P = eP^*$ holds with arbitrage equalizing prices across countries. The real exchange rate is the ratio of price levels $e = P/P^*$. Money market equilibrium implies $M_S/P = L(Y, r)$. Solving for the price level, $P = M_S/L$ and $P^* = M_S^*/L^*$ in the foreign country implying

$$e = M_S L^*/M_S^* L.$$

The exchange rate depends on relative home variables

$$e = e(M_S/\overset{+}{M_S^*}, \ Y/\overset{-}{Y^*}, \ r/\overset{-}{r^*}).$$

An increase in the supply of home money M_S relative to M_S^* depreciates the exchange rate. An increase in Y raises money demand and appreciates the currency. An increase in r lowers the demand for cash and depreciates the currency.

EXAMPLE 13.20   *Long Term PPP*

PPP would hold if all goods were freely traded, countries produced and consumed the same products, and exchange rates were free. William Crowder (1996) presents evidence that a long run equilibrium relationship holds between US dollars and UK pounds from 1900 to 1991, with a weaker relationship between Canadian and US dollars. Over long time spans, P and eP^* move together.

Aggregate Supply and Demand

Aggregate supply and demand ASAD introduce inflation in the macro model. The aggregate demand curve shows combinations of the price level P and income Y where there is ISLM equilibrium.

A decrease in the price level P raises the real money supply M_S/P and shifts LM to the right. A fall in the price level from $P = 1$ to 0.91 shifts the LM curve as in Figure 13.8 with Y rising from 10 to 10.5 along the IS curve.

The aggregate demand curve AD in Figure 13.15 shows this relation between income Y and the price level P. Along AD there is ISLM equilibrium. The AD

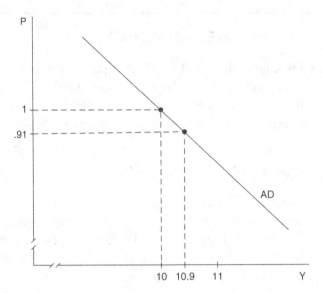

Figure 13.15
The Aggregate Demand Curve
The AD curve slopes down since a falling P raises the real money supply M_S/P increasing income Y in the ISLM model. Moving down the AD curve, r rises and w falls. Expansionary policy shifts the AD curve right.

function is $P = 2.8 - .18Y$ in the example. Expansionary fiscal and monetary policies shift AD right.

The upward sloping aggregate supply curve in Figure 13.16 relies on reactions to price changes. Multiply the price level P by real output Y to find nominal output $Y_N = PY$. When prices rise, firms perceive profit opportunities and raise output. The AS curve $P = .1Y$ assumes every 1% increase in P results in a 1% increase in Y.

Firms wanting to increase output offer a higher wage w, increasing the quantity of labor supplied. Ultimately workers may realize the price level is increasing and the real wage w/P is constant.

The ASAD economy has an equilibrium at the intersection of the AS and AD curves. In Figure 13.16 price $P = 1$ and income $Y = 10$. If the economy is near full employment, the AS curve is more vertical.

Inflation and the BOP

The price level affects the trade balance through the price adjusted exchange rate $e_p = eP^*/P$ making the BOP function

$$BOP = B(\dot{e}_p, \bar{Y}) = 0$$

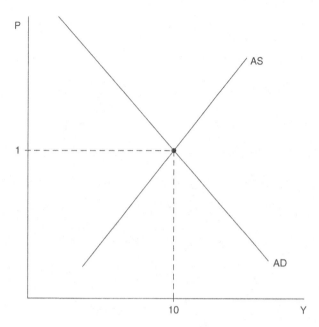

Figure 13.16
The Closed ASAD Economy
The aggregate supply and demand ASAD model determines the price level P and national income Y. The AS curve slopes upward if firms and workers, respond to rising prices and wage with increased activity. At full employment, the AS curve is vertical.

A higher price level P raises the relative price of home products and lowers BOP. Higher Y raises import spending M and lowers BOP.

The *FF curve* in Figure 13.17 shows combinations of P and Y where $BOP = 0$. An increase in P lowers the BOP and requires a reduction in Y to raise BOP.

The marginal propensity to import is the additional import spending per dollar of income. If the marginal propensity to import is constant, the average propensity to import M/Y is constant also. In the example, $M/Y = 0.14$. If $e = P^* = 1$ the FF curve is $BOP = 1.4/P - .14Y = 0$. Figure 13.17 shows the equilibrium where the AS, AD, and FF curves intersect in the ASADFF model.

Expansionary fiscal or monetary policies shift the AD curve to the right as in Figure 13.18. Output and the price level increase causing a BOP deficit in the move from point A to B. The 10% increase in Y and 10% inflation in the example could be the result of increased money supply M_S or increased government spending G, or both. The BOP deficit at point B requires adjustment either through depreciation with a flexible exchange rate, or a decrease in the money supply with a fixed exchange rate.

Depreciation would shift the FF curve in Figure 13.18 out to point B. With a fixed exchange rate, the BOP deficit leads to decreased money supply and a return to point A.

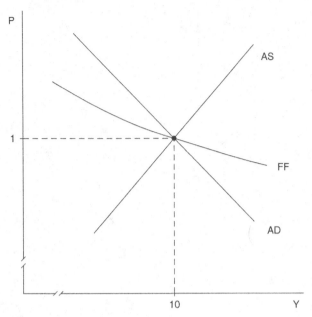

Figure 13.17
The ASADFF Model
The FF curve shows combinations of P and Y where $BOP = 0$. A higher P is offset by a lower Y to keep $BOP = 0$. The open economy equilibrium P and Y are determined where the AS, AD, and FF curves intersect.

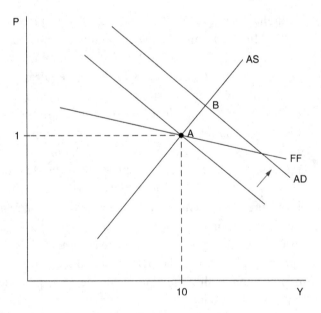

Figure 13.18
Expansionary Policies in the ASADFF Model
Expansionary policies shift the AD curve right, moving the economy from point A to B and raising the price level P. Output Y increases except near full employment. With a flexible exchange rate, the currency depreciates and the FF curve shifts out to point B. With a fixed exchange rate, the nominal money supply M_S decreases and the AD curve shifts back to point A.

Policy Viability for the Open Economy

Table 13.1 summarizes the macro effects of monetary and fiscal policies. Positive output effects assume the aggregate supply curve slopes upward. Near full employment, however, the Y effects are small or zero.

There are sound reasons governments should shy away from active fiscal and monetary policy to manage the macro economy:

- Nominal interest rates changes disrupt investment planning
- Inflation uncertainty disrupts trade and investment
- Traders and inverstors becomes preoccupied with arbitrary government policy
- Any successful policies have opposite effects on other countries
- Positive impacts rely on slack or unemployment in input markets
- Near full employment output will not increase

For many reasons, active macroeconomic policy is unproductive. Simply put, government spending projects should pass a benefit/cost test. Taxes should be set according to goals of income redistribution. Monetary policy should target zero inflation.

Section D Problems

D1. Explain how an increase in the foreign money supply affects the exchange rate.
D2. Show the effects of expansionary policy on output and the price level in a closed economy with full employment.
D3. Show what happens in the ASADFF economy with a revaluation.
D4. Show the effects of money supply contraction on output, the price level, and interest rates with a floating exchange rate versus a fixed exchange rate.

CONCLUSION

Macro policy tools are ineffective in influencing trade, investment, and exchange rates. Macro policy caters to the special interests influencing the political process.

Table 13.1 Macro Policy and Inflation

	e	Y	r	π	i
Monetary expansion					
Floating e	↑	↑*	↓	↑	↓ (or ↑ but less than π)
Fixed e	0	0	0	0	0
Fiscal expansion					
Floating e	↑	↑*	↑	↑	↑ (more than r ↑)
Fixed e	0	↑*	↑**	↑	↑ (more than r ↑)

*Close to zero near full employment
**Larger than with floating e

Policy makers use macro policy to their own benefit. Governments can play a positive role by redistributing income in a transparent political process and supplying money with no inflation. The basic lesson of international economics is that competitive markets are efficient and should be free of microeconomic trade policy and microeconomic fiscal and monetary policies.

Terms

Absorption	ISLM closed economy
Appreciation	Liquidity demand
ASAD closed economy	Monetary policy
ASADFF open economy	Monetary model of the exchange rate
BOP function	National income
Crowding out	Neoclassical macro production function
Depreciation	Overlapping generations model
Competitive devaluation	Perpetuity bond
Economic growth	Political business cycle
Fiscal policy	Real exchange rate
Fixed exchange rates	Ricardian equivalence
Floating exchange rates	Saving rate
Inflation	Sterilization
Investment function	Twin deficits

MAIN POINTS

- The microeconomic foundations of macroeconomics are the neoclassical production function, optimal saving in the overlapping generations model, and optimal investment.
- The ISLM model includes the investment-saving IS product market and the liquidity-money LM market. The ISLM model determines the interest rate and output consistent with equilibrium in the product and money markets. Holding the price level constant, the ISLM model shows the effects of fiscal and monetary policies.
- The open economy ISLMBP model includes the balance of payments and allows adjustment in the floating exchange rate or money supply with a fixed exchange rate. The effects of monetary and fiscal policies differ in an open economy.
- The monetary model of the exchange rate focuses on money markets across countries. The aggregate supply and demand ASADFF model includes inflation and shows that any positive policy effects are dampened by inflation.

REVIEW PROBLEMS

1. Similar to Figure 13.1 diagram the production function $y = 10k^4$ with $k = \$1000$. Indicate income per capita y and the wage w when $r = 6.3\% = .063$. Sketch the production function.

2. In the economy of Problem 1 suppose the growth rate of labor is 1% and the saving rate is σ is 20%. What information is required to determine whether the economy is growing?

3. The economy of Problem 1 grows until the capital labor ratio k is constant at the steady state $k^* = 2188$. Find the steady state income per capita y^s. Given the steady state interest rate $r^s = 4\% = .04$ find w^s.

4. Explain the labor and capital market changes in Problem 3. Use changes in supply and demand to illustrate what happens in the two markets as the economy grows.

5. Explain the changes in y, w, and r due to:
   (a) a decrease in the saving rate
   (b) improved technology
   (c) foreign investment
   (d) immigration

6. In the overlapping generations OLG model, suppose the wage is $50,000 and the interest rate is 10%. Diagram the intertemporal budget line. Find consumption in retirement if $40,000 is consumed while working.

7. If the interest rate in Problem 6 falls to 5% explain what will happen to the saving rate and consumption in both periods.

8. Find the level of saving that would equate consumption for both generations in Problem 5 when $r = 10\%$.

9. Explain what happens in capital and labor markets when the interest rate rises and the economy moves down its IS curve.

10. Suppose there is a decrease in the money supply M_s in the ISLM model. Explain adjustments in the capital and labor markets.

11. Explain the labor and capital market effects of an increase in taxes T. Show the adjustment in the ISLM model along the production function and the IS curve.

12. Show and explain the effects of an increase in taxes in an open ISLMBP economy with
    (a) a flexible exchange rate
    (b) a fixed exchange rate

13. Show and explain the effects of a decrease in the money supply in an open ISLMBP economy with
    (a) a flexible exchange rate
    (b) a fixed exchange rate

14. Show how an increase in foreign income Y^* affects output and the price level in the ASADFF model. What happens to real and nominal interest rates?

15. Contrast the effects of a decrease in the money supply on output in the ISLMBP and ASADFF models.

16. Show the effects of expansionary policy on output and the price level in an open economy with full employment.

17. Explain adjustment due to a sharp devaluation in the ASADFF model.

18. Explain why depreciation and inflation occur together in the ASADFF economy.

READINGS

Nelson Mark (2001) *International Macroeconomics and Finance*, Blackwell. A short advanced text on theory and application.

Robert Hall and David Papell (2005) *Macroeconomics: Economic Growth, Fluctuations, and Policy*, Norton. Macro text with an international slant.

Maurice Obsfeld and Kenneth Rogoff (1997) *Foundations of International Macroeconomics*, MIT Press. A thorough advanced text.

Gustav Cassel (1921) *The World's Monetary Problems*, Constable. A classic on money.

Francisco Rivera-Batiz and Luis Rivera Batiz (1994) *International Finance and Open Economy Macroeconomics*, Prentice-Hall. The complete source for the ISLMBP model with its many possibilities.

Hints and Partial Answers

Chapter 1

A2. Domestic supply rises.

A4. With identical supplies, the country with lower demand exports.

C2. XS increases.

D2. In the US, $S/M = 3/2$.

Review

2. Japanese XD rises.

4. Russian XD·rises.

6. XD^* from ROW rises.

8. XD from US falls.

10. Venezuelan steel costs $450.

12. Avoid mercantilist arguments.

14. Consider resource availability, technology, and climate.

Chapter 2

A2. 105 on the M axis, 135 on the S axis, $MRT = 105/135 = 0.78$.

B2. The economy specializes in M.

C2. Producing S has higher opportunity cost with growth biased toward M.

D2. The cost of living is lower inside an FEZ.

Review

2. The 1986 PPF has the point $(M,S) = (625,2200)$.

4. See Figure 3.2.

6. $tt = M/S = 1.2$ and the gains from trade are 21%.

8. Growth biased toward exports means more trade and higher income.

10. Differences are created by local customs, laws, and input costs.

12. Agricultural output and exports drop.

Chapter 3

A2. Which industry can better influence politicians?

B2. Domestic quantity supplied is greater with a quota.

C2. There is no incentive to trade if prices are equal.

D2. Consider the increasing geographical areas.

Review

2. P rises to $1.5 \times \$30 = \$45$.

4. $D = 100 - P = S = -10 + P$ and $P = \$55$.

6. Price is $50 and total loss is $500.

8. Imports are $D - S = 30$ and $P = \$40$.

10. The economy specializes in M but the tariff reduces M output.

12. Less local interests imply less protectionism.

Chapter 4

A2. Offer curves do not cross.

A4. Foreign offer curve falls toward its import axis.

B2. Similar to A2.

C2. H 4%, F 6%, H 5%, ...

D2. At 6%, the P series runs $20, $21.20, $22.47, ... , $35.82.

Review

2 and 4. Foreign offer curve falls toward import axis.

6. Tariff expands domestic production.

8. Foreign reaction function is horizontal at 4%.

10. Reaction functions lie along the axes.

12. A tariff on M pulls OPEC offer curve in toward its import axis.

Chapter 5

A2. The PPF is $220 = 4S + 5M$, $M/S = 4/5$ and output of S is 27.5.

B2. $M/S = 5/4$ at home.

C2. Upper limit to tt is $.01 > tt$.

C4. 114 on the A axis.

D2. Labor became less productive.

D4. Total M expands to $52 = 260/5$.

Review

2. Delta is the intermediate country and might produce both goods.

4. F specializes, producing 60 S and exports half.

6. Consumption with trade at home is worth 72.5 M and H gains more.

8. $ew^* = \$8.80$. $tt = 0.7$ and $w = \$12.32$.

10. $(3/5)(w/w^*) > e > ...$

12. $L^*/L = 5$ for good 2, and H exports it.

14. The lower limit is $e > 0.0053$.

Chapter 6

A2. *MR* for *M* is $150. For the 5th unit of *L*, *MRP* = $2.25.
B2. S_L should be higher.
C2. *k* = 1.
C4. F exports M.
D2. Unemployed *L* implies less labor intensive production.

Review

2. Demand rises in the market for *M* capital.
4. *r* should be less than *r**.
6. *K* input rises to 0.3.
8. *K*/*L* = 0.28.
10. *H* is labor abundant.
12. The endowment point lies between *M** and *S* expansion paths.
14. If *L** = 100, (*K*,*L*) = (200,50)
16. (*M*,*S*) = (400,500) in *H* and (300,600) in *F*, *tt* = 1

Chapter 7

A2. Temporary losses can be offset by future profit.
A4. Foreign *P* would be lower than home *P*.
B2. Aggregation simplifies theory but hides information.
C2. Unspent income is loaned to others.
D2. Protection is not productive.

Review

2. *P* rises to $800.
4. Foreign revenue is $192.
6. US: *wL*/*rK* = $209/$134 = 1.56 and *w*/*r* = 1.4.
8. *DF* runs from $10 to $3 on the demand curve.
10. Equilibrium high output for both, SA could pay Russia to remain.
12. PPF expands with bias toward *M*.

Chapter 8

A2. Find emigration from F.
B2. Incoming *L* raises *K* productivity.
C2. A 5% increase in skilled labor raises unskilled wage to $8060.
D2. Production of high tech goods & business services fall in DC.

Review

2. Consider other influences on supply and demand.
4. Immigration impacts labor intensive production.

6. US has comparative advantage in these activities.
8. Investment in US raises US wage.
10. The specific factor model can predict the effects.
12. Mexico is abundant in unskilled labor and scarce in capital.
14. FTZs are free from protectionism.

Chapter 9

A2. Consider standard techniques and specific inputs.
B2. Consider the pollution tax revenue.
C2. North PPF is biased toward S. Trade raises wages in South.
D2. Do the countries oppose free trade and free factor mobility?

Review

2. Each plant produces the same output.
4. Less TV output and higher prices.
6. Domestic firms would ask for the same favor.
8. North exports services in exchange for manufactures.
10. CU would be tough with free migration.
12. Some states would have government budget deficits and inflation.

Chapter 10

A2. Import elasticity is $15/17 = 0.88$.
B2. The BOT, DI, and KA increase. NII falls in the future.
C2. Which country is growing, which stable and wealthy?
D2. PI and KA increase now.

Review

2. XD, P, q_{imp}, and M all move in the same direction.
4. $S/M = 5/12.50 = 0.4$.
6. $BOT = -\$744$, ...
8. Investment flows are US debits.
10. Some countries are in recessions while others are in expansions.
12. There is no necessary links.
14. Export taxes would decrease exports.

Chapter 11

A2. Demand for euros is affected now.
A4. BGS is positive during the contract period, negative during pass through.
B2. Limit exchange of foreign currency.
C2. Work through excess supply and demand.
D2. Real return drops to $97.

Review

2. Yen prices are 495 and 562.5.
4. Supply of euro falls.
6. Change in export revenue is 2%. BOT rises.
8. Central bank is selling assets that should rise in value.
10. Central banks were buying marks, yen, and pounds.
12. Profit is $320.51.

Chapter 12

A2. Interest payments are $160 million.
A4. *NII* is −$0.94 billion. A3 and A4 are *NII* of the US in 1990.
B2. Shift S_{won} or D_{won}.
C2. Banks want to maintain value of their notes. Supply slopes upward.
D2. $P/P^* = 0.000625$, $/peso = 1/1500$.

Review

2. XD for loans falls.
4. Explain which is riskier.
6. Consider forward exchange market.
8. KA rises by $5 million. BOT will rise.
10. Demand for dollars falls.
12. Work through the credit market.
14. Wealth prefers stability.

Chapter 13

A2. Use production function $y = 1137k^3$ to find k.
A4. Consumer optimization requires tangent optimal indifference curve.
B2. Consider the change in the quantity of capital demanded.
B4. Higher taxes shift the IS curve.
C2. Saving is the key.
C4. The decreased M_s shifts LM curve left.
D2. AS cannot pass full employment output Y_{full}.
D4. AD shifts with the money contraction.

Review

2. In the closed economy, capital growth equals total saving.
4. Remember the labor force L grows.
6. Start with total income in retirement.
8. What is not saved in youth is consumed.

10. The decrease in the money supply shifts LM.
12. The increase in T shifts IS.
14. The higher Y^* shifts the FF curve.
16. Separate fiscal and monetary policies.
18. Consider changes in AD.

Acronyms

ASEAN	Association of Southeast Asian Nations
APEC	Asia-Pacific Economic Cooperation
BOP	Balance of payments
BOT	Balance of trade
BGS	Balance on goods and services
CA	Current account
CIA	Covered interest arbitrage
DI	Direct investment in the BOP
DC	Developed country
EU	European Union
FDI	Foreign direct investment
FTAA	Free Trade Area of the Americas
FX	Foreign exchange
GATT	General Agreement on Tariffs and Trade
GDP	Gross domestic product
GSP	Generalized System of Preferences
IMF	International Monetary Fund
IRP	Interest rate parity
ITC	International Trade Commission
KA	Capital account
LDC	Less developed country
MNF	Multinational firm
NAFTA	North American Free Trade Agreement
NII	Net investment income
NBER	National Bureau of Economic Research
NIC	Newly industrialized country
NTB	Nontariff barrier
OECD	Organization for Economic Cooperation and Development
PI	Portfolio investment in the BOP
PPP	Purchasing power parity
SDR	Special Drawing Rights
TS	Trade in services in the BOP
VER	Voluntary export restraint
WTO	World Trade Organization

References

Aizenman, Joshua & Eileen Brooks (2005) Globalization and task convergence: The cases of wine and beer, *NBER Working Paper*.

Alavi, Jafar & Henry Thompson (1988) Toward a theory of free trade zones, *International Trade Journal*

Amaya, Naohiro (1988) The Japanese economy in transition: Optimistic about the short term, pessimistic about the long term, *Japan and the World Economy*

Amuedo-Dorantes, Catalina, Cynthia Bansak, & Susan Pozo (2005) On the remitting patterns of immigrants: Evidence from Mexican survey data, *Federal Reserve Bank of Atlanta Economic Review*

Anderson, Kym & Hege Norheim (1993) Is world trade becoming more regionalized? *Review of International Economics*

Arndt, Channing & Thomas Hertel (1997) Revisiting 'The fallacy of free trade', *Review of International Economics*

Aw, Bee Yan & Mark Roberts (1986) Estimating quality change in quota-constrained import markets: The case of US footwear, *Journal of International Economics*

Ayanian, Robert (1988) Political risk, national defense and the dollar, *Economic Inquiry*

Baldwin, Robert (1971) Determinants of the commodity structure of US trade, *American Economic Review*

Baldwin, Robert & Glen Cain (2000) Shifts in relative US wages: The role of trade, technology, and factor endowments, *Review of Economics and Statistics*

Ballie, Richard & William Osterberg (1997) Central bank intervention and risk in the forward market, *Journal of International Economics*

Batra, Ravi (1992) The fallacy of free trade, *Review of International Economics*

Batra, Ravi & Daniel Slotje (1994) Trade policy and poverty in the United States: Theory and evidence, 1947–1990, *Review of International Economics*

Beard, T. Randolph & Henry Thompson (2003) Duopoly quotas and relative import quality, *International Review of Economics and Finance*

Beeson, Patricia & Michael Bryan (1986) Emerging service economy, *Economic Commentary*, FRB Cleveland

Ben-David, David (1993) Equalizing exchange: Trade liberalization and income convergence, *Quarterly Journal of Economics*

Ben-David, David & Alok Bohara (1997) Evidence on the contribution of trade reform towards international income equalization, *Review of International Economics*

Berman, Eli, John Bound, & Stephen Machin (1998) Implications of skill-biased technological change: International evidence, *Quarterly Journal of Economics*

Bernard, Andrew & Bradford Jensen (1998) Exceptional exporter performance: Cause, effect, or both? *Journal of International Economics*

Bernhofen, Daniel M. & John C. Brown (2005) Comparative advantage gains from trade: Evidence from Japan, *American Economic Review*

Bohara, Alok, Kishore Gawande, & William Kaempfer (1998) The dynamics of tariff retaliation between the United States and Canada: Theory and Evidence, *Review of International Economics*

Branson, William & Nikolaos Monoyios (1977) Factor inputs in US trade, *Journal of International Economics*

Broadberry, S.N. (1987) Purchasing power parity and the pound-dollar rate in the 1930s, *Economica*

Brook, Douglas A. (2005) "Meta-Strategic Lobbying: The 1998 Steel Imports Case", Business and Politics, Article 4. *http://www.bepress.com/bap/vol7/iss1/art4*

Brown, Lynn (1986) Taking in each other's laundry: The service economy, *New England Economic Review*, FRB Boston

Bryan, Michael & Susan Byrne (1990) Don't worry: We'll grow out of it, *Economic Commentary*, FRB Cleveland

Caprio, Gerard & Patrick Honohan (1999) Restoring banking stability: Beyond supervised capital requirements, *Journal of Economic Perspectives*

Card, David (1990) The impact of the Mariel boatlift on the Miami labor market, *Industrial and Labor Relations Review*

Casas, Francisco & Kwan Choi (1985) The Leontief paradox: Continued or resolved? *Journal of Political Economy*

Cha, Baekin & Daniel Himarios (1995) The internationalization of the US wage process, *Review of International Economics*

Childs, Nathan & Michael Hammig (1987) An examination of the impact of real exchange rates on US exports of agricultural commodities, *The International Trade Journal*

Clerides, Sofronis (2005) Gains from trade in used goods: Evidence from the global market for automobiles, *CEPR Discussion Paper # 4859*

Cline, William (1997) *Trade and Income Distribution*, Washington: Institute for International Economics

Cole, Harold & Lee Ohanian (1999) The Great Depression in the United States from a neoclassical perspective, *Quarterly Review*, FRB of Minneapolis

Crowder, William (1996) A reexamination of long run PPP: The case of Canada, the UK, and the US, *Review of International Economics*

Davis, Donald & David Weinstein (1995) Intra-industry trade: A Heckscher-Ohlin Ricardo Approach, *Journal of International Economics*

Davis, Donald & David Weinstein (1998) Economic geography and regional production structure: An empirical investigation, *Federal Reserve Bank of New York Staff Reports, #40*

Deardorff, Alan & Robert Stern (1984) The economic effect of complete elimination of post-Tokyo Round tariffs. In *Trade Policy for the 1980s*, William Cline, ed., Washington: Institute for International Economics

DeLong, Bradford & Larry Summers (1990) Equipment, investment and economic growth, *NBER Working Paper #3513*

Dinopoulos, Elias & Mordechai Kreinin (1988) Effects of the US-Japan auto VER on European prices and on US welfare, *The Review of Economics and Statistics*

Dollar, David & Edward Wolff (1988) Convergence of industry labor productivity among advanced economies, 1963–1982, *The Review of Economics and Statistics*

Dollar, David & Edward Wolff (1993) *Competitiveness, Convergence, and International Specialization*, Cambridge: MIT Press

Eckels, Alfred (1998) Smoot-Hawley and the stock market crash, 1929-1930, *The International Trade Journal*

Edwards, Sebastian (1999) How effective are capital controls? *Journal of Economic Perspectives*

Eichengreen, Barry (1991) Historical research on international lending and debt, *Journal of Economic Perspectives*

Eichengreen, Barry (1999) *Toward a New International Financial Architecture: A Practical Post-Asia Agenda*, Washington: Institute for International Economics

Engel, Charles (1999) Are we globalized yet? *Economic Letter*, FRB San Francisco

Engel, Charles & John Rogers (1994) How wide is the US border? *NBER Working Paper #4829*

Falzoni, Anna, Giovanni Brunno, & Rosario Crino (2004) Foreign Direct Investment, Wage Inequality, and Skilled Labor Demand in EU Accession Countries, *Centro Studi Luca d'Agliano Development Studies Working Paper #188*

Fang, Wenshwo, Yihao Lai, & Henry Thompson (2005) Exchange rates, exchange risk, and Asian export revenue, *International Review of Economics & Finance*

Feenstra, Robert & Gordon Hanson (1997) Direct foreign investment and relative wages: Evidence from Mexico's Maquiladoras, *Journal of International Economics*

Feenstra, Robert & Gordon Hanson (1999) The Impact of outsourcing and high-technology capital on wages: Estimates for the United States, 1979–1990, *Quarterly Journal of Economics*

Fischer, Stanley (1999) On the need for an international lender of last resort, *Journal of Economic Perspectives*

Frenkel, Jeffrey & Kenneth Froot (1990) Exchange rate forecasting techniques, survey data, and implications for the foreign exchange market, *NBER Working Paper #3470*

Garten, Jeffrey (1998) In this economic chaos, a global central bank can help, *International Herald Tribune*, 25 September

Gartner, Bruce (1987) Causes of US farm commodity programs, *Journal of Political Economy*

Goldberg, Linda & Keith Crockett (1998) The dollar and US manufacturing, *Current Issues in Economics and Finance*, FRB of New York

Goldberg, Linda & Michael Klein (1999) International trade and factor mobility: An empirical investigation, *Staff Reports*, #81, FRB New York

Golub, Stephen (1995) Comparative and absolute advantage in the Asia Pacific region, Working paper, FRB San Francisco

Griffen, James & David Teece (1982) *OPEC Behavior and World Oil Prices*, London: Allen & Unwin

Grilli, Vittrio & Andrea Beltratti (1989) US military expenditure and the dollar, *Economic Inquiry*

Grossman, Gene & Jim Levinshon (1989) Import competition and the stock market return to capital, *American Economic Review*

Grubel, Herbert & Peter Lloyd (1975) *Intraindustry Trade*, London: MacMillan

Gylfason, Thorvaldur (2004) Natural resources and economic growth: From dependence to diversification, *CEPR Discussion Paper*

Hakkio, Graig & Douglas Pearce (1985) The reaction of exchange rates to economic news, *Economic Inquiry*

Hanson, Gordon (1998) Regional adjustment to trade liberalization, *Regional Science and Urban Economics*, 419-44

Hansen, Wendy & Thomas Prusa (1997) The economics and politics of trade policy: An empirical analysis of ITC decision making, *Review of International Economics*

Harris, James & Michael Todaro (1970) Migration, unemployment and development: A two-sector analysis, *American Economic Review*

Haskel, Jonathan & Matthew Slaughter (2002) Does the sector bias of skill-biased technical change explain changing skill premia? *European Economic Review*

Hickock, Susan (1985) The consumer cost of US trade restraints, *Quarterly Review*, FRB New York

Hickock, Susan & James Orr (1989) Shifting patterns of US trade with selected developing Asian economies, *Quarterly Review*, FRB New York

Huber, Richard (1971) Effect on prices of Japan's entry into world commerce after 1858, *Journal of Political Economy*

Hufbauer, Gary, Diane Berliner, & Kimberly Elliott (1986) *Trade Protection in the United States: 31 Case Studies*, Washington: Institute for International Economics

Hunter, Linda (1990) US trade protection: Effects on the regional composition of employment, *Economic Review*, FRB Dallas

Irwin, Douglas (1988) Did late nineteenth century US tariffs promote infant industries? Evidence from the tinplate industry, *NBER Working Paper* #6835

Karrenbrock, Jeffrey (1990) The internationalization of the beer brewing industry, *Review*, FRB St Louis

Kasa, Kenneth (1997) Understanding trends in foreign exchange rates, *Weekly Letter*, FRB San Francisco

Kaufman, Henry (1998) Preventing the next global financial crisis, *Washington Post*, 28 January

Kelly, Kenneth & Morris Morker (1998) Do unfairly traded imports injure domestic industries? *Review of International Economics*

Knetter, Michael (1989) Price discrimination by US and German exporters, *American Economic Review*

Kouparitsas, Michael (1997) A dynamic macroeconomic analysis of NAFTA, *Economic Perspectives*, FRB of Chicago

Kreinin, Mordechai (1984) Wage competitiveness in steel and motor vehicles, *Economic Inquiry*

Krugman, Paul (1998) Saving Asia: It's time to get radical, *Fortune*, 7 September

Leamer, Ed (1980) The Leontief paradox reconsidered, *Journal of Political Economy*

Leamer, Ed (1984) *Sources of International Comparative Advantage: Theory and Evidence*, Cambridge: MIT Press

Lee, Jong Wha (1994) Capital goods imports and long run growth, *NBER Working Paper #4725*

Lee, Jong Wha & Phillip Swagel (1994) Trade barriers and trade flows across countries and industries, *NBER Working Paper #4799*

Lewis, Ethan (2004) How did the Miami labor market absorb the Mariel immigrants? *FRB Philadelphia Working Paper 04-3*

Lipsey, Robert (2000) The role of foreign direct investment in international capital flows, *NBER Working Paper #7094*

Maneschi, Andrea (1992) Ricardo's international trade theory: Beyond the comparative cost example, *Cambridge Journal of Economics*

Marjit, Sugata (1994) The fallacy of free trade: Comment, *Review of International Economics*

Markusen, James & Randall Wigle (1989) Nash equilibrium tariffs for the United States and Canada: The roles of country size, scale economies, and capital mobility, *The Journal of Political Economy*

Marshall, Alfred (1926) *The Official Papers of Alfred Marshall*, London: McMillan

Marston, Richard (1998) Pricing to market in Japanese manufacturing, *Journal of International Economics*

Maskus, Keith (1985) A test of the Heckscher-Ohlin-Vanek theorem: The Leontief commonplace, *Journal of International Economics*

McCallum, Bennet (1989) Targets, indicators, and instruments of monetary policy, *NBER Working Paper #3234*

Mishkin, Frederic (1999) Global financial instability: Framework, events, issues, *Journal of Economic Perspectives*

Moran, Theodore, Edward Graham, & Magnus Blomström (2005) *Foreign Direct Investment Promote Development?* Washington: Institute for International Economics

Panagariya, Arvind, Shekhar Shah, & Deepak Mishra (2001) Demand elasticities in international trade: Are they really low? *Journal of Development Economics*

Polachek, Solomon (1997) Why democracies cooperated more and fight less: The relationship between international trade and cooperation, *Review of International Economics*

Rassekh, Farhad (1992) The role of international trade in the convergence of per capita GDP in the OECD: 1950–1985, *International Economic Journal*

Rassekh, Farhad (1994) An evaluation of Batra's "Fallacy of free trade" *Review of International Economics*

Rassekh, Farhad & Henry Thompson (1993) Factor price equalization: Theory and evidence, *Journal of Economic Integration*

Rassekh, Farhad & Henry Thompson (1997) Adjustment in general equilibrium: Some industrial evidence, *Review of International Economics*

Rassekh, Farhad & Henry Thompson (1998) Micro convergence and macro convergence: Factor price equalization and per capita income, *Pacific Economic Review*

Ray, Ed (1991) Foreign takeovers and new investments in the US, *Contemporary Policy Issues*

Reinert, Kenneth & David Roland-Holst (1998) North-south trade and occupational wages: Some evidence from North America, *Review of International Economics*

Revenga, Ana (1992) Exporting jobs? The impact of import competition on employment and wages in US manufacturing, *The Quarterly Journal of Economics*, 255-84

Richardson, David & Chi Zhang (1999) Revealing comparative advantage: Chaotic or coherent patterns across time and sector and U.S. trading partner? *NBER Working Paper #7212*

Rogoff, Kenneth (1999) International institutions for reducing global financial instability, *Journal of Economic Perspectives*

Romer, Paul (1994) New goods, old theory, and the welfare costs of trade restrictions, *Journal of Development Economics*

Rousslang, Donald & Theodore To (1993) Domestic trade and transport costs as barriers to international trade, *Canadian Journal of Economics*

Ruffin, Roy (1988) The missing link: The Ricardian approach to the factor endowments theory of trade, *American Economic Review*

Ruffin, Roy & Farhad Rassekh (1987) The role of foreign direct investment in US capital outflows, *American Economic Review*

Sachs, Jeffrey (1995) Do we need an international lender of last resort? Princeton University, Frank Graham Memorial Lecture

Schott, Peter (2004) Across-product versus within-product specialization in international trade, *Quarterly Journal of Economics*

Seshan, Ganesh (2005) The impact of trade liberalization on household qelfare in Vietnam, *World Bank Policy Research Working Paper # 3541*

Shapiro, Matthew (1987) Are cyclical fluctuations in productivity due more to supply shocks or demand shocks? *NBER Working Paper #2147*

Smith, Alasdair & Anthony Venables (1988) Completing the internal market in the European community, *European Economic Review*

Stern, Robert & Keith Maskus (1981) Determinants of the structure of US foreign trade, *Journal of International Economics*

Stiglitz, Joseph (1997) Dumping on free trade: The US import trade laws, *Southern Economic Journal*

Sweeney, George, T. Randolph Beard, & Henry Thompson (1997) Quotas and quality in international trade, *Journal of Economic Integration*

Tarr, David & Morris Morkre (1987) Aggregate costs to the United States of tariffs and quotas on imports, in *The New Protectionist Threat to World Welfare*, Dominick Salvatore ed., Amsterdam: North-Holland

Thompson, Henry (1986) Free trade and factor price polarization, *European Economic Review*

Thompson, Henry (1987) Do tariffs protect specific factors? *Canadian Journal of Economics*

Thompson, Henry (1991) Simulating a multifactor general equilibrium model of production and trade, *International Economic Journal*

Thompson, Henry (1994a) An investigation of the quantitative properties of the specific factors model of production and trade, *Japan and the World Economy*

Thompson, Henry (1994b) NAFTA and industrial adjustment: A specific factors model of production in Alabama, *Growth and Change*

Thompson, Henry (1995a) Factor intensity versus factor substitution in a specified general equilibrium model, *Journal of Economic Integration*

Thompson, Henry (1995b) Free trade and income redistribution in some developing and newly industrialized countries, *Open Economies Review*

Thompson, Henry (2001) International trade with three factors, goods, or countries, *Keio Economic Studies*

Toledo, Hugo (2005) Coca substitution and free trade in Bolivia: The pending crisis, *Review of Economic Development*

Toledo, Hugo & Henry Thompson (2001) Bolivia and South American free trade, *The International Trade Journal*

Trela, Irene & John Whalley (1995) Internal quota-allocation schemes and the costs of the MFA, *Review of International Economics*

Upadhyaya, Kamal & Henry Thompson (1998) The impact of the exchange rate on local industry, *Economia Internazionale*

Wacziarg, Romain & Jessica Wallack (2004) Trade liberalization and inter-sectoral labor movements, *Journal of International Economics*, 411-39

Walter, Ingo (1983) Structural adjustment and trade policy in the international steel industry, in *Trade Policy in the 1980s*, William Cline ed., Washington: Institute for International Economics

Weidenbaum, Murray & Tracy Munger (1983) Protection at any price? *Regulation*, July

Wickham, Elizabeth and Henry Thompson (1989) An empirical analysis of intraindustry trade and multinational firms, in *Intraindustry Trade: Theory, Evidence, and Extensions, ed. Peter Tharakan*

Williamson, Jeffrey (1996) Globalization, convergence, and history, *Journal of Economic History*

Wong, Kar-yiu (1995) *International Trade in Goods and Factor Mobility*, MIT Press

Xu, Zhenhui (1996) On the causality between export growth and GDP growth: An empirical reinvestigation, *Review of International Economics*

Xu, Zhenhui (2000) Effects of primary exports on industrial exports and GDP: Empirical evidence, *Review of Development Economics*, 307-25

Subject Index